BETWEEN SUNDAYS

G

BETWEEN SUNDAYS

BLACK WOMEN AND
EVERYDAY STRUGGLES OF FAITH

MARLA F. FREDERICK

UNIVERSITY OF CALIFORNIA PRESS
Berkeley · Los Angeles · London

University of California Press
Berkeley and Los Angeles, California

University of California Press, Ltd.
London, England

© 2003 by the Regents of the University of California

Library of Congress Cataloging-in-Publication Data

Frederick, Marla Faye, 1972–
    Between Sundays : Black women and everyday strug-
gles of faith / by Marla F. Frederick.
        p.   cm.
    Includes bibliographical references and index.
    ISBN 0–520–23392–1 (alk. paper) — ISBN
0–520–23394–8 (pbk. : alk. paper)
        1. African American women—Religious life.
I. Title.
BR563.N4 F73   2003
277.5'6'083'082—dc21   2002152990

Manufactured in the United States of America

12   11   10   09   08   07   06   05   04   03
10   9   8   7   6   5   4   3   2   1

To My Parents
L. C. and Carolyn Frederick

CONTENTS

PREFACE

"Spirituality is so central to scholarship on women's culture and women's liberation that we can't discuss liberation or empowerment for women without also discussing women's spirituality."

Dilla Buckner, "Spirituality, Sexuality, and Creativity:
A Conversation with Margaret Walker-Alexander"

To study African American women's spirituality is to embark upon a project that is at once tangible and yet distinctly intangible. For those in theological studies, it is to assume a priori knowledge about the realm of the spirit and how this life of the spirit is manifested in the flesh. For those engaged in the social and anthropological study of religion it is to assume very little about the spirit and yet everything about its manifestation in the flesh—namely, how people act out in society a particular understanding of spirituality. My own research attempts to mediate between these two perspectives by focusing on the social and political aspects of religious commitment while resisting the reductionism of the spiritual to the material inherent in that perspective.

Between Sundays explores the role of spirituality in the cultural production of activism in the lives of African American women in northeastern North Carolina, a poor, rural area of the U.S. South. "Spirituality" provides a space for creative agency, which gives voice to the multifaceted ways in which women interpret, inform, and reshape their social conditions. These social conditions—often characterized by limited access to job opportunities, community health, health care, and equitable schooling—are the day-to-day concerns that influence and are influenced by women's spirituality.

This work developed out of intellectual frustration. It seemed that much of social science approached spirituality and issues of faith from a vantage point that reduced religion to a series of signs, symbols, rituals, and structures. Outside of theology, there was little that seemed to validate the experiences of believers by seeing the actual *work* that their faith produced. Much of the literature, as anthropologist Frances Kostarelos points out in her book *Feeling the Spirit,* has viewed the faith of black people as "otherworldly and compensatory beliefs and practices that help poor blacks adapt to social and economic hardship and injustice" (2). This type of functionalist approach is not only condescending but also fails to come to terms with the complexity of religious faith. In my time among women believers in Halifax County, the heart of much of their endeavors centered around what they considered their "relationship with God" or a desire to "please God." Whether they were protesting hog industries trying to locate in their communities or defining new boundaries for their sexual relationships, a considerable factor in their decision-making process was their understanding and perception of what they believed the immaterial world had to say about the material world. In these instances it seemed evident that questions of religion and questions of power were intimately connected in a way that demands scholarly reassessment.

As I have worked to produce such a text, a number of people both inside and outside of the academy have contributed enormously to this endeavor. I have benefited from the support of an absolutely incredible network of brilliant and caring people. For them I am eternally grateful.

Early training and intellectual maturation at Spelman College made this work a priority for me. Dr. Gloria Wade-Gayles, as mentor and professor extraordinaire, along with a host of other women (and some men) who make up the Spelman community taught me the importance of listening to and thinking about African American women's lives and histories. Central to coming to a knowledge of oneself—as all of Dr. Gayles's students learn—is a commitment to "claim your space" in a world that could otherwise render you silent and invisible. This work on numerous levels is a testament to that lesson. Dr. Johnnetta B. Cole, as sister anthropologist, along with Dr. Darryl White allowed me to see the enormous value of anthropology in studying the life experiences of everyday folk. From the earliest days of our Introduction to Anthropology course, with Dr. White's lectures and Dr. Cole's excavation of the material, I knew there was something about the discipline that would keep me coming back.

Many colleagues and friends at Duke University, including Charles Piot, Lee Baker, Karla Holloway, and Irene Silverblatt, as dedicated members of my dissertation committee, helped me to establish critical intellectual ground in earlier versions of this manuscript. Enthusiastic about the dissertation, they insisted that this work be published. Their support has been completely invaluable. In additon to my time spent at Duke, I had the unique opportunity to benefit from the rich intellectual communities that make up the "Research Triangle." Scholars in the Department of Anthropology at the University of North Carolina at Chapel Hill formed my second academic home as I worked with the UNC-based North Carolina Public Spheres Project. Many thanks to Dorothy Holland (who served double duty on my dissertation committee), Cathy Lutz, Don Nonini, Lesley Bartlett, Thad Guldbrandsen, Enrique Murrillo, Jr., and Kim Allen, who were my colleagues on the project. Discussing with them issues of economic restructuring, democracy, and public spheres has contributed in obvious ways to my thinking about the role of faith and activism. They all have helped to make theory and practice a reality in my academic endeavors.

I spent a significantly rewarding year as a Visiting Fellow at the Center for the Study of Religion at Princeton University. While there, I received insight, critiques, and support for my work from several scholars: Marie Griffith (tons of "thank yous"), Robert Wuthnow, Peter Paris, Lisa Matterson, Penny Becker, Leslie Callahan, Regina Langley, Tammy Brown, and a number of scholars and graduate students who participated in our weekly symposium. What a year! I also owe tremendous thanks to the faculty and staff of the Department of African American Studies at the University of Cincinnati for their support and to my students who eagerly read versions of several chapters and offered wonderful critiques. As I worked on final edits for this book, Dr. Jacquelyn Grant and the Womanist Scholars Program at the Interdenominational Theological Center provided me with invaluable time and resources to complete the project and begin laying a foundation for my next one.

Independent of formal affiliations several scholars read my work as friends. I am especially grateful for the wisdom and keen insights of Chauncey McGlathery, Angela Sims, Tomeiko Ashford, Tonya Tarpeh, Madeline McKlinney-Sadler, Rodney Sadler, Sylvia Lim, John L. Jackson, Stacy Torian, Tonya Armstrong, and J. T. and Enid Walker.

Deep thanks also to my editors at the University of California Press, Reed Malcolm and Kristen Cashman, whose enthusiasm for the project inched me *closer* to my deadlines. Special thanks to Kay Scheuer whose detailed reading of the text during copyediting caught numerous errors that my eyes must have been trained to miss!

My research would not have been possible without the openness and support of the women from Halifax who invited me into their homes and their lives. Thank you for sharing your stories with me. To my friends at CCT, you are incredible! Keep the struggle for black land, education, community, and self-actualization alive! There are many others in Halifax, teachers, city and county officials, business leaders, public and private sector workers, church members, who have been instrumental in helping me to understand the county. I greatly appreciate your willingness to participate in my research.

The study of spirituality would not have been as enriching had it not been for my early experiences of faith. To Rev. and Mrs. Randolph and my First Baptist Church family in my hometown of Sumter, S.C., thank you. To Rev. and Mrs. Davis and my First Calvary Baptist Church family in Durham, N.C., thank you. To my Impact family, thank you. Your encouragement over the years has made this journey of faith wonderfully rewarding.

In the face of my temptation to be consumed by the manuscript, my immediate and extended family, along with faithful friends, have reminded me that my *real* life reaches beyond the demands of my work. Much love to my irreplaceable circle of sister-friends, especially to Cerene Holley, Lisa Herring, April Jefferson, Melody Gardner, Terri Carson, Anita Pollard, Kimberly Grantham, Monica Rivers, and Traci Griffin. Such friends are God's greatest gift to women. Worlds of thank yous to my extremely nurturing family of grandparents, aunts, uncles, nieces, nephews, and cousins. Thank you especially to my parents, L. C. and Carolyn Frederick, and my sisters and brothers-in-law, Fredereka and Kelvin McDuffie, and Brenda and Al Sept. Your boundless love and support give me freedom to grow.

Finally, I am most grateful for the many times that I am reminded of unseen guidance.

INTRODUCTION

Lynne was disgusted just thinking about her daughter dating a preacher.[1] "The idea that she could even consider it makes me sick! After all that I've told her and all that she's been exposed to." Lynne's frustration was evident in the tone of her voice and the contortions of her face. Nearly the first half of our interview seemed to center on her disapproval of her daughter's romantic choice. For Lynne, preachers and their theologies are the main problem with black communities in Halifax County, and by extension the majority of other black communities. While her daughter, a distinguished judge in another part of the state, no longer lives in Halifax, Lynne's distrust of the ministry reaches far beyond the confines of this rural area. She could not help but go into a detailed description of the short, well-groomed, rhetoric-spouting minister. He had thoroughly irritated her upon their first meeting. For Lynne, self-indulgence—a preoccupation with image, authority, and money—causes ministers to hinder the type of progressive impact that the church could have. Women who participate in the church, in Lynne's estimation, have their lives and frustrations with the social order curtailed into benevolence instead of anger.

In a memoir that Lynne helped a young high school student write, the idea comes across clearly. The student's celebration of his grandmother's influence in his life seems at least a partial reflection of Lynne's own misgivings about the church. "My grandmother is my superstar," he writes. "She is such a woman of mystery and strength. Always there for us. Always making a way for us. God seems to guide her every purpose. Then again, she could be a tower of anger and despair . . . Her voice muted by the culture, by the church and by her beliefs in God." The final lines echo the hours of interview time I spent with Lynne. Based upon her lifetime of fighting injustice in the county and beyond, she believes that when the response should be indignation the church instead channels women's voices into prayers for peace and acts of benevolence. For years she has worked to get women involved with her type of politics—bold, confrontational, impolite, *honest*. The daughter of well-respected farmers severely mistreated by the government, she was molded into an activist from an early age. She counts her success in converting women to her views as slow but steady—her own politics and beliefs (especially about God) sometimes making her more of an eccentric than a leader in this small community. Nevertheless, she is revered and respected as a woman who stands her ground and comes to the aid of those in need. For the past several years she has diligently cared for her ailing parents, making sure that her mother receives her nighttime bath and that her father takes his medicine and eats healthy meals to regulate his diabetes. Her mother's wanderings in the middle of the night and ornery mood swings leave her drained and frustrated—experiencing the type of exhaustion only those who have cared for Alzheimer's patients understand. Though she remains concerned with the problems of society, most of her time now is consumed by household responsibilities. Nevertheless, she still tries to dedicate some of her labor to outside efforts.

She once married a death-row inmate and traveled across country on the back of a truck with a bullhorn to publicly ridicule the inhumanity of the death sentence. The disproportionate use of capital punishment for black and poor inmates makes the punishment that much more intolerable to Lynne. I could only imagine the slim possibility of any of the women of faith that she described taking such a bold and outrageous step—not just carrying the bullhorn across the country, but marrying the likes of a death-row inmate—completely jeopardizing the image of "respectability" so valued in most churches. This particular campaign of Lynne's, however, dated from nearly twenty years ago. Her most recent action was one in a list of smaller protests that highlight her keen sensitivity toward situations she perceives as unjust.

She sent a petition around town to have a man kicked out of the community. After receiving notice from the courts that he was required to pay child support for his two young daughters, he had posted a sign on both sides of his small red pick-up truck saying that he would never pay anybody's child support. Enraged by his intolerable rejection of his fatherly responsibilities, Lynne decided that he was no longer welcome. She responded with a petition: "We, the Citizens of Tillery, hereby no longer welcome William Thomas [pseudonym] in our community. His actions do not reflect our community's spirit. They are offensive and abusive towards women and children and we will not tolerate it . . ." Some people signed, some did not. In this small, closely knit town on the outskirts of the county seat, almost all the residents are members of one of the seven churches that line the main street. Some thought it "un-Christian" to send around a petition reviling the name of someone in the community; others thought it "un-Christian" of him not to pay his child support and thus found themselves justified in signing.

Although seemingly harsh, Lynne's critique of the church and the impact of faith upon how people respond to certain issues merits discussion. In our need as social scientists to discuss the significance of gender, race, and class for how people experience and act in the world, we neglect to consider seriously the impact of spirituality on such practices. Lynne's frustrations thus remind us of the profound influence of faith upon actions. Whether related to how people respond to signing a petition, or how people become involved in community work, or how they spend their money, or how they relate sexually to their partners, *among the faith-filled,* faith in God navigates how individuals respond to almost all of life's circumstances.

While Lynne was speaking more about the practice of faith outside of the church, her critique reflects concerns that others have long had over the inside workings of the institution. Lynne is one who finds the teachings and practices of the church stifling. Years ago she removed herself completely from the institution, renouncing her faith. Other women, while seeing and often sharing some of her concerns, have chosen to stay within the church *and* hold to their faith. Skeptics like Lynne wonder why women remain in an institution that often curtails their leadership and silences their voices. Women's ministerial leadership is often undervalued, and more often than not women are absent from powerful decision-making bodies in the church, like the deacon and trustee boards.[2]

During an interview I had with one female minister in the county, the clergywoman despairingly recalled her struggles to be recognized as a minister in the Baptist ministerial alliance. Because her own association refused to ordain her, she had to travel to another North Carolina association for ordination. Although she is now a recognized minister in the Baptist tradition, those who opposed her ordination find other ways to prove their point. When she visits churches pastored by them, they rarely extend to her an invitation to join with other clergy as pulpit guests. These small acts of intolerance toward women ministers along with the relative absence of women in the business and financial decisions of the church raise numerous questions among those concerned about equitable distributions of power in the church. Further, the abuse of women at the hands of "preachers that prey" as one minister terms it[3]—an allusion to some ministers' sexual improprieties—makes a discussion of women and faith even more urgent.

In spite of the problems within the church, women not only remain members, they worship, participate, teach Sunday school, usher on the ushers' board, give their tithe, form community outreaches, and in a large sense undergird the entire operation of the church.[4] It is common knowledge that regardless of race or socioeconomic background women form the backbone of most religious organizations in the United States. Leading womanist theologian Jacquelyn Grant suggests that male leadership in churches celebrates women as the "backbone" of the church in order to keep them in the "background."[5] Similarly, the simple title of Cheryl Townsend Gilkes's work on church women, *If It Wasn't for the Women,* leaves the reader with little doubt in answering the hypothetical: If it wasn't for the women, *there would be no church.* Yet while the inner dynamic of church life is often far from ideal, women continue to worship God and contribute to the overarching aims and missions of their local church bodies. They move beyond the problems and limitations of the church to full participation not because the church is perfect, but because their churches form valuable community networks that foster mutual support, nurture individual gifts, and validate individual identities. Furthermore, women participate because their faith is real—complicated but real.

The presence of women reflects at some points their acceptance of male-centered theologies of female subordination, as well as their larger commitments to the community in which the church resides and their social relationships within the church. Most important, however, their commitment reflects a level of faith that encourages a desire to be a part of what they consider God's work wherever and however it is taking place. Often this work takes place within the church; even more frequently, however, it takes place in everyday situations outside of the church. Women's expressions of faith reflect what I refer to as their spirituality—their understanding of God and God's work in their day-to-day lives. Spirituality in discernible ways embodies both the personal and public areas of life. In this book I discuss women's experiences of faith that reach beyond the preparation and execution of the Sunday morning worship service, what takes place "Between Sundays."

RESISTANCE AND ACCOMMODATION

Lynne's critique raises several issues. First, her suggestion that faith and the church work against women's radical expressions of anger and indignation reflects part of a larger debate within the study of African American religion. Theologians and scholars of religion have for years debated the accommodation versus resistance practices of "the black church," as dynamic and varied as these historic institutions are. Much of this debate, however, focuses on the ways in which the church fights against the racist practices of society. Very little of the discussion turns on questions of sexism within the church itself. Resistance and accommodation are seen largely as subjects for the analysis of racism, not sexism. Nevertheless, the history of the resistance/accommodation debate illumines a discussion of how the church serves as a source of strength and empowerment for people of faith.

The social unrest of the sixties led to revisionist work which attempts to incorporate the ideals of black social power within an understanding of black religious traditions.[6] Over the past several decades there has been a shift in focus from viewing black faith as one embedded in escapist theology[7]—a compulsion to find joy and peace in the world to come—to viewing it as a faith which acknowledges the power of practitioners to not only endure, but also resist structures of oppression. This revisionist work began to reconceptualize the relationship between religion and social protest, ultimately demonstrating how religion serves as a means of both "social relief and social protest."[8]

Some even suggest that it is precisely this tension between accommodation and resistance that sets African American religious practice apart from the varieties of influential African and European traditions.[9] Gayraud Wilmore, a scholar of African American religion, notes that black religion "began in Africa, was mixed with European Christianity in the Caribbean and Latin America, and was further molded by and recoiled from American evangelical Protestantism on the slave plantations of the South," and suggests that "an exceedingly elastic but tenacious thread binds together the contributive and developmental factors of black religion in the US as one distinctive social phenomenon," its radicalism.[10] While one can acknowledge the validity of this position, it is nevertheless important to point out that the tradition of accommodation is equally salient in the history of African American Christianity.[11] Many African Americans were not radicalized by their beliefs and practices. Furthermore, much of African American religious experience has involved some degree of capitulation or accommodation in the face of unequal structures of power. Which view one holds is largely predicated upon how one defines accommodation and resistance. Lest we forget, numerous black churches and church members opposed any involvement by the church in the Civil Rights Movement and the Black Power Movement. These were seen as social concerns and not necessarily the responsibility of local church bodies.

While not wanting to leave the terms "accommodation" and "resistance" entirely behind, I nevertheless feel that they largely fail to capture the complexity of the everyday lives of the practitioners I know. Although for the most part seen by critics like Lynne as accommodating to structures of oppression, women's lives are not easily placed on a binary continuum measuring political or apolitical activity alone. Instead, they manifest a diversity of belief, an often contradictory set of commitments, and a depth of religious engagements that defy easy either/or labels.

Evelyn Brooks Higginbotham, a historian whose work on African American women has opened new and interesting ways of understanding women's history at the turn of the twentieth century, argues that such attempts at dichotomizing the faith experiences of women believers elide the varied dynamics of black faith. "Arguments over the accommodationist versus liberating thrust of the black church miss the range as well as the fluid interaction of political and ideological meanings represented within the church's domain. Equally important, the artificiality of such a dichotomy precludes appreciation of the church's role in the 'prosaic and constant struggle' of black people for survival and empowerment."[12]

Eugene Genovese similarly argues that even in the historical interpretation of African American slave experiences one must try to challenge the "mechanistic error of assuming that religion either sparked the slaves to rebellion or rendered them docile."[13] Instead one must examine the "creative impulse" among slaves that allowed them to "blend ideas from diverse sources into the formulation of a world-view sufficiently complex to link acceptance of what had to be endured with a determined resistance to the pressures for despair and dehumanization."[14] Both Genovese's notion of the melding together of ideas and Higginbotham's understanding of the "'prosaic and constant struggle' of black people for survival and empowerment" are important in creating a paradigm for interpreting African American women's spirituality.

STRUCTURE AND AGENCY

Second, Lynne's suggestion that the church *itself* has hindered black progress raises questions of how institutions or structures affect people's activism or sense of agency. How free are women to work against not only the sexist language of the church, but the racist baggage of institutions like the school system, or corporations that employ minority laborers in low-level and often dangerous positions? Do institutions have the final say, or are women able to work within and against structures to effect change? Furthermore, what is meant by agency? Must agency be limited to only that which engages politics? Or when we say "agency" are we also referring to the ways in which women through empathetic and caring activities create communities of strength and healing?

There are everyday forms of resistance that people use that do not necessarily require organizing for direct protest; nevertheless, they demonstrate opposition to the status quo or to practices with which they disagree.[15] The pastor's refusal to welcome female ministers into his pulpit, though sexist to many, is one such example of "small acts" of resistance. Although he cannot prevent women's ordinations, he hinders their participation on a level that he can manipulate.

Sometimes, however, people take little interest in resistance per se and begin channeling their energies in other directions. In these instances confronting the institution is not the ultimate goal of those who feel limited by institutional barriers. The tradition of self-help so ensconced in African American religious history has been about the establishment of schools, community centers, orphanages, senior homes, and other places of refuge and development. The day-to-day activities in these facilities work against outside forces of oppression through education, training, and nurturance. The act of creating thus becomes their demonstration of agency. Creativity, then, *is* their form of resistance. Women who work in these places do not resist politically or with confrontation; instead, in the midst of struggle, they create lives and sustain communities and develop opportunities for success. In her work on women community workers, Cheryl Townsend Gilkes points out the ways in which black women serve and restore their communities through education and activities that affirm their social traditions and validate their history.[16] Given the obstacles these women must overcome to participate, these acts, though not always protest-oriented, are nonetheless agentive.

In trying to tease out the relationship between structure and agency, anthropologists Sherry Ortner and Nicholas Dirks along with historian

Geoff Eley expand on the idea of "practice theory."[17] This theory of practice "hold[s] together all three sides of the [theoretical] triangle: that society is a system, that the system is powerfully constraining, and yet that the system can be made and unmade through human action and interaction."[18] Examining power often causes one to see it either as a tool of the social system in recreating inequitable social relations or as a form of resistance by which people respond to oppression. The tendency to overdetermine either position decreases one's ability to see the ways structures and agents are often intimately connected in processes of power replication. Within a practice framework, there is an attempt to merge structure with agency and draw attention to the power relations that operate within social systems.[19]

In her work on evangelical women and submission, R. Marie Griffith addresses this concern by looking at the myriad ways in which women's prayer lives move them to places of submission as well as spaces of resistance.[20] Religious doctrine often encourages women to submit to pastors and husbands, who are understood as having religious authority over them. Yet while women submit, they simultaneously resist requests or petitions that appear to them antithetical to biblical principles. As women negotiate these tensions, they experience transformation. By unraveling the complexity of evangelical women's submission, Griffith works to create a theory of practice that holds together all three sides of Dirks et al.'s theoretical triangle.

Spirituality's role in resolving these theoretical tensions is recognized in its creative agency. Women respond to the day-to-day issues in their lives by transforming not only institutions, but also themselves. Thus, much of spirituality's work takes place on the public level, with women openly contesting unjust laws and practices and creating communities of love and support, as well as on the individual level, as women redefine their personal goals and boundaries, deciding with whom they will or will not engage in sexual activity and how they will or will not distribute their money.

THE BLACK PUBLIC SPHERE

Finally, Lynne's emphasis upon the type of power that the black church has to effect change in the community highlights the significance of the black public sphere. Such a sphere, where critical debate about issues relating to African American public life takes place, has historically been found in the black church.[21] Thus, the financial resources, facilities, and security of the church have all contributed to making it a central component in organizational and protest efforts. The need for the church to perform this function has been tied directly to the United States's history of racism and exclusion.

African Americans, experiencing exclusion from public debate, have historically cultivated space in black churches, women's clubs, and various social and political organizations to address openly and critically issues pertaining to themselves.[22] The black public sphere was central to the organizing efforts of African American women at the turn of the last century.[23] Such a space allowed for not only the discussion of critical issues, but also the distribution of resources and establishment of schools and care facilities in the black community. The significance of a black public sphere today, however, hinges on whether or not racism in a post–civil rights era is perceived by blacks as a real threat to African American progress. Differences in locale, economic progress, social mobility, and educational attainment each inform this perception. While many feel that racism is a major problem facing African Americans, a growing number of civic and religious leaders are beginning to reject race as an explanation for the concerns challenging African American communities. This growing conservative chorus, moved largely by calls for individual responsibility, points to the passage of civil rights laws and an expanding African American middle class as evidence that race is declining in significance. While William Julius Wilson popularized this phrase with his 1978 book focusing on the significance of class in social inequality, numerous conservative and neo-conservative thinkers, such as Shelby Steele, John McWhorter, and Thomas Sowell, along with conservative-leaning television preachers who point to the power of the holy spirit to circumvent the challenges of race, have adopted this idea to direct attention away from a need to organize around race and instead exercise personal ingenuity or faith to progress in contemporary America. Louis Farrakhan's "Million Man March" aimed at getting black men to assume "personal responsibility" for their current social condition is a key example, according to historian Robin D. G. Kelley, of the type of "culture wars" that are being fought in American politics today.[24]

Recognizing this shift, Steven Gregory and Michael Dawson, both empathetic to current challenges of racism, argue that the black public sphere reached its functional climax prior to desegregation.[25] Based on his research in New York, Gregory explains that since the seventies, the black public sphere has been reorganized and its ability to place explicit emphasis upon the problems of race has been compromised. Class restructuring along with the growth of post-1960s governmental bureau-cracies, organized to address race issues, have preempted such discus-sions.[26] The emergence of diverse ethnic communities and a focus on multiculturalism have further complicated the idea of race and racialized politics in urban centers. In these new discussions, "race," which refers to socially constructed categories based historically on a system guar-anteeing the inequitable distribution of power and economic benefit, has been subsumed by discussions of "culture," which refers more loosely to differences in history, language, religion, food, dress, and other learned ways of knowing. My own research indicates, however, that a black public sphere today in Halifax County has not been drastically reor-ganized. While some rural areas, like many urban centers, have experi-enced a substantial increase in Spanish-speaking migrant and factory workers, Halifax County and rural regions like it have not experienced the type of drastic increases in ethnic communities that would seriously reshape their historic racial demographics. Public politics are still largely framed as "black and white," although class increasingly complicates this binary.

Evidenced by the interdependence that women have with institutions like black churches, civic organizations, and grassroots activist organi-zations, black public spheres create important and effective means for women to express righteous discontent with unjust social orders. The sustainability of the black church in Halifax County as a vibrant black public sphere, however, is largely dependent upon its ability to maintain a critical discourse around race, sex, and economics in the face of com-peting discourses.

RETHINKING SPIRITUALITY

Spirituality is central to my inquiry because, for the African American women I came to know, it often motivates their social interactions and is directly connected to their everyday political and economic realities. These realities limit and define the issues they bring before God, the choices they make, and the ways in which they live out their spirituality. If religion and its constituent parts convey "order" and the saliency of social institutions, spirituality conveys creativity, the ability to invent, to reinterpret, to move beyond some of the limitations of ritual and static notions of religiosity. The agency that spirituality confers allows for ac-tive work in the public areas of life as well as the more private areas.

The way people use the term "spirituality" evokes countless ideas about what spirituality is. For some a more general understanding of spirituality focuses exclusively on the individual without a connection to institutions and institutional responsibilities. Writing about feminist spirituality, for example, Cynthia Eller explains that many (predominately white) women involved in this movement disconnect themselves from religious institutions in order to concentrate more fully on their new-found connection with the universe.[27]

This type of spirituality runs counter to the idea of spirituality held by most religious traditions, which rely on shared text, shared doctrine, and shared institutional protocol. While noting that individualism dictates many forms of Christian spirituality, Robert Wuthnow complicates the idea of spirituality in his work on Christian support groups.[28] These smaller groups, which often take the form of at-home Bible studies or before-work prayer meetings, encourage members collectively toward deeper spiritual growth by stressing the biblical text and encouraging participation in a larger church body. Nevertheless, these groups also often fall prey to what Wuthnow terms a growing form of secular spirituality:

> At one time, theologians argued that the chief purpose of humankind was to glorify God. Now it would seem that the logic has been reversed: the chief purpose of God is to glorify humankind. Spirituality no longer is true or good because it meets absolute standards of truth or goodness but because it helps us get along. We are the judge of its worth. If it helps us find a vacant parking space, we know that our spirituality is on the right track. If it leads us into the wilderness, calling on us to face dangers we would rather not deal with, then it is a form of spirituality we are unlikely to choose.[29]

In a sense what Wuthnow is questioning is the growing individualism found in various forms of Christian spirituality, the idea that the goal and aim of God is to meet individual wants and needs socially, professionally, or financially. Like more traditional Christian orthodoxy, which rejects such individualism, much of the feminist movement proper rejects the growth of feminist spirituality because it is similarly seen as apolitical and narcissistic. According to Eller, "Criticism of feminist spirituality as insufficiently political has come in several guises. Probably the most common critique is that spirituality is overly personal and can therefore never address the concerns of women as a class. Feminist spirituality is at best a waste of time and at worst a serious distraction from more important political pursuits; it may help individual women, but it does not have the power to change the status of all women."[30] These issues of individualism raise significant questions about the reach and influence of

spirituality. For the women I interviewed, nurtured in black church traditions, spirituality tries to make broad appeals to the common good of
society as well as addressing the personal needs of women. In a sense for
those who feel that their faith is becoming more focused upon themselves, there is a constant edge of concern, a feeling that they at least
"should be" doing something more for others, that their faith walk
"should include" larger sacrifices, both political and social. For others,
authentic Christian spirituality is a mandate to community involvement
and political activism. Continuously in struggle with the varied dynamics of their faith, the women that I interviewed actively work at balanc-
ing spirituality's social, political, and personal mandates in their lives.

   This idea of spirituality also moves beyond romantic notions of an exclusively political and radical black faith because it allows for what some
refer to as desires that may seem "antithetical to power"—for love, for
tenderness, for communion.[31] Women's refashioning of their world may
not always coincide with traditional interpretations of radical politics;
nevertheless, the communities they create and the life changes they inspire speak to the agentive possibilities of their faith. Historians Evelyn
Brooks Higginbotham, Judith Weisenfeld, and Bettye Collier-Thomas, in
telling the life stories of women in the nineteenth and twentieth centuries,
address the general questions of faith (the need for grace, forgiveness,
faith, and peace) in black women's lives while simultaneously wrestling
with how these issues are complicated for women living in a society that
places immediate race, gender, and class obstacles before them. Though
their writings talk about activism as a way of exploring the relationship
between women's spirituality and the public sphere throughout American history, they also try to explain women's more personal concerns
about propriety and personal responsibility. Higginbotham and Weisenfeld look at how African American women at the turn of the century
worked within the National Baptist Convention, the Black Women's
Club Movement, and the Young Women's Christian Association
(YWCA) in order to effect change within both the church and the community. Their work with poor women and children often involved building schools and orphanages and teaching women the more domestic eti-
quettes of cleanliness and wifely responsibilities. Collier-Thomas
explores the history of struggle related to women ascending to the privileged position of minister, evangelist, or pastor. Her work includes not
only histories, but also sermons of women who preached in the late nineteenth and early twentieth centuries. In their sermons these women simultaneously critiqued social ills, such as slavery, Jim Crow, and lynch-

ings, while calling for Christian men and women to live holy and pleasing lives before God. Such biographical and autobiographical accounts address issues of how African American women have "made decisions, how their religious and moral values informed their participation in social issues, and how their spirituality interacted with their social conscience."[32]

These works, in exploring the activist nature of black women's faith, wrestle with the influence that the women's faith has on the less public areas of their lives, often their experiences as wives and mothers, where tangible and overt forms of power are less noticeable. In the pursuit of "respectability" in a society that deemed black women hyper-sexual jezebels or asexual matriarchs,[33] the Black Women's Club Movement of the early 1900s interjected key dialogue about marriage and sexuality which at the time served to redeem black womanhood from derogatory white social commentary. These issues, though seemingly private, weigh heavily in any discussion of black women's experience in a race- and gender-conscious United States. This more personal dynamic of women's lives is crucial in a holistic evaluation of faith. How does one's faith influence one's activism from without as well as one's activism from within?

Whereas Higginbotham, Weisenfeld, and Collier-Thomas explore the historic significance of spirituality in women's lives, this book looks at the role of spirituality in the lives of contemporary women. Given the close relationship between spirituality and activism in the history of black faith, how is this relationship manifested in the lives of contemporary believers whose experiences with unjust systems fall more under what sociologist Howard Winant calls a regime of racial hegemony—where racism is less overt—as opposed to one of racial dominance—where racism manifests itself in open displays of hostility and hatred?[34] How might the more personal dynamics of women's spirituality—those relating to marriage, family, and finances—demonstrate new forms of activism or old forms of gender oppression? Ultimately, how *does* spirituality inform women's experiences in a raced, classed, and gendered society such as the United States today?

SPIRITUALITY IN PRACTICE

Although literature on spirituality in the African American context of Christianity is largely focused on the political dynamics of faith, I argue that spirituality for the women I interviewed is more than a source of cultural identity and a means of expressing political allegiance, though both themes emerge in their life stories. Spirituality is about living through moments of struggle and moments of peace and ultimately acquiring a better life, a life that is filled with a deeper knowledge of God. This better life comes from the onset of not only public political confrontation but also personal affirmation and development over time. In setting the works of scholars of African American faith against interpretations of African American women's stories, I aim to show their areas of overlap and establish an understanding of spirituality sufficiently nuanced to interpret these women's lives and life experiences.

Spirituality is a process of engagement with God that informs the thoughts, motivations, and actions of individuals. There is a difference between religion or "religiosity" and "spirituality" as defined by the women that I interviewed. Though the two are not mutually exclusive, they ultimately convey different meanings. Unlike religion, which is often seen as embedded in structures and repetitive ritual practices, spirituality conveys process. Spirituality evokes the idea of maturation over time, not simply repetitive religious engagement. These women I know develop depths of spirituality over time and in relationship to the various circumstances of their lives. Spirituality is thus not something that just happens at a certain age and remains the same forever. Instead, it is a process that ebbs and flows with the development of individuals.

For the women I interviewed, spirituality is personal and experiential. It is, as one of them put it, that which "comes from inside the person and it's a reflection of how they live." Spirituality, said another, is reflected in a "person that's aware, a person that cares, a person that tries to practice being a Christian." It encompasses a process of thought, concern, and action that affirms one's identity as a Christian. One who is spiritual possesses a knowledge of "the Word," "what the Word says," and an awareness of the community and its concerns. Along with knowledge, "concern" is a recurring theme. One who is spiritual is concerned about others and is especially concerned about what God thinks. Finally, spirituality consists of action, reflected in how one treats others and how one follows "the direction of the Holy Spirit."[35]

Without any one of these components, one is simply religious but not spiritual. As Sylvia Jones, one of my respondents, explained, religious people "are the ones that's always, 'Praise the Lord. Hallelujah!' And will talk about you before you leave their presence." For her, when one's actions contradict what one has spoken, one is merely religious, thus demonstrating a lack of genuine concern for the individual. Likewise,

Carmen Moore spoke of religiosity as routine. "Religious to me is just going through the motions. You know, you are affiliated with this church. Some people say they're Baptists. Some people say they're Methodist . . . But, to me, you can be religious about going to church. You can be religious about getting involved in things in the church." Marie Carter reiterated a similar concern, comparing religiosity to her work schedule. "Religion is like I get up and go to work religiously *every* day—and you know routine. Religious I look at as routine. Spiritual is when you worship; you worship Him in spirit and in truth. Religion is something totally different."[36] In each of these scenarios the absence of a genuine concern about God and the things of God results in the routinization of religious practices.

It can be assumed that the presence of concern and action in the absence of knowledge can lead to empathetic activity but not to the acknowledgment of God necessary for spirituality. As Gloria McKnight told me, "I became spiritual about two years ago because I was in the church. I did the thing that 'Christian' people are supposed to do. You know religious people do this. But, I didn't have God in my heart." Likewise, the presence of thought and concern without action invalidates the earnestness of one's commitment to spirituality. As Carmen Moore suggested, "Faith without works is dead!"

"Religion," according to theologian Flora Wilson Bridges, "teaches humankind to appreciate God's love; but spirituality challenges human beings to directly experience the transformative power of God's love . . . Religion may enlighten the mind, but spirituality converts the entire existence."[37] This type of spirituality requires a mind, soul, and body connection, where the body acts out what it knows mentally and spiritually. Therefore, missing from the women's understandings is any reference to institutional practice. The women focus on the individual as bearer of that which is spiritual, not the church, nor rituals of the church. This is not to underplay the significance of the church in their spiritual development. Rather it emphasizes the significance of the individual believer's experience and actions once church is over.

Knowledge, concern, and action are central to any understanding of how these women respond to particular situations in their lives. True spirituality will involve all three elements. While spirituality for these women intersects with feminist spirituality in its search for a better understanding of self and a larger connection to the Creator, it in obvious ways stands apart from critical interpretations of feminist spirituality. For the women I interviewed in Halifax, spirituality is rooted in the biblical text and relies heavily upon shared notions of Christian orthodoxy. Furthermore, it means a constant wrestling with how one becomes active in and engaged with the larger society. Withdrawal for them is not an option. It further reflects women who, in the midst of struggle themselves, engage in struggle for others. They are not women of excessive privilege. Further, their ideas contrast with the secular spirituality that Wuthnow critiques. Although the women are not always removed from similar preoccupations with how God can specifically benefit their family, their finances, or their employment, largely because of their locale, they maintain an overall concern with the experiences of those in their community. The complexity of concerns that Higginbotham, Weisenfeld, and Collier-Thomas discuss demonstrates the dynamic nature of these women's experiences as black women of faith.

SPIRITUALITY IN CONTEXT

Spirituality is specific to particular groups—such as these African American women—when it is informed by shared historical or ritual experiences. It is informed first by an individual's relationship with God—nurtured by religious doctrine, holy scriptures, pastors, televangelists, and other mediators of faith. It is further informed by historical traditions—learned understandings of what it means to serve God. Finally, spirituality is informed by social relations—one's positioning in society, which in the United States is inevitably raced, classed, and gendered. These three contributing elements form vast and complicated systems through which women navigate their spiritual experiences.

In regard to an individual's relationship with God there exists a shared text, the Bible, and shared ritual practices, which create a Christian understanding of spirituality. This spirituality, however, is not homogeneous because of the varied ways in which people interpret scripture in order to inform or validate their positions. The complex of Christian denominations—Methodist, Baptist, Pentecostal, Presbyterian, Adventist, each with its own particular doctrines—bears witness to this fact. An individual's relationship with God is thus often negotiated in a filtering process through which one discerns that which is God, that which is self, and that which is the product of one's surroundings. In recent years the proliferation of "how to" material on building a relationship with God has created an amalgam of possibilities. The Bible and the preacher—previously believed to be the primary purveyors of faith—now compete with vast assortments of books, tapes, and television programming which create doctrinal and theological labyrinths. For women developing their relationship with God and understanding themselves as social actors, this contemporary environment creates a multifaceted worship experience that leads to constant reconstruction of their spiritual lives.

Historical traditions further inform women's spiritual lives by giving them a standard against which to measure their spiritual progress. These historical traditions are both personal and collective. In some women's personal lives, testimonies about how they came to know God as a child or their childhood experiences in church form much of their understanding. For others who develop their spiritual lives at later ages, their stories begin with "Well I didn't go to church as a child, but . . ." These women point to the avenues through which they were introduced to the church and how this experience may differentiate them from someone who grew up "in the church."

Collective histories include assumptions passed down about what it means to serve God, how one should behave in church, and what types of activities one should engage in as a believer. The history of black church activism thus inevitably informs women's understandings of what they should or should not do within and outside the public realm. These ideas establish guidelines for them to measure the success or failure of their particular church. It was not uncommon to hear women complain that their churches were not involved "enough." These women have high expectations regarding what they as individuals and the church as a collective should be doing in the community.

Finally, social conditions are the primary backdrop against which I understand women's notions of spirituality. Exploring the dynamics of racism, sexism, and classism at the turn of the twenty-first century helps us discern the forms of activism embedded in the spirituality that these women practice. Patricia Hill Collins argues that although African American women may all experience the intersecting oppressions of gender, race, and often class, their responses are varied. "The existence of core themes [race, class, and gender oppressions] does not mean that African American women respond to these themes in the same way. Diversity among black women produces different concrete experiences that in turn shape various reactions to the core themes."[38]

Deborah King articulates this diversity in terms of the concept of "multiple jeopardy." "'Multiple' refers not only to several, simultaneous oppressions but also to the multiplicative relationships among them. In other words, the equivalent formulation is racism multiplied by sexism multiplied by classism."[39] King's writing informs and challenges previous models that mainly focused upon race and gender oppressions and complicates the assumption that these oppressions occur in linear fashion. She suggests that "the relative significance of race, sex, or class in determining the conditions of black women's lives is neither fixed nor absolute but, rather, is dependent on the socio-historical context and the social phenomenon under consideration."[40]

I discuss the role of spirituality in the lives of the African American women I interviewed in light of these interactive models. Their responses to race, class, and gender politics are fixed neither by the innate nature of their identities, nor by the assumption of any monolithic set of rules that apply to spirituality. Nevertheless, a common thread binds their experiences in that all of the women encounter the politics of interrelated identities on a lived basis and draw from a spirituality rooted in the transcendent power of Christ as they navigate through their lives.

Spirituality is as much about the personal life as it is about public life. For the women I interviewed, spirituality pertains to the political matters of voting for qualified representatives and attending public meetings as well as to the personal matters of tithing, attending to elderly neighbors, and maintaining family relations. When one considers the nature of family relationships and the assumptions embedded therein as well as the societal influences upon these relations, it is evident that "the personal," as feminist studies note, "is political." The women I interviewed, however, rarely spoke about spirituality as synonymous with activism. In fact, they rarely spoke of themselves as activists. Instead, they saw themselves as "active in their church" or "helpful towards others," and rarely spontaneously appropriated the term "activism" in and of itself. Their insights challenge previous notions of spirituality by complicating the assumption that African American religious practice is amenable to simple characterization by motives of either protest or accommodation. Spirituality is not only about the political negotiated within the public sphere. It is also about the everyday negotiated within the private sphere.

ETHNOGRAPHIC POSITIONING

Limited scholarship has been done on the impact that African American religion has on the *everyday* lives of women like Juanita Cleveland, Sylvia Jones, and Yvette Stephens, three of the women I interviewed. In studying African American religion, most scholars have studied "the black church," or the impact of the religion as a whole on society. They have not as a rule focused on individual members of churches. When they do, scholars tend to chronicle the lives of *prominent* individual members, such as Howard Thurmond, Martin Luther King Jr., or Benjamin E. Mays, rather than everyday practitioners of the faith.

While much work has been done chronicling the lives of these elite figures and the history of the "black church,"[41] works focusing specifically on African American women within this church tradition have emerged only recently. Most of these works have come from theology, literature, and history. Womanist theologians, for example, have created a literature that looks specifically at the influence of prominent women within church communities.[42] Other scholars have examined specific social movements and noticed the intersection between women's faith and their involvement in these movements.[43] What is missing from this literature, however, is an ethnography that examines the ways in which contemporary African American women negotiate their day-to-day spiritual strivings. This work attempts to provide such an intervention based upon ethnographic research conducted among women of faith in Halifax County, North Carolina.

Recent criticisms in anthropology identify numerous shortcomings in the standard practice of writing ethnography.[44] Scholars criticize the notion of the "detached observer," one who merely writes about a particular society without any reference to his or her emotional or ideological commitments. Such criticisms arise largely out of anthropology's history of studying remote and distant societies in order to produce scientific documentation of these societies' functioning. Recent anthropology, largely informed by feminist and postcolonial critiques, has attempted to rewrite this style not only by altering the ethnographic form but also by raising questions about the very nature of anthropology's focus, "remote" societies. One response has been a turn toward analyzing one's own culture and thus establishing a type of native anthropology.

In their edited volume *Women Writing Culture* Ruth Behar and Deborah Gordon, along with their contributors, give constructive criticism of (largely white and male-dominated) anthropological history. They cite the ways in which women ethnographers are reclaiming a type of native anthropology relevant to the life experiences of women. Writing as a contributor to the volume, Graciela Hernández examines not only the extent to which African American women have been ethnographers, but also the extent to which they have written against the ethnographic grain that assumes the need for a detached observer. Her analysis of the work of Zora Neale Hurston points specifically to how women of color have studied their own cultures and have made rich and invaluable contributions to the field of anthropology.[45]

These critics also suggest that the notion of ethnographic "truth" is the greatest of misnomers. If there exists any grain of reliability in the ethnographic text, it must come, they argue, from the author's immediate and up-front acknowledgment of her limitations and of her ability to encapsulate only "partial truths." Though her research may be detailed and nuanced, it is also selective and narrowly focused upon her research agenda. James Clifford and George Marcus argue that "even the best ethnographic texts—serious, true fictions—are systems, or economies, of truth. Power and history work through them, in ways their authors cannot fully control . . . Ethnographic truths are thus inherently *partial*— committed and incomplete."[46]

In endorsing this view, I thus need to make clear my own biases. As a practitioner of the faith, I made my inquiry into the spiritual lives of women in a deliberate effort to unpack the dynamics of a lived experience that I have witnessed since childhood. My earliest memories of the Christian faith and church are enmeshed with the lives of a plethora of women. Certainly men were present and men were active, but the women in the church lend me the greatest sense of recall. I remember these women as if they are present today. Their lives and dispositions were always varied. They were the ones who took care of bereaved families and prepared for the repast after a funeral or provided dinner after a special Sunday service. Mrs. Evans was extremely mean. In my home church she ran the kitchen and insisted that no one besides her and the kitchen staff enter. Miss Laura some folks called "crazy." According to Mama, she could never quite get it right after her parents died. I vaguely remember her interacting with the other women of the church before her parents' deaths, but most of my memory is of conversations that my mother had about her being checked into a home, or how she was staying in her parents' home without electricity or blankets. We would stop by on occasion—like other members of the church—to make sure that she had sufficient food, or blankets and a coat for the winter. Mrs. McKay, a tall, big-bosomed woman, had a very distinct voice. Although the rest of us sang hymns, she sang as though she were performing for the opera. After I graduated from high school and left for college, my mother called one day and told me that Mrs. McKay's son had come to move her to Tennessee with him and his family. Because she had been a widow for numerous years, they wanted her closer to them as she aged. Mrs. Goodine was always old, ever since I can remember. She wrote beautiful poetry and gave marvelous recitations. I never forgot the time she recited for the church during one of our annual Women's Day services a poem about growing old. Her refrain, "My get up and go, don' got up and went!" had the church in stitches. My sister and I mimicked her for days, laughing at her stark humor. These were the older women we knew.

The women my mother's age seemed less visible, but not because they were absent. Indeed, they sang in the choir, served as ushers and Sunday school teachers. However, this was not our main reason for seeing and interacting with them. We didn't sing in the adult choir, nor were we members of the adult usher board. Our interest was in their children. We simply wanted to know if Nolita and Lamont, Kristen, James, Kiesha, Chris, and Maxine had come with them to choir rehearsal so that we could play during their long meetings. The sanctuary, however, was forbidden for play because it was a holy place. In fact, it was even considered inappropriate for women to wear pants in the sanctuary for choir rehearsal and there was no "walking across the pulpit." This was sacred space for ordained clergy only—and the deaconess who changed the water pitcher and made sure there was a clean glass for the preacher on Sunday.

Then there was Mrs. Randolph, "the first lady of the church." I remember Mama saying that it "seems like Mrs. Randolph would wear a hat at least sometime." Hats then signified status, a standing apart with dignity that older women held. Though stockings and dresses were standard attire for all women, hats seemed of special significance for those who were older and those who held important church positions. For Mrs. Randolph to not wear a hat must have communicated to some that she had a complete disregard for her position, or at least a disregard for how they viewed her position. Whatever her "role," I knew it was special, but to me she was just sweet Mrs. Randolph, the woman with all the hugs I'd ever want and all the candy we could enjoy. She taught our Sunday school class and helped the children's choir prepare for our second Sunday debuts. We would come dressed in our choir uniforms, white shirts and navy blue skirts for girls and pants for boys, and with our hair freshly pressed or at least braided (for my mother). Having well rehearsed, we were ready to render to the congregation our mini-concert, two songs before the offering and one just before the pastor's sermon. "I Want to be a Sunbeam for Jesus" was our favorite song.

As I matured, so did my understanding of the women in my church. They were no longer confined by the simple descriptions of my childhood imagination, "nice," "mean," "crazy"; nor were their experiences limited to the categories convenient for my childhood mind, "wife of the pastor," "cook," "mother of Nolita." Instead their lives yielded new complexity. They were working women—inside and outside of their homes—women impacted by the economic restructuring taking place in the South and the rest of the country, Southern women defining and redefining locality, effecting and being affected by political change.

Most peculiar to my realization is the fact that they were women whose church experience and whose understandings of this experience informed many of the facets of their lives. They seemed to talk about God *more* as I got older. They seemed to talk about prayer *more* and faith *more* as I got older. Somehow they linked and intertwined these concepts with the varied aspects of their lives. They talked about God and work, faith and family, prayer and community. Yet, maybe it wasn't time that changed them, so much as my own development over time. I began to hear with new understanding.

Certainly, the eyes of a child see in ways that are peculiar to her or his positioning in the world. What is obvious to children is sometimes hidden from adults and what is clear to adults is frequently baffling for children. Position and positionality are key. Clifford and Marcus are correct in arguing that positionality informs one's data and thus ultimately influences one's interpretations. "Partial truths," truths that come from one's own vantage point and one's own collective set of information, are the best that we as ethnographers can ascertain.

While conducting research, I came to realize the "paradox" of these partial truths. Because of my background in the church, I was in position to see clearly into the mysteries of my research topic; yet, at the same time, I was in a corresponding position to "miss" the objective nature of my study. My personal belief in God and the resurrection of Jesus allowed me to see and understand in many instances the leaps and walks of faith that believers practiced. However, the activities of faith bear tangible, sociological consequences, which if unexamined can go unnoticed. As both an insider to the faith that informs these women's lives and a critical scholar, I attempted to make observations from "two sides of the coin," sides seen by some as mutually exclusive. In other words, I was forced to wrestle with the question of how one holds faith and reason in balance. When the two conflict, which side wins and for what audiences? Can both faith and reason exist simultaneously in this quest for knowledge?

The experience of my childhood and the dynamics of my own faith journey point ultimately to the type of ethnographic work that women of color in anthropology have been conducting for decades, the type of anthropology that is part autobiography, part ethnography, or "autoethnography." In their compilation of essays, entitled *Black Feminist Anthropology,* editor Irma McClaurin and other black female anthropologists outline the methodological and theoretical benefits and challenges that come to fore when conducting research in communities that resemble one's own.[47] Their insights force us, as anthropologists, to write more honest ethnographies, as well as more socially responsible ethnographies, taking seriously the life and life experiences of women of color in the United States and the African Diaspora. By positioning themselves within the text, ethnographers are able to explore the combinations of power and agency operating in women's lives.

In addition to the personal tensions my research raises, I found both benefits and limitations to conducting research from the perspective of an insider. During my months of field research, the limitations were most evident in the type of information that was given. Drawing out details of women's salvation experiences and why they believe was at times difficult because they assumed my knowledge of the subject and my ability to translate their tenets of faith. They did not feel compelled to explain what salvation is or how they received it. In many cases I had to ask detailed questions in order to gain an outsider's understanding. Many women also assumed my comprehension of their personal theology or the role of the church in their lives. Granted some of this information is known, but how they articulate their experience and why they as individuals adhere to certain doctrines are important for systematic analysis.

There were, however, benefits to serving as both an observer and an active participant. When I visited worship services, I was often familiar with the style and practice of worship. In addition, speaking with people and understanding their ceremonial language was not difficult, or dislocating. When greeted with "Praise the Lord" or "God is good," I was comfortable in reciprocating with my own praises to God. These responses often curtailed suspicions about who I was and whether I was a believer.

Salutations alone, however, could not secure entry into a small and intimate community of people that did not know me. The women whom I interviewed hold membership in several different Baptist churches in Halifax County. In these churches, as in most, social relations are key in establishing contact with people. Some of the women I met had no prior knowledge of me or my research. I was not formally introduced to them. I simply appeared in their church one Sunday and attended their weekly

Bible study where we eventually met. Other women were introduced to me during the course of my research with the North Carolina Public Spheres Project. This collaborative research project brought me to Halifax County and served as my initial introduction into the social, political, and economic conditions of the area.

METHODOLOGY

My field research in Halifax County was divided into two major periods. The lengthier portion was conducted through my work on the North Carolina Public Spheres Project, which is based in the Anthropology Department at the University of North Carolina at Chapel Hill. This research extended over an eleven-month period between March 1997 and February 1998. The second portion of my research was conducted during the summer of 1998 with the assistance of a Race and Gender research award from the Women's Studies Program at Duke University. I spent this time focusing specifically on spirituality in the lives of some of the people that I had come to know during the first half of my research.

The Public Spheres Project, funded by the National Science Foundation, looked at the impact of economic restructuring on forms of democracy in North Carolina. The project explored the political economy of North Carolina, the ways in which the public sphere is defined, and the levels of inclusion and exclusion of persons based upon the categories of race, class, and gender. Through library research, attendance and participation at public meetings, and interviews with over sixty residents of Halifax County, I gathered material on public sphere activism and the political economy of the county. Over the course of the year, I attended bi-monthly meetings of the county commissioners, monthly meetings of the three county school boards (Halifax County, Weldon City, and Roanoke Rapids boards), weekly meetings of the Concerned Citizens of Tillery (a grassroots social change organization), and quarterly meetings of the Runnymede Community Association (a local association working for adequate water and sewer systems in its area). I also volunteered for CCT, aiding the members in writing their newsletter, facilitating mass mailings, organizing meetings and their annual conference on black land loss. Volunteering with CCT played an invaluable role in helping me to grapple with the issues affecting Southerners who live in rural locations.

This research informed my project by elucidating the larger context of the lives of the women I interviewed. Over the same period of time, I attended weekly Sunday morning worship services at numerous churches throughout the county. In addition, I attended the weekly Bible study for two of these churches. It was here that I came to know several of the women I later interviewed. I participated in both the vacation Bible study and the monthly prayer service held by one church and interviewed some of the women that I became acquainted with during these meetings.

While participation and observation are central to my research, in-depth interviews form the bulk of my data. During the week, I conducted interviews for the Public Spheres Project. These interviews included twenty "drama of contestation," ten "lifetime participation," ten "lifetime non-participation," and twenty "informal" interviews.[48]

The second portion of my research, conducted in August 1998, included more in-depth interviews with women and pastors about religious practice. I chose August because it is Homecoming Month for most of the churches in Halifax County, a time when family and friends who have moved away return to celebrate their church's anniversary. This timing allowed me to attend several of their annual revivals in addition to the weekly Sunday morning services. I conducted informal interviews with several women and pastors during this time, then narrowed my in-depth interview pool to eight women. Narrowing my focus enabled me to do a more thorough examination of each woman's experience of faith over the course of her life.

My initial goal was to choose women who demonstrate a profound commitment to the life of the Spirit. Yet, establishing a criterion for determining this requirement was difficult at best. Instead, I relied on something less profound, women's willingness to talk with me and their demonstrated interest in institutions associated with God (i.e., church, Bible study, and auxiliary ministries). Both factors helped me assess their level of spiritual commitment. In the end, however, it was their openness in talking about the life of the Spirit that contributed most to the success of my research. They welcomed my inquiries and spoke with enthusiasm about what they believe God is doing in their lives. They also spoke candidly about their failures and successes on their journey. I am grateful for their willingness to trust me with their life stories.

During this phase of the research, I conducted long semi-structured interviews. I used a structured set of questions to ascertain each woman's age, marital status, educational background, present occupation, and year that she joined her church. However, I used more open-ended questions to gather information about the women's spiritual journeys. For example, I asked them to "tell me about your conversion experience." This question allowed each woman to clarify first whether or not she has had

a "conversion experience," and if so, the process that she engaged in
order to complete it. I also asked each woman to tell me about a time
when she felt that she had to draw upon her spirituality for guidance.
This left each woman open to talk about work, family, or other experiences that significantly affected her Christian development without my
assuming a priori what these experiences may have been. In a majority
of cases, women talked about issues pertaining to their families. Each interview lasted approximately two to three hours. These women, their life
stories, and my interaction with them for over a year form the basis of
my analysis. Needless to say, their lives, though varied, are intertwined
within the social network of Halifax County and the public spheres issues on which I conducted research as part of the North Carolina Public Spheres research group.

OVERVIEW

The chapters in *Between Sundays* explore the spiritual lives of women
from one Sabbath to the next. Thus, each chapter bears the name of a
day of the week, alluding to the possibilities of what any given woman
could be faced with on any given day. On Monday I situate the women
I interviewed within the social and economic history of their communities. Changes in the political economy of Halifax County are not gov-
erned exclusively by this region of northeastern North Carolina or by
North Carolina generally, but are intimately connected to national and
international trends. These trends often influence local politics, public
school decisions, and economic development. I discuss these current
trends in light of notions of "progress" set forth by business and government leaders. This discussion illuminates the problems and contradictions of economic development and politics in Halifax and their effect on the social life of its citizens. Although discourses of progress
dominate much of the public domain, "progress" does not necessarily
describe the lived experience of a large section of the populace, which is
largely made up of poor people and people of color. My discussion addresses the issues that influence my informants' lives and the lives of
people in their communities.

On Tuesday I look at how spirituality operates as a transformative
power in women's interactions with others. I argue that women's expressions of spirituality range from gratitude and empathy to righteous
discontent. Gratitude arises from the ability to perceive a spiritual reality
beyond the material world. This expression generates hope in the midst

of despair and thanksgiving in the midst of fortune. But while it might generate hope, gratitude does not necessarily result in active community engagement. It is the feeling of empathy that allows people to express compassion for those in the community. Living in an area largely burdened with poverty, the women engage in activities such as elder care and the nurturing of teenagers, to meet the immediate needs of those dispossessed. Yet, when they aid women and children in the area who need assistance, are these actions merely "accommodating" to systems of oppression, by not overtly confronting the systems that perpetuate such inequality?

On Wednesday I wrestle with what is commonly understood as resistance and the experiences of women who go to the heart of institutional practices and demand change. I suggest that women's level of activity in the larger public is contingent upon their ability to channel righteous discontent with the prevailing social order into a viable, responsive alternative public sphere. For most, a black public sphere located historically in the black church forms this space. Other spaces, like the Concerned Citizens of Tillery, have also been created to help facilitate this political involvement. Tuesday and Wednesday, thus, mutually address the question of accommodation and resistance in public life. How do women's interactions with others conform to and contradict the paradigm of accommodation and resistance set forth by scholars of African American religion? My research reveals that women struggle with this tension, though rarely employing the terminology. They talk instead about their history in and present commitments to the Civil Rights Movement, their experiences with job-related racism, their attempts to protect their granddaughters from sexual assault, their fight to keep their neighborhoods free of industrial pollution, and the challenges facing senior citizens in their community. Their spirituality leads them to view their lives as ongoing commitments to the lives of those in their community.

On Thursday I look at the shifting nature of the black public sphere in the African American community, particularly in relation to the black church. Given on the one hand Steven Gregory's analysis of the "restructuring" of the black public sphere in inner-city New York and, on the other, Evelyn Higginbotham's assertion of the historical significance of the black church to women's activism, how should one rank the black church's role as a significant alternative public in the contemporary South? Moreover, in today's high-tech, transnational world of television ministries, does the black church and its message of liberation carry the same type of authority historians have traditionally ascribed to it? The introduction of television ministries is creating a black church that is as much influenced by the Sunday-to-Sunday service that worshippers watch on television as it is by the Sunday morning worship service. While this medium often encourages forms of personal empowerment in the world, it is also dominated by themes of individualism, materialism, and a form of multiculturalism that elides a serious critique of racism.

With the influence of television ministries, women's sense of spiritual commitment is as much centered on the transformation of the individual as on the transformation of society. While on Tuesday and Wednesday I discuss the ways in which spirituality affects women's engagements with others and their responses to social systems, on Friday and Saturday I discuss the fact that much of the transformative power of spirituality lies in its ability to influence individual women's more intimate renegotiations of self. Management of personal income (giving, tithing) and views of sexual intimacy (abstinence, fidelity) are central to these renegotiations. Financial management reflects gratitude for God's benevolence, whereas intimacy reflects the value placed on the body as the temple of God. Although these changes affect others, they are not spurred by desires to affect others, but rather by desires to change oneself, or acknowledge changes one believes God has made within.[49]

The forms of activism studied range from public and overt forms of protest/revolution to more subtle forms of resistance. The women I interviewed were at differing phases in the process of changing themselves and their communities. Their struggle and their experience with power often center on a reconfiguration of self that also implies a reconfiguration of society.

Interspersed throughout the text are "revivals." In the traditional church sense of the word, revival is a time where old, decaying situations are rejuvenated with life, where people, those who have "backslidden" and those who have become complacent from the monotony of church work, are renewed and inspired. I use this term as a metaphor for the type of writing that distinguishes these short vignettes. During "revival," I write more openly and expressively about the types of day-to-day exchanges that I had with the women, many of whom became friends and confidants. These "revivals," I hope, bring to life their realities in a way that elicits greater appreciation for the complexity of these women's spiritual lives.

How we understand African American religion is significant because it speaks to a number of different ways of conceptualizing power. Traditional ideas which focus on other-worldly models have proven insufficient in evaluating the lives of believers. Revisionist work is challenged by the emergence of a media theology that focuses almost exclusively on individual transformation with less regard to overt social protest and resistance. To evaluate African American religious practice thus requires a more nuanced approach, one that looks at spirituality as the intersection of individual transformation and social protest—one that acknowledges the profound agency of individuals, as well as the limits of that agency, in deconstructing, creating, and recreating social realities.

My focus upon spirituality in the anthropological study of religion is a response to the relative absence of discussion about the power of the nonmaterial world over the material world. Studies in power which deal only with the dynamics of race, class, and gender often miss such important facets of people's lives. Thus, to study the lives of the women that I interviewed without also studying the role of spirituality in their lives would be to miss a key component of their motivation for acting in the world. Spirituality helps us to gain a more complex understanding of religion as well as a more complex understanding of power.

STRANGE MEETINGS

With her Bible left open to her scripture of meditation for the morning, Ms. Cleveland hurried out the door to begin her twenty-five-minute commute to work. She works in a county adjacent to Halifax as a clerical assistant in one of the county offices. She has been commuting from her modest three-bedroom home in Weldon every day for about ten years, ever since her husband passed.

It had been about seven months since I completed the final stages of my research, and upon my departing Ms. Cleveland told me that I was welcome to stay with her any time I came back to the area. Unfortunately, an occasion came all too soon. I had come to town the night before for Aunt Eula's homegoing service. She died earlier in the week from a massive asthma attack. Aunt Eula and Uncle Charles had adopted me into their family from the beginning of my time in Halifax County. I came over for meals, went shopping with Aunt Eula, stayed up late at night talking about family, church, and relationships. I stayed with Aunt Eula and Uncle Charles during the summer while I conducted follow-up interviews for this project. Aunt Eula gave great advice and listened exceptionally well. We talked about everything from family to church to sex. Ours was an open relationship. Although she never had children of her own, countless people considered her a surrogate mother, and for some like me, she was like a grandmother. Although she was in her late seventies, her death was both a great shock and a tremendous loss.

For most in this area there is little challenge given to the notion of life after death or the existence of a creator God. One's funeral is only a comma in the cycle of life. Everlasting life begins after one has departed the physical body to spend eternity at home with God. During church services, I have even heard some worshippers boldly thank God for their being in the "land of the dying" on their way to the "land of the living." Aunt Eula's was truly a *homegoing* service.

This particular visit to Halifax County demonstrated to me again the interconnectedness of the women I interviewed. I met all eight of them in different settings, but their lives were not separate and unrelated. In fact, they are joined in unexpected ways through various social activities and church meetings.

The morning was slow. Ms. Cleveland's orderly and peaceful home provided just the respite I needed to deal with the challenges of the weekend. She wanted me to sleep in that morning because of my travel the day before and because we had stayed up talking long after both of our bedtimes. In spite of our late night, her television came on at 6 A.M., interrupting what was for me a sound night's rest. The morning news stayed on for at least an hour as I tossed trying to find the quickest avenue back to sleep. Mississippi senators are trying to find a way to reduce the number of teenage pregnancies. Donna Shalala is in China, criticizing the Chinese government for human rights violations. They in turn rebuked U.S. human rights violations. The weather will be sunny, but cool, mid 50s. Then, silence. For twenty minutes I thought she'd left the house. When the television returned to its original volume, I realized that she'd only turned it off to have her morning "quiet" time with the Lord.

The first Sunday I stood up in Shiloh Baptist Church in Weldon as a visitor was the Sunday I met Juanita Cleveland. I had only been in town for a couple of weeks, but when I met her I felt as though I had known her for years. Her small frame and exuberant personality seemed a contradiction, such power coming from such a tiny body. She came up immediately after service to welcome me to her church. As I accepted her welcome, she immediately proceeded to ask me what brought me to the area. I told her that I was conducting some work for a project at UNC–Chapel Hill, but that I wanted to attend a church while I was in the area and several people suggested Shiloh Baptist. She gladly accepted my explanation and continued the conversation by inviting me to Bible study on Thursday nights. That Thursday I went.

When I walked in the door, Ms. Cleveland was in the front leading the devotional time. She smiled and acknowledged me as a visitor to the eleven or twelve people present. Compared to the church's large Sunday morning services, Thursday night Bible study is somewhat small and intimate. This intimacy allowed me a greater opportunity to talk with some of the other members and interact more closely with Ms. Cleveland. Though she is at least a generation older than I am, our conversations over the next several months led to a friendship that produced a willingness on her part to share with me the dynamics of her faith walk.

Ms. Cleveland did not attend Aunt Eula's funeral because she thought she did not know her. Only after I returned that evening with a copy of the obituary did she realize that she did "know" Aunt Eula. She'd seen her "probably at one of the church services around here." The funeral service was beautiful. Friends viewed the body before the family procession inside the church. After all were seated, only standing room remained. Because seating was limited, I did not sit with the family. Instead I sat with Ms. Sylvia, who had come along to support me.

I met Ms. Sylvia during my first visit to Halifax County, while those of us involved with the UNC project were making our final decisions about counties in which to conduct research. We knew of the work Ms. Sylvia's organization, the Concerned Citizens of Tillery (CCT), was doing protesting corporate hog "farming," organizing to help save black farmland, providing healthcare for seniors, and forming coalitions with other grassroots organizations. When three of us from the project arranged a meeting with CCT organizers and drove up to their office, Ms. Sylvia was the first to greet us, arms open wide. While George, the director, seemed more concerned about our research agenda, Ms. Sylvia took greater interest in learning about us. "Where are you from?" "How long have you been in the area?" The conversation flowed easily. My relationship with Ms. Sylvia grew over the course of my subsequent research and volunteer work at CCT. For several months, I wrote articles, critiqued letters and news briefs, prepared mail, picked up seniors for meetings—all the time working alongside Ms. Sylvia.

When I saw her once again at the funeral, she was disheartened by my loss. Although Ms. Sylvia had more than enough work to do, after learning of Aunt Eula's passing she wanted to attend the funeral. "Friends mean more than work," she explained. So, she drove thirty minutes from Scotland Neck to sit and hold my hand. I couldn't help but remember her telling me that "folks in this county will put a baby's birth on hold to attend a funeral." I was glad that she put whatever it was on hold to sit with me. I cried a river. After a while, I ceased wiping tears and allowed the water to simply roll down my cheeks. Ms. Sylvia hugged me and told me that it would be okay. She'd only met Aunt Eula once when she came over to the house for our interview, but she knew how special she was to me. She had seen us together!

From the moment they met, the conversation between Aunt Eula and Ms. Sylvia was nonstop as they learned of their shared struggle with breast cancer. Aunt Eula told about her mastectomy; Ms. Sylvia, her lumpectomy. They discussed the devastation that followed and the strength they had to discover in order to proceed with life. I was taken by the detail they gave to such a "private" surgery. Only in the last few years has there been direct public attention to the issue of breast cancer and the number of women who battle it. Even the pastor of the church could not bring himself to say the words "breast cancer" as he gave Aunt Eula's eulogy. He spoke instead of how she was such a source of encouragement, particularly to women who'd experienced the same type of "women's surgery" that she had. Aunt Eula had given other women hope.

After the funeral, I introduced Ms. Sylvia to some of the people I knew from Aunt Eula's church. She soon left and I went to the interment that followed in the church cemetery. The cemetery was located at the end of a dirt path leading from the back door of the church. It is obvious that the site was once a quiet haven, a place of solemn mourning, before the interstate was built. Now, the noise from the freeway almost overshadowed the respectful transference of Aunt Eula's remains.

The sadness of the interment for me was calmed only by memories of Aunt Eula saying that she would one day "go home to be with the Master!" Her use of the term "master" was in no way connected with an earthly master. She was referring to God, Master of the universe, the one who had walked with her through this earthly life and would one day embrace her in the life to come.

The burial was quick. The pastor reminded us that we would all return "ashes to ashes and dust to dust." The family placed roses on the casket and prayer was offered by one of the ministers. Back inside the church, the atmosphere took on a different feel. I remembered Ms. Moore, one of the women from Tillery, once stating how African American funerals are always followed by the "repast." "Folks always want to know 'where you gonna feed?'" Aunt Eula with her foresight and zeal for life had let everyone know how she wanted the repast to be. "In celebration of my life," the obituary read, "extended family and friends are invited to share with my family for dinner and fellowship in the dining hall of Mt. Sinai Baptist Church. At this time, you may share one with the other and reflect upon the fond memories that we all have experienced." As her words showed, she seemed not to fear death, but rather to mark it as that moment where time would cease and eternity would begin.

The dining hall was crowded, too many people for the relatively small but new extension to the nearly one-hundred-year-old church. While I was talking with friends, one of the women from the church signaled for me to come help in the kitchen. More hands were needed to serve the family. The women from Aunt Eula's prayer group, including Vivian and Yvette, also served.

Almost two years before, Aunt Eula held the group's second prayer breakfast at her home. I remember struggling out of bed that Saturday morning to make it over in time for 7 A.M. prayer. Aunt Eula was so excited about the group. Despite my late evening, I couldn't disappoint her by not showing up. The group consisted of approximately ten African American women, the majority of whom appeared to be in their mid-forties or early fifties; three senior women, including Aunt Eula and her older sister; and one white male in his mid-thirties. He worked with several of the women at one of the local plants. During work breaks he had shared with them his wife's struggle with bone cancer and asked that they pray for them and their two small children. Aunt Eula was particularly concerned about him because of her own experience with cancer. The amount of time spent praying for one woman's son and this lone man's wife and family made the morning particularly memorable. Yvette gave thanks for her new husband, and Vivian, with her daughter sitting next to her, simply asked for prayer for her family. I would come to understand only later the burdens of her heart that morning.

As I talked with the dozens of people at the repast, these memories emerged only sporadically. I stayed at the church to help clean up as most returned home or went back to work. The women's work made the space a women's space, and one they turned into a haven for sharing. Vivian and Yvette diligently worked with the others, at times stopping to laugh and reflect upon things that happened earlier in the week at work or at church. More solemn moments were spent talking about how much we would all miss Aunt Eula and how surprised we were at her passing. One of the deacons lingered helping to fold chairs and mop the floor. He also took responsibility for discarding the garbage, though cleaning the dishes and cooking were clearly demarcated as "women's work."[1] The women gave instruction to the teenagers as well, and together we cleaned, repackaged, discarded, and stored the remaining food items and utensils. I asked if this group of women were the main people to work the kitchen during church functions. Pointing instinctively to those standing around and laughing at the thought of another group existing, Shirley, one of the women in charge, confirmed my assumption.

Although the funeral was at noon, we stayed until well past four cleaning and straightening the kitchen and dining area. That afternoon was thus an opportunity to spend time with three of the women who informed my inquiry. I had not thought of seeing so many of them on one day—Yvette, Vivian, and Sylvia. Even more of the women I interviewed might have been at the funeral had other demands not intervened. Diane, for example, was preparing for a trip to Washington, D.C. She, like Sylvia, works with CCT. They and the Black Farmers and Agriculturist Association (a national organization that grew largely out of the efforts of several CCT members) were off to Washington to protest the restitution amount that the government proposed giving black farming families for their years of discrimination at the hands of the United States Department of Agriculture.[2] Diane was leading the youth component of their protest. The bus taking everyone to D.C. was scheduled to leave at 3 A.M. the following morning so that they could begin their campaign as soon as government offices opened.

Although Carmen Moore has participated in such organizing efforts, she was not leaving with the bus for Washington. She works a full-time job as an instructor at the Halifax County Community College. She too was not at the funeral. Ms. Moore and I did not meet through the church. Instead Diane suggested that I meet her. Diane, Ms. Moore, and Sylvia have worked for years on projects at the Tillery Community Center. Last fall Ms. Moore participated in a rally for U.S. Representative Eva Clayton, helping to raise funds and grassroots support for her reelection campaign.

Marie, the seventh woman I interviewed, participates in electoral politics as well, though on the local level. She successfully ran for a seat on the Halifax County school board, becoming one of the first African American women to serve on the board. She credits her election to the support of her family and church community. I was first introduced to Marie at one of the county school board meetings. I only came to know of her faith through an interview that I conducted with her for the UNC project.

Gloria, the eighth consultant to the project, I met at Shiloh Baptist. She and Ms. Cleveland faithfully attend the church's weekly Bible study, and I came to know both of them in this context. Gloria and I often shared Bibles, but I only began to really appreciate the importance of her contribution when I attended a women's conference sponsored by T. D. Jakes's ministry in July, the month before I returned to Halifax County to complete my research. The Georgia Dome was packed with over 50,000 women who had traveled from far and near to attend the "Woman Thou Art Loosed" conference and hear Bishop Jakes, a nationally recognized pastor and television minister, who has been leading a ministry for women since the early 1990s. I had attended one of his conferences nearly a year earlier with a friend in Dallas and had returned to this one because I was invited by friends in Atlanta. During one of the intermissions, I walked onto the mezzanine to scan the book tables. Gloria spotted me from across the room and came to speak. I knew then that I wanted her to participate in this research. Our meeting in such an enormous setting could not have been merely coincidental.

While I interviewed numerous women in Halifax County, I narrowed much of my research analysis to the lives of eight women: Juanita Cleveland, Carmen Moore, Yvette Stephens, "Ms. Sylvia" Jones, Vivian Dawkins, Diane Little, Gloria McKnight, and Marie Carter (all pseudonyms). Ms. Cleveland and Ms. Sylvia, both in their sixties, are the oldest participants. Ms. Moore is in her fifties. Diane, Vivian, Gloria, Marie, and Yvette are all in their late forties. Because they were closer to me in age and at least a decade younger than my own mother, I felt comfortable calling them by their first names. The women attend a variety of churches, some rural, others middle-class town congregations; all, however, are Baptist. Their lives come together in the midst of the often complicated and stressful social, political, and economic world that is Halifax County.

PROPHETIC ENGAGEMENT

MONDAY

"OF THE MEANING OF PROGRESS"

Understanding the Social, Political, and Economic History of Halifax County

"How shall man measure Progress there where the dark faced Josie lies?"

W. E. B. Du Bois, "Of the Meaning of Progress,"
The Souls of Black Folk

In his seminal anthropological tale of "dreams deferred" in the hills of Tennessee, Du Bois summons a call for meaning. What is progress? At the turn of the century he was engaged in educating former slaves who longed for knowledge and a better life. They came to his one-room schoolhouse en masse because it was the only school open to blacks in their rural region. When his time there expired, he moved on. Upon visiting ten years later, he found that little had changed. The people were still overworked, underpaid, their hopes discouraged by the passage of time. Finding the one-room schoolhouse dilapidated, Du Bois laments the ominousness of progress: "My log schoolhouse was gone. In its place stood Progress, and Progress, I understand, is necessarily ugly."[1]

At that time the industrial revolution was the promise of progress. Yet, this isolated region offered nothing of progress for the masses of African Americans who remained in an area where the social order of the day held them as second-class citizens and laborers unworthy of hire or competitive wages. Their desire for knowledge was great, but rising above the conundrum of their situation was difficult at best. Upon his return, Du Bois mocked the notion of progress. Industry, reconstruction, and education were to bring about a "New South," but in these rural regions life proved cyclical and unyielding. "Progress" was a word full of irony.

Du Bois's caustic proclamation that progress is "necessarily ugly" resonates with the realities—though not with the images—of progress just a hundred years later. The South today is presented as a "New South." In many regards it *is* the "Sunbelt" of the United States.[2] Cosmopolitan centers such as Atlanta, Houston, Memphis, and Birmingham are just a few of the areas that have experienced rapid growth and economic expansion since the 1970s.[3]

In North Carolina this notion of progress is no less taken as true. As in the rest of the South, the desegregation of public school systems and the advancement of African Americans, Latinos, and other minorities to key positions of leadership symbolize breaks from the past. In addition, the movement of industry has made middle-class suburban life a reality for many native Southerners and those relocating to the area. A key element in this pattern has been the steady growth of a black middle class, particularly around more metropolitan areas such as Raleigh, Durham, Charlotte, and Fayetteville. Absent from this presentation, however, is any discussion of the rapidly growing divide between North Carolinian haves and have-nots. Disparities over school funding, failed attempts at democracy, and radical disparities in income distribution are only some of the factors that give the lie to this notion of progress. In Halifax County, Aunt Eula's home, struggles develop constantly over issues of schooling, government spending, and industrial labor. William Chafe, a North Carolina historian, asserts that the changes the state has undergone have resulted in a "progressive mystique." He suggests that there is an overlay of progress that eclipses the reality of regression across the state. According to him, the progressive mystique "involves a set of ground rules that support the notion of North Carolina as a more civilized, enlightened and tolerant place than the rest of the Old Confederacy . . . This 'progressive mystique' has served as an exquisite instrument of social control, defining the terrain of political discussion in such a way that African Americans, factory workers, and field hands have found it virtually impossible to break through the veil of civility and insist on change."[4]

This chapter explores issues of inequality in Halifax County in relation to the rise over the last thirty years of neoliberal ideology and its touting of free-market capitalism. It is within this context that the spiritual lives of the women I interviewed create a complex fusion with their material reality. As religion historian Judith Weisenfeld keenly notes, any study of religion in America is an "understanding of religious experience as embedded in social contexts. While the most intimate, direct, and personal religious experience can be examined productively as merely an individual event, no person fails to be influenced by the powerful social forces within which she finds herself."[5]

By exploring the meaning of "progress" as it relates to economic development, education, and electoral politics, this chapter provides a broad view of the political and economic climate of the county in which the women I interviewed live and work. How does the contrast between the ideal of "progress" and the reality of stagnation impact their communities? In other words, where do these women, their families, and their friends work? What influences do state and industry economic decisions have on local communities, given neoliberal rhetoric's focus on free-market competition? And finally, how do "progressive" people explain the continuance of racialized inequality in government and electoral politics?

ENTERING HALIFAX COUNTY

I made my first official trip to Halifax as an ethnographer on a lazy Sunday afternoon to look for housing. One of my friends from Durham called her old friend from church, Eula, to let her know that I was coming and to see if she could help me locate a place to live. Wanting to take in my surroundings, I cruised more slowly than required. Because Halifax County is situated at the cusp of two major intersecting highways, there are numerous ways to enter it. One route, Interstate 95, stretching between Florida and Maine, runs through the center of the county. It is the major interstate carrying people and cargo up and down the East Coast. Alternately, Highway 158 runs east and west, eventually cutting across I-95 just about twenty miles south of the Virginia border. It is one of the main highways leading from the center of the state to the far-eastern counties of Northampton, Hertford, and Gates.

I entered Halifax County from Durham County, to the southwest. Traveling I-85 north, I exited in the town of Norlina and drove east on Highway 158 for nearly an hour until I reached Littleton. The sign "Speed Limit 35" immediately slowed my momentum, causing me to take inventory of the surroundings. Although I had driven through a vast expanse of trees and fields with scattered houses along the way, I was now entering a township with a small conglomeration of buildings, houses, and one lone gas station on the main street. The railroad track on my left separated the north end of town from the south. I pondered the likely racial history of that divide, assuming that at least a portion of the history might still hold true today.

As I left the township, headed for Roanoke Rapids, I again entered a vast expanse of trees and fields—much of it farmland or remnants of old farm life: haystacks, a few animals, and dilapidated barns. The two-lane road was relatively straight, though dangerous for passing because of the constant entrance of log trucks. When I finally reached Roanoke Rapids, I knew that I had entered the county's central city; a spread of fast-food restaurants, shopping centers, and a little blue sign for the local hospital signaled my arrival. Mobile home dealerships as well as automobile showcases lined the busy thoroughfare and several of the side streets. Roanoke Rapids was the "urban attraction" for the surrounding towns, the place where folks buy groceries, clothes, shoes, cars, insurance and enjoy entertainment.

My relatively scenic initial entry into Halifax County helped me gain my bearings for what would be a year of traveling long miles to and from appointments. I arrived at Aunt Eula's with little trouble. She welcomed me into her home, offered me lunch, and then insisted that we begin looking for apartments while it was still early. When we finally returned to her home, she made a surprising suggestion: that I stay with her and Uncle Charles. She would get an additional phone line and help me re-organize the guest room to make it conducive for my work. Appreciating her sincere generosity, yet realizing the space that I would need to compile research and possibly conduct interviews, I gratefully declined. I soon located a nice one-bedroom apartment in the central city and embarked upon my work.

While Aunt Eula provided me with my first tour of the area, subsequent meetings with community leaders, church members, and business leaders provided me with opportunities for "re"entering the county. One such meeting with a local official named Dave Cummings gave me an appreciation of both the economic and the social history of two of the major communities, Willowdale and Shepherdscreek (pseudonyms), near the homes of Carmen Moore, Diane Little, and Sylvia Jones. The history of these towns belies first impressions of a reasonably prosperous rural area.

During my meeting with Cummings, he offered to take me on a tour. While driving through Willowdale, he explained the history of the municipality's development. Two towns, Croswood and Pinedale, decided to merge into one city, Willowdale, in the early 1900s. Today the part that was once Croswood is predominantly white, while the section that was Pinedale is predominantly black. The two areas of Willowdale are joined by a widely set main street that allows for parking down its center. Approximately 3,500 people live in Willowdale. The majority of factories and mills are located in the black section of the town. When desegregation occurred in 1971, the schools of Willowdale were reshaped, some turned into county administration buildings and one changed from a predominantly black public middle school into a high school. Most white students in the town upon integration, however, began attending private segregated Christian academies.

As we passed through the black section of Willowdale, Cummings pointed out the sewing factory and the mill located on the main street. "The only difference," he commented, "between that [working in the sewing factory] and slavery is that they've taken us out of the fields and put us in the mills—so we're picking corporate cotton." Referring to the fact that black women make up well over 95 percent of the floor laborers, he said "We're still in cotton." As we continued to talk about industry in Halifax County, Cummings explained, "When you're poor and unemployed, you don't have a lot to say about what happens in your community. Unless you get someone elected to represent your issues." He believes that he is that kind of leader, one concerned about the plight of everyday folks who work in factories and on farms.

As we drove, we talked more about local politics and the history of racialized redistricting in Halifax County. Cummings explained that there are seven municipalities: Hobgood, Scotland Neck, Enfield, Halifax, Weldon, Roanoke Rapids, and Littleton, all of which are predominately white. In addition to these municipalities, which have locally elected city governments, there are smaller communities, like Tillery, whose small populations do not mandate elected officials. While nearly 53 percent of the county's 55,617 residents are African American, they are predominantly residents of the county and not the municipalities. City electorates thus generally reflect the seven municipalities' white populations. The women I interviewed lived in or around these municipalities. In recent years the imbalance of city representation has caused major political fallout in several of the towns. Although we did not spend a significant amount of time talking about this fallout, Cummings and I both knew that in Enfield town government had for a period ground to a halt because of it.

We initially planned to end our tour at noon, but when he discovered that his afternoon meeting was canceled, Cummings asked if I wanted to see another section of the county. I agreed and we left once again, this time in my car. He drove as I took notes.

We went in the opposite direction, through Enfield and into Hollister (the district of William Dale, one of the first African Americans to be elected to the Halifax County Board of Commissioners). The Haliwah-Saponi Native American community is largely situated in this area of the county. As we traveled, Cummings pointed out a number of homes where Haliwah-Saponi families reside. Their presence in the county complicates the black/white binary of the area, though many residents question the group's claims to authentic Native American lineage. Some believe that they are just black folks who do not want to self-identify as black, while others believe that members of the tribe are positioning themselves to capitalize on federal money recently released to Native American communities. Latino migrant workers, brought in to work on local farms, are also gradually changing the area's demographics. A few East Indian and Asian families have also moved into Roanoke Rapids, mostly due to professional relocations. Along with Haliwah-Saponi, these groups make up the one percent "other" listed in Halifax's racial demographic records.

The vast majority of the land that we passed was owned by Larry Welch, one of the richest, if not *the* richest man in Halifax County. According to local opinion, Welch gained his wealth by buying land that went into foreclosure. When people could not pay their taxes, Welch, because of personal connections, knew immediately and placed a bid on the land.[6] This practice led to Welch's disproportionate ownership of land in the rural region.

Land ownership and use, however, have become not only local concerns but also national and international ones. Lumber companies and vertically integrated hog operations as well as the traditional sewing, rubber, and textile companies have brought about distinct changes in the county's traditionally "rural" landscape. Although the county has a long history of industrialization, dating back to the turn-of-the-century mills which settled the Roanoke Rapids area,[7] poultry and hog industries located there today—some within miles of Ms. Sylvia's, Ms. Moore's, and Diane's homes—bring a new set of social, political, and economic dynamics to the region. For some the changes signal progress; for others they signal new challenges to *real* progress.

In Halifax County "progress," as related not only to economic development, but also to education and electoral politics, is the buzzword among elected officials, economic development officers, and some residents. The term, however, must be examined in relationship to the county's history and burgeoning social problems.

HISTORICAL ECONOMIC PROGRESS

Since the turn of the last century, state legislators and business leaders have often touted North Carolina as the center of progress in the U.S.

South. Industrial development, highway expansions, and the presence of major research universities have paved the way for such claims. After seizing political power in 1896 from a joint Republican and Populist alliance called the Fusion Party, white Southern Democrats embraced progressivism as their commitment to the industrial and educational development of the state.[8] Overtly communicated in their plan, however, was an insistence upon white supremacy. Historians and political scientists studying the era have pointed out "the relative powerlessness of workers and the absolute exclusion of blacks from political life."[9] "Progressivism" as it was defined masked "the fact that the state's power holders, even as they invested in educational and transportation improvements, were serving the interests of a narrow economic elite."[10]

In rural North Carolina this discourse of progress holds particular weight because of the region's historical dependence upon agriculture. In most counties in eastern North Carolina, agriculture has been the bedrock of economic stability.[11] To this day farming still contributes millions of dollars to Halifax County's revenues, making it the number one producer of cotton in the state and the number two producer of peanuts. Despite these figures, agriculture is no longer the primary source of employment for residents. Downturns in farming sent industries, looking for cheap and dependable labor, into rural areas en masse. Wealthy capitalists built small factories in many rural areas including Halifax County. According to one study, "the decline of North Carolina's agricultural economy in the 1950s provided industrial employers with a ready supply of labor, workers [in the South] who expected wages far less than what Northerners were demanding. Unemployment, and thus available labor, was greatest in the rural counties of east and west."[12]

As markets became more sophisticated and globalized in the 1980s, national and multinational corporations began to invest less in North Carolina's rural areas. This move of industry was fueled by shifting demands of business executives and the presence of low-wage workers in other countries. With corporate globalization some speculated that "the Sunbelt outlook may turn cloudy."[13] In anticipating the present growth of this problem, Linda Flowers, an ethnographer of the region, stated:

> Economists point to the increased difficulty rural areas are likely to face in attracting and retaining outside companies, largely because the attitudes and many of the policies historically conducive to this end now work somewhat against it: cheap, abundant labor aggressively advertised, low corporate taxes, right-to-work legislation, anti-unionism, gov-

ernmental cooperation, and the like. Exploitations on which Southern manufacturing has always been dependent may now be coming home to roost. The same low taxes that traditionally have made us attractive to industry also keep us poor: our schools, especially, as well as, in some ways, our quality of life. Companies that can pick and choose will likely relocate where they can have the best of both worlds: cooperation from state and local governments, but, also, good schools and cultural enrichment . . . Furthermore, "low wages—long an inducement for companies seeking to escape high labor costs in the unionized North," are now relatively less important "as more . . . companies leave the country altogether for low-wage nations . . ." Few companies native to the state and few coming in can be said to thrive independently of international competition.[14]

Paul Luebke makes the same point: "The kinds of low-skill, low-wage factory jobs that manufacturers once gladly brought to rural counties were becoming scarce. Now employers could pay far lower wages in Latin American or Asian countries."[15] Furthermore, the automation of certain industries has steadily forced workers out of jobs. This present climate of stagnating industry investment coupled with the ever present demand for jobs has made it increasingly important for local officials to "lure" industry into the area. Pressured by high unemployment rates and growing citizens' needs for things such as adequate water services, paved roads, and adequate housing, officials, adopting the discourse of neoliberalism, promise the benefits of business-friendly economic development ventures.

The neoliberal discourse that generates much of this discussion, however, has led to a backgrounding of issues related to social justice. Organizations like CCT, where Ms. Sylvia and Diane work and where Ms. Moore sometimes volunteers, insist that discussions of workers' rights and job safety are today overshadowed by attempts to appeal to potential industry. Instead of speaking of fair wages and safe working conditions, officials talk in terms of making sure that local workers outproduce workers in other countries and maintain a competitive edge in the global market. These officials equate progress more with revenue and tax base than with a leading concern about equitable pay and job safety. Given the area's variegated economic and racial history, many of these silences reify racial divides already present between blacks and whites.

RACIAL DIVISION AND PROGRESS

Political and economic divisions, as theorists of race have taught us, reinforce and naturalize racial categories that have no biological legitimacy.[16] The U.S. South has undergone two major periods of reconstruction in terms of race over the past 150 years. The first occurred during the 1860s and '70s, the second during the 1950s and '60s. These periods held potential for major advancement in race relations and racial equality. Yet historians cite both movements as having fallen short of their potential because of the relationship between race and economics. This relationship is evident throughout the history of slavery, the First Reconstruction, and the Second Reconstruction.

Slavery and the removal of Native Americans from their land formed the foundation of the Southern economy. While "the wholesale importation of African slaves to English colonies in America did not begin until the latter part of the seventeenth century, an estimated 15 to 20 million slaves were brought to the Americas between the fifteenth and nineteenth centuries."[17] As historians have argued, "without the labor provided by the African slaves and their descendants, the economic development of the South in the particular form it took would have been severely retarded, if not impossible."[18] Slavery provided free labor in the South and drastically impacted social relations. Although the majority of white Southerners were not slave owners, their social position was determined by their relationship to enslaved blacks. This racial hierarchy continued well into the postbellum years and was especially evident during the Great Depression, when both blacks and whites faced the challenges of limited resources.

While the social and economic hierarchy of slavery informed race relations in the South, industry and access to jobs largely defined relations in the North. When free and fugitive blacks moved north during the antebellum period, they often met with white resistance. In nearly every antebellum Northern legislature and constitutional convention, fears were expressed over blacks entering occupations formerly dominated by whites—porters, truckmen, sawyers, mechanics.[19] This type of negative response was evident in conflicts that erupted between the 1840s and 1860s between blacks and whites, many of whom had recently immigrated from Europe. These conflicts demonstrate that racial tension and injustice were not phenomena particular to the South. The nation as a whole suffered from racism fueled by changing economic conditions.

Life for African Americans in the South was to take a dramatic turn as the post–Civil War period ushered in the First Reconstruction (1865–1877). Aid from the Freedman's Bureau assisted former slaves with the purchase of land in order that they might establish independent farms. Blacks during this period of Reconstruction were granted economic, political, and social rights previously denied. The passing of the Fifteenth Amendment allowed black men access to the polls, though black women were still excluded, and several black representatives were elected to state and national legislatures. North Carolina, for instance, elected its first African American state and federal legislators during this period. Reconstruction, however, proved short-lived.

The 1890s marked the beginning of a nadir in American race relations. Historians note the rise of a reactionary mentality among whites that feared the emergence of a free and powerful black class. Between 1884 and 1900 more than 2,500 lynchings of black men and women were recorded.[20] A marked increase in economic and political power among blacks set off a backlash that reverberated in new legislation. According to legal scholar Derrick A. Bell, "Historians for some years have engaged in vigorous debate as to whether the flood of black disenfranchisement provisions placed in state statutes and constitutions during the decades after 1890 served as a fait accompli for work already accomplished by violence and intimidation, or whether affirmative legal steps were necessary to supplement the courts' silent acquiescence in stripping from blacks rights granted in the Fourteenth and Fifteenth Amendments."[21] Supreme Court decisions included the 1896 *Plessy v. Ferguson,* which upheld the ideology of "separate but equal," and the 1898 *Williams v. Mississippi,* which validated Mississippi's disenfranchisement plan. States including North Carolina, Texas, and Georgia, without convening constitutional conventions, passed legislation through referenda that had similar effects.[22] This retreat from fair legislation marked the beginnings of Jim Crow, which left many disenfranchised in the political system that was supposed to protect the rights of the disadvantaged.

Ongoing hostilities in the South, along with opportunities for industry work in the North, resulted in the heavy northern migration of blacks between the World Wars. These migrants settled in places like New York, Detroit, and Chicago.[23] From the mid-1940s to the late 1960s, nearly 4.5 million more blacks left the South than migrated to it.[24] Ms. Sylvia was among those who headed north for better economic opportunity. Her return to Halifax is a part of a "return migration" pattern of older generations back to the land and homes they left nearly thirty years prior.[25] The movement north did not result in any dramatic shifts in the employment or treatment of blacks in the South. With the stagnation of industrial job opportunities there, most rural blacks continued the mode of tenant farming and sharecropping that had characterized much of African American employment since Emancipation. Several of the women I interviewed grew up sharecropping or were children of parents who worked as sharecroppers. Many of the African Americans in Halifax County are among those who remained in the South managing their own farms or working as tenant farmers on white-owned farms.

The years surrounding the Second Reconstruction were marked by shifting social and economic patterns. The Civil Rights and Black Power Movements of the 1950s and '60s actively challenged the racial status quo in both the South and the North. The demolition of Jim Crow laws, the *Brown v. Board of Education* decision, and the passing of the Civil Rights Act of 1964 and the Voting Rights Act of 1965 helped to institutionalize needed structural change across the South. Increased industrial expansion led to the creation of 17 million new jobs in the South between 1960 and 1985 (compared to 11 million in the West and 13 million in the Midwest and Northeast).[26] This, along with the entry of women into fields formerly occupied by men and the increase in Latino and Asian populations, complicated social and economic structures in the South that had previously endorsed white and male-dominated political and economic hegemony. An imagery of "The New South" began to emerge during the 1970s which challenged former notions of the South as "backward" and racist.

Whether or not the imagery shift reflects "real" shifts in the practices of the South is still open for debate. While the South's industrial base has increased due to the relocation of Northern industry and the steady pool of available labor, questions remain about the distribution of jobs and disparate earnings among employees, particularly in rural areas.

ECONOMIC DEVELOPMENT AND PROGRESS

In an interview, Steve O'Donnel, one of Halifax County's chief economic development specialists, spoke optimistically about the "progressive" nature of certain areas of the county. He attributed the progress of these areas to the fact that they seemed most open to growth whereas other areas seemed more resistant to growth and industrial development. O'Donnel described the predominantly white Roanoke Rapids city council as progressive because they put "a great deal of emphasis on moving forward and putting things in place to make them very competitive and to move forward in their economic development efforts." In his experience, attracting business investment is not an easy process. "Economic development encompasses a lot of different areas, product development is one of them. Not only does it involve going out and finding somebody to come in and build or establish a company and provide jobs and tax base for the county, but it also means that you know, you've got to develop your product." For O'Donnel the products include a shell building (an already completed building waiting to be occupied by an interested party), the already operating industrial park, and a trainable workforce able to compete with global production rates. This latter part, he insisted, is key in "selling" Halifax County to interested corporations.

O'Donnel saw community opposition in the predminantly black outlying areas to the efforts of the economic development commission as unwarranted. He cited two occasions on which communities spoke out against certain industries developing in their area. One industry, he explained, was "going to provide 180 jobs. These people were going to make a minimum of $15/hour. Their tax base was going to be about $30 million." Another industry would "invest 50 jobs . . . minimum, average annual salary was like $18,000/yr." He later indicated that the first industry was recognized by the EPA as producing environmentally hazardous material and the second industry was a human feces recycling plant. These, however, were for him manageable issues. Focused mainly on the potential for economic growth and not on the danger or discomfort of the predominantly black communities in which these industries would locate, O'Donnel expressed dismay that citizens did not want the plants. "The mindset is, 'I know what I know. Don't confuse me with the facts. You're lying to me. You're trying to put something on me that I don't want. And you work for the government, so you're wrong. And you're mean and you're bad and you're going to do something that's going to destroy my way of life . . .' That's the mindset. And you can't overcome it. You absolutely can't overcome that."

Those in opposition to the efforts of O'Donnel's committee, however, were most often members of the Concerned Citizens of Tillery (CCT) or the Center for Women's Economic Advancement (CWEA)—regional, grassroots, nonprofit organizations that describe themselves as advocates for local communities and industrial workers. Ms. Sylvia, Ms. Moore, and Diane are active members of these organizations. Members of CCT and CWEA did not define progress or development in the same way as O'Donnel, the development officer. For George Givens, director of CCT and a leader in the community, the issue centered around safe and nonexploitative industry. In deciding which industries to support, Givens explained that he must always examine the difference between "what they're bringing into the community and what they're taking out." He,

Diane, and Ms. Sylvia were three of the main leaders standing in opposition to the industries that O'Donnel mentioned.

According to them, the discourse of progress employed by O'Donnel and other economic development officials omits the critical assessment of industries needed to protect workers. Not only have some of the industries presented environmental health issues, but the means through which they enter the county often do little to challenge racial and gender inequity. Because eastern North Carolina is the place where the majority of African Americans in the state live and the area with one of the longest histories of sharecropping, a large portion of the low-skilled and semiskilled workers are African American. These workers and their descendants are the ones most negatively affected by the market-driven notions of progress employed by local officials. Such notions often lead to unfavorable work conditions.

"I just don't want my daughter to have to work in one of these plants," explained one poultry plant worker that I met through CCT. "They have already done enough damage." Although she said that the work brings a steady income, the effect on the body has been great. "White women" she insisted do not have to work under such harsh conditions. At one point she told the story of a white woman who came to work on the floor cutting chickens. The routine is for one person to cut off a particular portion of the chicken (leg, thigh, head) as it passes on a conveyor belt. A manager stands behind the worker at intervals with a stopwatch to ensure that workers are cutting at production rates. After watching the woman struggle with her job, the manager decided to find her another job, saying that floor work was "too hard for her" and that she "didn't belong there." White women, my informant insisted, are most often placed behind desks to do paper work. Black women, contrarily, are seen as able to bear the burdens of this physical labor. The idea of black women as able-bodied "mules of the world," in Zora Neale Hurston's phrase, those who do the hardest, most demeaning work and receive the least credit or compensation, figures increasingly in criticisms of divisions of labor in the United States. This is also a growing critique of the types of jobs being transferred outside of the country to poor women of color.

One former plant employee and advocate for women workers in eastern North Carolina indicated that the line speeds have increased over the last several years. "The lines go so fast, the processing lines go so fast that that's why people are developing carpal tunnel, because they're doing repetitive motion work so fast. Workers who worked at the plant before the lines were going this fast said that you didn't have problems like that . . . that people did not get injured as quick or as fast as they do now. So, we're pushing for a national lines speed." The increase in the line production speed is consistent with the influence of globalization and the creation of competitive labor markets in other countries.[27]

Another employee and member of CCT related how she and her husband supported eleven children by working in a local factory for 27 years, never making over $10 an hour. Although they were glad to see the end of sharecropping with its low wages and uncertain pay schedule, industry work created for them another type of hard labor.[28] "How we got that money, it's because we worked, we pulled hours and hours and hours and hours and hours. We didn't get that money just going down and touching that button, we pulled them hours, and them was rough hours, it was a manpower job." She was a rubber splicer at a local factory working throughout the day with heated material and heavy, high-powered machines. "We worked seven days a week. Seven days a week, and then sometimes they want you to come in earlier or stay over. But about two years before I come out of Solo [pseudonym], we just lived in Solo, all of us lived in Solo, seven days a week. And then like I said, they want you to stay over four hours, either come in four hours early or two hours early like that. And so they will tell you, 'If you don't want to work, there are plenty more peoples out there.'"

The threat of losing a job with a steady income while caring for children and often aging family members is the main reason why black women in particular in this rural region endure the harsh realities of their working conditions. When I naively asked why women and not men "put up with" these conditions, two women that I interviewed responded almost simultaneously, "because they have families to feed." Often carrying the weight of raising and providing for a family by themselves, black women are still "de mules 'uh de world"; Hurston's statement carries an eerie truth decades later.

African American women are disproportionately represented not only in poultry plants, but also in the local rubber and sewing factories. Their presence in these industries again reflects that hard physical labor is part of their jobs. These types of high-risk, high-production industries have grown most in areas of semi- to low-skilled workers.[29]

Lisa Jackson, an organizer with CWEA, explains that the goal of CWEA is "to create a community of women free from all oppressions where they can earn a decent wage, where they can become enablers of others, where they can believe in themselves to control their situations." The women that Jackson supports are most often women in the sewing or poultry industries who have been injured on the job and are seeking disability. "The [poultry] plant has been in the area for 21 years . . . and what I've seen in the last seven years [since working here] is that it's totally destroying the community, the African American communities, because you have women who can no longer sustain their households, can't do anything, but take medicine."

As a former employee in the sewing factory and an advocate for women factory workers, Jackson is well acquainted with the incidence of carpal tunnel syndrome common to women in these types of high-production jobs The fast-paced repetition of tasks and the risks of operating heavy equipment are often direct causes of their injuries. When asked who generally works in these types of floor positions, Jackson responded that in the poultry plant "they have three shifts and it's 98% African American women." Women in the rubber industry indicated the same type of disproportionate representation of African American men and women in their plants. One woman explained, "All the white people was in the office." African Americans worked the floor. "When I left there on third shift, no white peoples. On second shift, I think about two . . . You don't got no black peoples down in the office down there. You got to stick them down on the floor to do manpower work. Or else, go." Factories competing for an edge in the global market are most suspect for requiring rigid production rates in these types of assembly line jobs.[30]

For these factory workers *meaningful* progress comes in the form of state regulation of production lines and the establishment of living wages. Organizations like CCT and CWEA have argued not for the removal of plants, but for the fair and equitable treatment of employees. Some workers, in fact, wrestle with getting involved in organized protests because of the scarcity of jobs and the realization of their own dispensability. "Progress" is thus a contested term defined one way by economic development officers looking to increase the county's tax base and another way by black women laborers desiring to protect their bodies, their jobs, and their families.

EDUCATIONAL PROGRESS

As the county's push for development continues to bring a certain type of industry (i.e. hogs, poultry, and prisons) into the rural and predominantly African American section of Halifax County, more appealing and lucrative industries (i.e. paper, textiles, and energy) have located in Roanoke Rapids. The location of these industries alone has brought about a form of de facto segregation that has evident consequences in the school system. "In the early twentieth century, textile magnates donated land and money for the construction of a Roanoke Rapids town school; in exchange, they secured business education and industrial arts classes and a future white labor pool. One-room school houses, with significantly fewer resources at their disposal, spread haphazardly throughout the county. Segregationists took advantage of arbitrary historical boundaries to declare racialized school districts."[31] This racialized polarity of white municipalities and schools vis-à-vis a predominately black county and county school system remains intact despite desegregation laws and the fluctuation of industry in and out of the county. In fact, Halifax County, with three school systems, is one of only a handful of counties in North Carolina that have not been forced by the state legislature to merge their schools into one large county system. Reasons for maintaining the old predominantly white system in Roanoke Rapids include fears about the loss of "community," a desire to attract industry into the area with the lure of "at least one" good school system, and an ambivalence among African American leaders in the county who fear that merger will bring about complete white dominance in both the city and the county school systems. Rhetorics of "progress" continue in spite of the reality of racial segregation.

Segregation reinforces the sharp disparities in resource allocation and pupil performance in the three systems. Despite Halifax's status as one of the state's low-wealth counties, the three school systems are variably affected by the county's low-wealth status. The Halifax County and Weldon school districts, 86 and 92 percent African American respectively—where most of the women I interviewed send (or have sent) their children to school—are near the bottom of the state's school rankings, while Roanoke Rapids is in the middle percentile. "In 1996, on the SAT scores of [the] 121 [North Carolina] school systems, Weldon placed last and Halifax 117th, while Roanoke Rapids ranked 43rd. In fact, two of the four schools in Weldon were among the fifteen lowest performing in the state that received 'assistance teams.'"[32]

The inequalities between the county's school systems reflect the differences not only between the tax bases of the town and the county but also between the class backgrounds of parents in both areas. The city exacts a considerable industrial tax from the textile and paper industries.

Likewise, the presence of middle-class and working-class families who can afford a voluntary tax boosts Roanoke Rapids's ability to acquire needed resources and proficient teachers able to meet the varied needs of students. Halifax County school officials know that it is too much of a burden to ask parents to pay additional tax to improve their school system when economic demands are already overwhelming. Several of the women spoke of the financial strains that they or their families and friends experience in the county. Developing a county school tax according to them is not a viable option.

Because of the sharp disparities between the systems, residents of Roanoke Rapids are overwhelmingly opposed to the idea of merger. The "'M' word," as one white official called it, has led to serious debate in the city. Residents are careful not to couch their concerns in terms of racial typologies. Instead they speak in terms of the preservation of "community," "tradition," and "family."[33] An administrator in Roanoke Rapids argued, "It [the reality of separate school systems] has nothing to do with trying to set ourselves apart and say, 'We're better than you,' or anything like that, it has more to do with a certain, a loyalty and a feeling of more like family and not wanting to be swallowed up in a larger entity so that we would lose our own identity."

The idea of maintaining "community" and "tradition" was evident during the city's centennial celebration, where events centered around the Roanoke Rapids Graded School District and its founding. The parade moved from one end of Main Street to the other, ending in front of the city's only high school where a joint band and choir concert initiated the weekend's events. During the celebration I and approximately seven other African Americans sat in the packed auditorium while the band and choir entertained the audience with songs which paid tribute to the South, including "Dixie." Nostalgia about the school and the town's history poured from the memories of school board members, faculty, and older graduates of the high school as they rendered their salutations. Their traditions and memorabilia consisted of a hodgepodge of old Dixie, without any mention, let alone critique, of its racist past.

The celebration encouraged romantic ideas about the overall "progress" of the area. As evidenced by the presence of former students (now local doctors, lawyers, educators, and council persons) and by its current academic ranking, the system has been successful in educating youth and sustaining the community. In the eyes of the residents of Roanoke Rapids the school system is progressing.

Thus, to merge the system with Halifax or Weldon would seem to many whites in the city antithetical to progress. As one official stated, merging the systems "would be like mixing hot and cold water." You would have only a "lukewarm school system." According to one influential school official,

> Merging would no doubt help the Halifax system, but it would damage Roanoke Rapids' city system, and then I think the doctors and lawyers would leave the city to pay for education elsewhere . . . We know [Halifax] schools are in trouble, but I would hate to see the only school that is halfway right be taken over by the county . . . I'm not sure what to do. I don't know if it would bring to ruin the manufacturing out in Roanoke Rapids, or what it would do. That's our biggest tax base in Roanoke Rapids. That's where all the jobs and manufacturing is in Roanoke Rapids. And those folks won't come into Halifax County and put their kids in the county schools. So what would it do economically for the county?

Thus there are concerns not only about educational investments in the students of the area but also about protecting the area's economic viability. The intermittent debate over merging Halifax's segregated systems illustrates the conflict between economic interests and racial integration. To opponents of merger, progress means having at least one "good" school system to present to potential industry looking to locate in the area. More than one official pointed out that locating industry in the region would be difficult if there were no "good" school systems for industry heads to send their children to. When moving to Halifax, the argument goes, industry leaders want to ensure that their children are gaining the type of quality education that will make them competitive with children in other parts of the country. Such business concerns engender support for sustaining the segregation of the school systems. The reasoning is that, if not "progress" in the sense of integration, the county will secure progress in terms of economic development.

While white citizens of Roanoke Rapids express opposition to merger, African American leaders in the county school system express ambivalence. It is important to note that though African American leaders are uncertain about the benefits of merger, they are not in direct opposition to it. Unlike their counterparts in Roanoke Rapids, black school leaders in the county have seriously considered the benefits of merger, yet have ceased to push for it because of direct opposition from Roanoke Rapids. For years the push for merger has engendered severe controversy and a deep concern about the impact of merger on the children. Marie Carter, whose children attended the county school system, commented,

We wouldn't want to subject our children to a lot of hostility just to say that they're in a better, or, they're getting a better opportunity. For instance, last year was the first time that we've had black students to go to private schools . . . Would I send my kids there? No. It might be better. They might get better educated . . . But I would not send my children there. And the reason I say that is because it has always been a white only school. Just because you have a minority there, it might change the outlook, but not necessarily the inlook. See what I'm saying?

Leaders fear not only the possible negative effect of merger on the children, but also the loss of black leadership. Since the early 1990s the Halifax County school system has secured a predominantly African American school board. As one of the first black women elected to the Halifax County school board, Carter was directly part of the struggle for African American leadership in the predominately black system. The turn in power on the school board has brought with it the hiring of an African American superintendent and an increasing number of African American employees in the system. According to several informants, whites wanted to retain leadership in order to ensure that whites would benefit financially from the system as teachers, administrators, and contractors for school renovations. Merger would challenge the new power that African Americans have on the school board.

As an alternative to merger, African American board members in Halifax County have suggested that equal funding be provided for each school system. This they believe would assist in bringing up school test scores and attract highly skilled and motivated teachers. During one of my months in residence, the problem of teacher shortages became crystal clear when I tutored the high school daughter of a couple who allowed me to talk with them about water pollution in their area. After my discussion with her parents, the high school student asked me to assist her in math. Highly intelligent and expressive, she wanted me to become her algebra tutor because the state-sponsored End of Grade tests were around the corner and she was uncertain of her preparation. As I explained one of the equations, I asked if her teacher gave the class the same explanation. She responded that her math teacher is really a biology instructor and does not know how to explain the material clearly. The school district was short on teachers and needed to reassign them in order to cover the necessary classes. Now in her sophomore year, this student had not had a real math teacher since entering the high school. This problem is not uncommon in the county. George Givens explained earlier that during his tenure as an English teacher he was asked to teach science for one school term because of the shortage.

It is problematic to hold the school system or the students solely responsible for educational performance, yet this has been the practice of much of the state's enforcement effort. The county school board has responded to the issues first by lobbying the state for greater funds and second, by requiring student uniforms in an effort to increase students' focus on their schoolwork. As already indicated, the county has been named one of the state's "low-wealth" districts and as such is supposed to receive special state aid for equipment such as upgraded computers in classrooms and renovated facilities. After studying the practice of wearing school uniforms, the school board held meetings throughout the county at various schools and asked parents to vote. Overwhelmingly parents approved uniforms. Instead of merger, parents and school board members are taking the more conservative approach of pressing for internal change, rather than external equity.

In this turn of events progress has been redefined, not in terms of "integration" but rather in terms of internal improvement. Integration, it is inferred, is not necessarily best. As parents and school officials redefine "progress," the children are the ones whose progress will determine their ultimate success.

ELECTORAL PROGRESS

As I continued to survey changes in the county, debates over "progress" became evident in yet another area, that of electoral politics. The issue of progress comes up in debates about the makeup of the school board and in discussions of city and county officials. Actual progress in electoral politics, or the absence thereof, affects whether there is progress or regression in a host of other county decisions—for example, board appointments, the placement of infrastructure, and the location of paved roads. For this reason, African Americans in the county have long pushed for representation not only on local city and town council boards but also on the county commission. Progress, however, has three major challengers: historic white political and economic dominance, majority tyranny, and conflicting political agendas among African American representatives.

The idea of a "good ole boy" network operating in Halifax County resonated throughout interviews with residents. "It's a good ole boy network . . . controlled by a few people," explained one white business owner as she talked about her apprehension at getting involved in county politics. When asked to explain her comment she stated, "I mean that there are a few people involved that get things done behind the scenes and that's how things get done. I don't know of any involvement by women . . . The only African American involvement I know of is by people who have always been politically active, not by like regular citizens." As she finished I asked what gave her such a view of Halifax— "Forty-six years of watching!"

While she described Halifax County as a safe and comfortable place for her to grow up, her overall opinion as an adult is that people in the county have a "very narrow view" and change is difficult to introduce. This type of resistance to change is the bedrock of complaints filed by those who want a more representative government. In recent years the county has seen growth in the number of African American officials in both city and county government. Those boosting the progressive nature of the county are quick to point to these increases when talking about how far Halifax has come in race relations. Yet these seats were hard won, and even with success other struggles ensue.

Halifax County elected its first African American county commissioner in 1982 only after black residents filed a federal lawsuit in Superior Court. According to the residents who filed the petition, the at-large system of elections ensured that whites would win. Although blacks voted in the elections, they were still held captive by employer/employee relationships. Black employees of white farmers were either afraid of voting in the election or afraid of not demonstrating their loyalty to white bosses and their friends. Black employees were often "asked" to place campaign material in their yards for white candidates. According to one black resident, William Dale, who ran for commissioner against a powerful white landowner and businessman, "I couldn't defeat him because he owned most of the land in Halifax County, most of the black folk in Halifax County. All the material and everything . . . everybody in the county had Buddy's material in front of their house. And I told them, 'Don't take it down, leave it there. But when you get in the precinct, you can ignore that and vote for me.'"

When the results came back, Dale had won the election, but only after shrewd maneuvering to secure votes. The class-action suit later filed would help to preclude the need to garner black support in such necessarily subversive ways. Race-based precincts allowed blacks in Halifax to place their issues at center stage and elect a representative they believe represents them.

Cummings spoke of fear not only of losing one's job but also of having problems with bank loans. Speaking to why blacks do not become more involved in electing candidates and running for office, he stated, "Often times people have to look at their economic situations when they're getting involved with anything." To put it differently, people fear they lack the resources to withstand possible retaliation. Once as an elected official he countered the majority white board, forcing them to deadlock on a decision to appoint the head of a county department. He, the other African American board member, and one white board member opposed the suggested candidate in favor of an African American female candidate. When the deadlock continued for over a week, one of the board members contacted Cummings's boss requesting that he relay to Cummings the seriousness of his position—that he could lose his job. Fortunately, Cummings's supervisor did not side with the disgruntled board member; yet the influence of such board members and other political leaders has intimidated many who would potentially enter politics or support certain political efforts.

Since the mid-1980s, when the class-action lawsuit was filed, four blacks have been elected to the county commission, and two African Americans have chaired county departments—the Department of Social Services and the Health Department.

The election of blacks to the county commission and the city council alone, however, has not in and of itself guaranteed substantial change or progress. Minority representation alone, as legal scholar Lani Guinier illustrates,[34] does not ensure that the concerns of the minority will be heard. One must contend with the imbalance of power on boards. In North Carolina in 1997 major conflicts arose surrounding 4–3 or 5–4 majority/minority, white/black splits on boards or councils.[35]

Guinier terms this type of voting pattern the "tyranny of the majority"; the majority rules without the checks and balances of minority input because of their sheer numerical advantage. In fact history demonstrates that whites more often than not support white candidates and blacks more often than not support other black candidates.[36] Tyranny of the majority means that minority representation exists but there is rarely sufficient numerical representation to ensure that the issues and concerns of the minority are brought before the council, heard, and finally acted upon.

One of the six major townships in Halifax County, Enfield, ceased operating for nearly twelve months in 1997–1998 because of internal racial strife. Three African American elected officials began a boycott of the regular town council meeting because they felt that the concerns of African American residents were not being addressed by the majority white board. In this scenario the progress implied by their election was short-circuited by the fact that they were treated as mere tokens on the board. Unable to form a majority voting block, these elected officials complained that they could not secure paved roads, fair electricity prices, and a host of other amenities for their constituents in majority black communities. A journalist at one news magazine called these majority/minority votes which end in an actual boycott of meetings "quorum busters."[37] Likening the boycotts to legislative filibustering, the article states that "in all these places, race is the defining factor. The boycotting members share similar grievances related to the inadequate provision of services to minority communities."

Finally, as well as historical white domination and contemporary majority tyranny, the conflicting agendas of African American representatives affect electoral progress. The divide between African American political representatives is most often described as a rift between the "old guard" and the "new guard." The rift stems from opinions as to whether political conflict is best resolved through direct confrontation with the established system or by gradually working within the system. In Halifax this tension is most evident in the split between the prevailing three African American organizations, the Halifax Coalition for Progress, the local chapter of the NAACP, and the Halifax County Black Caucus. The first, led by people like John Dixon and Conley Davis, older community leaders who were heavily involved in the Civil Rights Movement, is seen as the "old guard," the second is perceived as more moderate, while the last is seen as the most radical and confrontational of the three.

Present-day differences in ideology are traced back to the decision to file suit against the state regarding the Halifax County Board of Commissioners. According to Dale, who was one of the original plaintiffs, John Dixon and Conley Davis were "against the suit in the county" because they preferred working through the system. The younger, more radical group of leaders were setting a precedent for the county by filing a petition in federal court suing the county. The NAACP and the Black Caucus both supported the suit and aggressively petitioned for the creation of minority districts to usurp the power of whites in the at-large elections. Although the groups still work together on major issues, the precedent set by this history dictates a frequent division in their approach to politics.

DEFINING PROGRESS

The ongoing struggle for justice and equality in Halifax County is a struggle over projects that reflect different ideas of progress. For African American workers in certain types of high-risk industries, school children in need of adequate training, and minorities entitled to fair representation, progress is an ideal yet unfolding. During my twelve months of ethnographic inquiry, the word was often used by local officials and school board members to distance themselves from a troubled past, which they characterized as one of racism, poverty, and isolation. Their position was, "We are not where we used to be, nor are we where we want to be, but we are moving forward." School board members express this idea when discussing segregation. Economic development officers express it when discussing the arrival of new industry. City officials express it when discussing citizens' access to public goods and the recent presence of African Americans on the county commission. Yet, this rendering of progress is confounding.

Because of their long struggle for equal rights and fair pay, African Americans and those sensitive to the plight of industry workers in eastern North Carolina do not consider Halifax County necessarily progressive. Progress for them is defined by the success of citizens who have organized *against* unwanted industry. For CWEA it is assessed according to their success in lobbying for state regulation of processing lines in poultry plants. Progress for them does not simply mean more industry, it means safer industry.

In regard to Halifax County school children, progress is that which ensures their best academic preparation in a competitive world. While at one point progress was understood as mandatory integration, school officials today, including Marie Carter, question the necessity of integrated schooling given the hostility of Roanoke Rapids toward integration and the recent election of blacks to the Halifax County school board. The newly hired black superintendent and board members are trying to map out a path of progress that effectively sidesteps forced integration, while at the same time providing equitable learning for students in the predominately black school district.

African American city and county officials are attempting to force open more doors of opportunity for African American leadership so that the county can live up to its rhetoric of progress. As they work against the historical limitations of white dominance, progress will be defined by the degree to which such historical strongholds give way to new ideas, new economic opportunities, and minority leadership.

GRATITUDE AND EMPATHY

Living in one of the poorest counties in the state, the women I interviewed are surrounded by poverty, poor schooling, and abandoned elderly people. "Progress" for them and their communities is often an ideal in the making. How women respond to these conditions is informed both by their material conditions and by their faith experiences.

While legislative changes have been made to ensure equitable schooling for all students in the county, schools remain largely segregated with variably distributed resources. Likewise, although particular areas of Halifax County have benefited from the movement of industry into their communities, other areas have had to struggle to maintain their environmental health in the face of industrial expansion. Some community members have taken jobs created by the arrival of new industry, while others still struggle to make ends meet, working for low wages and few if any benefits.

Women decide to engage in various forms of activism at different stages in their lives. Nevertheless, they maintain throughout a level of personal involvement in the everyday experiences of those in their communities. Their decisions to engage in public activism are not necessarily made at moments of crisis, but are instead based upon a series of unorchestrated interpretive moments that occur over the course of their lives. These moments result in outward expressions of gratitude, empathy, and what Evelyn Brooks Higginbotham aptly calls "righteous discontent." Gratitude and empathy help women of faith create communities of love and mutual support, while righteous discontent aids in making women public actors (elected officials, protest organizers). The degree to which the African American women I interviewed engage in this type of public activity is determined by their ability to express and channel their righteous discontent into supportive, alternate public spheres, or into a black public sphere where issues affecting African Americans are constructively debated in open forum.

ACTIVISM'S BOUNDARIES

Discussions of activism often give little account of the transitions between activist and apparently nonactivist moments in people's lives. There is an assumption that activism is public and can be measured within a certain block of time. Other life experiences, by their omission from analysis, are seen as nonactivist or nonresistant moments.[1]

That women see their spirituality as central to their life experiences speaks to the power of spirituality to transform meaning and create action. Spirituality is thus embedded in the "timeless" spaces. It is that which gives meaning to life's experiences, both its joys and sorrows. Spirituality is at work when historians, social scientists, and journalists are busy looking for and documenting the public "moments" of resistance.

Because women's spirituality changes over time, it is difficult, if not impossible, to argue that there is a "private" spirituality and a "public" spirituality, whereby one exchanges one for the other, or changes from outside-oriented activist to private introspective worshipper. The boundaries are not that neat, nor are the categories that stable. There exist instead various manifestations of spirituality over the course of time. This is to say that both time and space impact how one interprets spirituality and how one chooses to live it out. Based upon their experiences in a constantly changing society, women's spirituality ebbs and flows with the passage of time. In some moments their lives take on dynamically public forms. In other moments women become less engaged in that which is measurable in public, while still contributing to the process of change.

Given this, spirituality affords the opportunity to examine women's lives over time in order to understand how and why they engage in public displays of collective activism or individual resistance at particular times in their lives. These moments in and of themselves, as noted, are not the only moments of activism. Furthermore, the transition between public and private moments is as important as the moments themselves in understanding women's activist agendas. How women interpret their life experiences between moments of hyper-public engagement dramatically affects their decisions to engage or not to engage in public activity. Spirituality is not then that which simply sparks one toward activism, as one might be led extemporaneously to "speak in tongues" or engage in "shouting" or celebratory dancing. Instead, spirituality offers a space through which one can interpret one's life experiences and respond according to one's understanding of faith. These interpretive moments yield three predominant outward expressions: gratitude, empathy, and righteous discontent. Highlighting these expressions is not to suggest that women do not experience a broad *range* of emotions in relationship to their life's experiences. Indeed, a host of emotions—sadness, joy, peace, anger, disappointment, frustration—are all variously embedded in the overarching expressions of gratitude, empathy, and righteous discontent.

Gratitude, for example, reflects an ability to turn experiences of struggle into prayers of thanksgiving for "making it through." Women in my research expressed feelings of immense gratitude at God's seeming benevolence toward them. In looking at birth, death, financial stability, tragedy, and a host of other life experiences, interviewees rendered an overarching sense of gratitude for God's intervention during these moments. Empathy, or an ability to feel another's pain, was also a common expression for the women that I interviewed. Their proximity to neighbors and their close family ties often led them to experience a deep sense of loss at another's misfortune. Refrains such as "but for the grace of God," or comments about assisting "the least of these" reflect their kinetic relationship with others in the community. Gratitude and empathy often became motivation for acting graciously on behalf of others. Righteous discontent, or indignation, on the other hand, emerged differently from gratitude and empathy. Although it was often sparked in both public and private spaces, the life of such indignation is fed by public interaction with others usually in a church- or community-based black public sphere.

DISTINGUISHING BETWEEN INTERPRETIVE MOMENTS

Understanding Gratitude

> I was here alone and I guess it was probably like about September or October and I was here about 12 or 1 o'clock that night. I had said my prayers and got in the bed and all of a sudden the Holy Spirit started dealing with me and I got up out of the bed and started saying my

prayers again and I started singing. I just walked through the house praising the Lord that night. Nobody was in the house but me, now. I'm home alone. I'm single then. And I just walked all that morning crying and just praising God for the things He had done for me. [There] was no sadness. There hadn't been nothing terrible that had happened in my life. It was like I was at a peace that God said, "I done gave you everything you asked for. Now you know it's just my time. It's time for you to give me some time." And that went on until about five o'clock that morning and I had to be to work at seven. And I went to work all day and felt good all that day. I had been praising the Lord and I had done prayed and sung and prayed ALL NIGHT LONG—from about 12 or 1 o'clock 'til five that morning.

Sheer gratitude for life and its provisions is a consistent theme throughout my interviews. Yvette is not an exception. Each of the women expressed immense gratitude to God for some level of progress in her life. Yvette, who grew up picking cotton and shucking peanuts, believes that God has abundantly provided for her daily needs, sometimes more than she has ever expected. As a child, she lived with her parents and seven siblings in a small green house on what was to her a huge farm. "[There] was about eight of us and we lived in that house on that farm. I think it had a kitchen. My mama's room that was the living room and bedroom all together. And upstairs we had one great big opening and the four girls slept on that end [motioning toward the right] and the four boys slept on that end."

Now living in a three-bedroom brick-underpinned trailer home with her husband, Yvette believes that she has traveled quite a distance from her modest beginnings. At seventeen, like too many other young women in rural areas, she gave birth to a child and had to withdraw from high school during her junior year. Since her "shot-gun" wedding, she has earned her GED and remarried. Gratitude for Yvette is based upon her ability to measure positively the change that has taken place in her life since childhood.

She and other women express an enormous amount of gratitude for the intervention they believe God has granted, whether by bringing salvation to a loved one, restoring a broken relationship, providing the necessities of life, or simply being present during a difficult moment. Gratitude, however, is not only a spontaneous expression; it is also a learned response to God's benevolence. Despite the harsh conditions of Halifax County, it is not difficult to find people gathered in churches Sunday after Sunday giving thanks to God for "God's goodness." Church services throughout the community have testimony periods and praise and worship moments during which parishioners are invited to stand and share with other believers the goodness that God has rendered throughout the week, the month, or the year. As I visited various churches, I witnessed countless exhortations by pastors, praise-team leaders, or choir directors for those gathered to praise God *"anyhow."* These formalized periods teach people a particular way to respond to life's adversities. Praise is offered as a form of gratitude for that which is regenerative, replacing worry, frustration, or disillusionment over that which is incommodious. Such testimonials are intended not only to benefit the person expressing the gratitude, but also to give encouragement to those listening.

For the women I interviewed God has been a consistent presence, even when their lives did not reflect a worthiness they deemed acceptable. "In spite of" the sentiment goes, "God has been good." Gratitude can be extended for anything from the mundane and ordinary to the ultimate expression of thanks for salvation. For Gloria, who had to relocate to North Carolina several years ago, one aspect of gratitude results from God's financial provision during the breakup of her first marriage. Standing as the sole provider for her two small children after leaving an abusive situation, in time she secured a job that allowed her to meet her financial obligations.

Although her sister loaned her extra cash and her brother placed her things in storage so that she could make an immediate exodus from Philadelphia, relocating presented a tremendous emotional and financial strain. When she returned to Halifax, she and her sons rented a trailer home affordable on her single income.

> Once I got here . . . I knew I was going to have a hard time finding a job, but I didn't know it was going to be that hard. I started working as a waitress . . . So, that was pretty good. It helped me get a car, you know. Save up enough money to get a car here. After that, I started feeling a little better about myself, but my self-esteem was still low. I wanted to go back to school, but I couldn't afford to go back to school. Didn't have transportation so that was another blow.

In time things improved. She found a job as a desk clerk and a part-time job at a grocery store.

> So, things started looking up for me, I did move forward to a better job, better paying job. I worked as a desk clerk. Then I got another job in the grocery store. I was beginning to [she pauses, taking time to clarify her thought]. My self-respect. My self-esteem. I felt a little more indepen-

dent. You know, I had a car. My money was startin' to look better, you
know. I got my own place. So I was really feeling good about myself.
And I didn't go down. I didn't have a down until after I got married.

While life seemed to provide her with all that she needed, her second
marriage proved to be one of her greatest trials. The difference in their
ages and life philosophies and the fact that they each had children from
previous relationships caused much tension. Yet, as she grew in faith, attending more Bible studies and talking with women at the church about
her marriage, she developed a different perspective. "Had you done it
this a way," or "had you done it that way," were the thoughts she used
to have when reflecting on her child-rearing, her marital decisions, and
her lack of formal education. Now, with her children grown and her faith
increased, she reflects differently.

> I have a job. You know, you have a home. You have money to fix it up
> like you want it, somewhat like you want it. Your daughter's in college.
> You thank God you can put her through, help her go through college.
> You know I had to look at those things, that God has blessed me with,
> NOW. And I knew who was pulling me down, and I knew it was Satan.
> And I had to rebuke him . . . Even riding down in the car, on the high-
> way in my car. 'Cause he was really doing a job with me. He was really
> playing with my mind.

When life is fairly good, one's children are in school, bills are paid,
and lodging is secure, gratitude is the "natural" state. To not be grateful, for Gloria, is an indication of the power of another force—according to her, Satan. The understood archenemy of God is at work pre-
venting her from expressing gratitude for God's benevolence. Even if
trouble remains, gratitude is expressed. This gratitude does not necessarily lead her to enter into public debate about the need for a living wage
or parental leave time. Instead, gratitude makes her discount the "I
should have" statements that may have caused her to think about alternative responses to her condition. Gratitude stands as an individual expression of thanksgiving to God, an appreciation for how God is intervening in her life regardless of the circumstances.

Gratitude concerning financial matters, while central to women's testimonies, reflects only one aspect of it. Safety and protection from "dangers seen and unseen" inspire many adulations of praise. Ms. Sylvia expressed gratitude for what she believes was God's intervention while she
was driving, God's "traveling mercies," as she explains. When I asked her

about the types of things for which she prays, she explained that she doesn't "pray for" things as much as she "gives thanks."

> Well, mostly, I give thanks. I thank God for my health. I thank God for my traveling mercies. I thank Him for my children, I thank Him for all the good things He has done for me and I would pray for the continuation of the same.[2]. . . I just let God know that I thank Him and when I do that I just feel good. I say, "Lord I just thank You for all the wonderful things that You've done for me." And sometimes I just start, I get right happy.

With this last statement she chuckled at the extent to which she gets carried away. The idea that she mostly "gives thanks" is a statement of her complete understanding of God as benevolent in her life. What she has, she has because God has granted it. Ms. Sylvia's gratitude, like Gloria's, is for her a "natural" expression. At this moment she began to tell me of two incidents in which she believes she would have died had it not been for God's intervention.

> I remember one night when I was in Philadelphia coming from church, just singing, and can't sing a lick . . . I had the green light . . . And all of a sudden a car with the red light facing it, with no lights, came through that intersection. I know that car had to be going, traveling about 70 mph, and if I had been, say, maybe four seconds earlier. . . . If I had been walking alone, I probably would have been in the middle of that intersection, and he would have hit me on my side and what could I have done.

As she went on to explain, "I was giving praise to God that I never walk alone. I'm never alone. And I felt that He proved to me, 'You ain't by yourself, girl.'" God was with her and had prevented her from sustaining injuries in what could have been a fatal accident. She expressed the same type of gratitude for God's intervention in another potential accident, this time in Halifax, "where 561 ends into 258 heading towards Rich Square." She was driving down the road *ironically* thinking that people should begin writing their own obituaries. As she was deciding how hers would begin, "all of a sudden," she looked up and saw a truck in her lane.

> So, lo and behold, the truck was, 18 wheeler, was in the lane I was driving in—because it was a two lane highway . . . He was trying to pass a car, and apparently with me coming over the hill and him coming out of a curve, with such a big vehicle, it was hard for him to get back [in the lane]. Well, me being whatever, I didn't believe he was in my lane, I

never broke my speed. So, finally I had to end up braking and I skid. When I skid to the shoulder, his, the back of his truck just came right in front of my car. And then I sat there . . . So, I felt that was a very spiritual moment, but I still don't understand that obituary business.

While women express gratitude for safety, financial provision, and health, the ultimate expression of gratitude is for salvation. Most of the women had a dramatic salvation experience in that there was a direct change from a past life into a "new life." Salvation involves for them a realization that God sent God's son, Jesus, to die for them and that Jesus' death and resurrection entitle them to a personal relationship with God. This type of evangelical conviction, traditional to most black Baptist congregations, gives them tremendous peace and comfort in the midst of many trying situations. Although most of the women I interviewed spoke in terms of a "born-again" experience, not all of them expressed their salvation in those terms. Two in particular associated their salvation with their general "spiritual growth," since childhood. The women who experienced a more distinct regenerative process, however, spoke with great passion of their gratitude for God's provision. Yvette described one dramatic moment in which she reflected upon the reality of her new spiritual state.

> I was pulled up at the bank and the song come on the radio, "The Blood." And I know that man thought I had probably had death in the family because I'm sittin' in front of the bank at that counter and was sittin' there and I just cried all I wanted to, right at the bank. It just made you think "God, you didn't have no sin and you would die for a nothing like me, a nobody." You know somebody that people look down on sometime, you know, and all the things that I had done and been through and you still shed that blood for me. Somebody that's not nothing but what? Filthy rags.[3] And I said, "Lord, I don't know why." And that He did He had did that for me.

The process of salvation, for Yvette, not only brings spiritual renewal, but also transforms her social status. "People," as she explains, sometimes "look down on" women like her—women without formal education, or who have had children out of wedlock, or who are without an outward show of wealth. Her experience of salvation, however, has not only changed her eternal condition, but has also dramatically influenced the way she experiences her "temporary" social condition, marked at times by society's rejection and erasure. "The Blood" was a testimony to the tremendous sacrifice of God and her (seeming) unworthiness of such sacrifice. Gratitude in this instance is for the ultimate gift of salvation. For Yvette there is no greater expression of love than God's gift of Jesus. God's ability to meet her in the most difficult and undesirable place in her life, a time, as she describes, when she is "filthy rags," is nearly unfathomable.

Yvette's expression of gratitude in private mirrored the expression of Juanita Cleveland one Sunday during service. As a frequent attendee of her relatively large Baptist church, I did not stand as a visitor on the Sunday that Ms. Cleveland welcomed visitors and read the announcements. As she concluded, closing her manila folder and heading toward her seat in the choir stand, she stopped for a moment simply peering at the congregation. She then proclaimed with tremendous conviction to the worshippers who had not yet moved with the Spirit of worship, "God is good! Jesus didn't have to die for you nor me. Hallelujah! God is good. ALL the time!" Her words garnered only a meek reply from the fairly solemn congregation. She then retorted, "I said, God is good! And I don't care whether you praise Him or not, I'm going to praise the Lord." This dramatic ending left congregants both stunned and in gleeful laughter, at which point they responded with an enthusiastic "Amen."

Gratitude is a profound expression in the lives of the women I interviewed. For some struggling to raise children with or without the support of a partner, gratitude becomes an expression of endurance. Faith that God will provide a means for getting food, restoring electricity, or reconnecting the hot water heater gives one strength not to give up when hopelessness seems inevitable. The experiences of the women I interviewed resonate with those of countless residents of Halifax County who wrestle with the failures of progress. Access to decent jobs, safe water supplies, and quality education for children constitutes only a fraction of the considerations that confront particularly poor and minority residents of the county. Gratitude in the midst of these circumstances is a reflection of both an expectation of God's blessing and a realization that God has historically provided for basic needs.

This same gratitude, however, does not necessarily translate into active engagement with an often hostile society. Gratitude alone does not render one knowledgeable enough, fearless enough, or organized enough to engage in active deconstruction of a political or economic system, even though one may know it is unfair in its hiring practices and its distribution of public goods. Gratitude even for the ultimate "gift" of salvation does not necessarily inspire one toward active engagement with the public sphere or direct protest. While gratitude can be a very active component in leading people to lives that seek social justice, it is by no means the standard by which one can measure people's political engagement. Many people who are genuinely grateful for various gifts, opportunities, or provisions in their lives are by no means engaged with public debate. Some social scientists have even argued that the experience of faith leaves people predisposed to a withdrawal from protest or from actively engaging a hostile public sphere. Lesley Gill, for example, suggests that in Bolivia the growth of fundamental Protestant churches has caused people to turn away from issues of material concern. "These relatively new organizations [fundamental Protestant churches] try to capture the imagination of the poor and unemployed by orienting the terms of debate around personal, religious, and lifestyle concerns. In the process, the language of class and class struggle disappears."[4]

Furthermore, the language of gratitude does not necessarily assist women in seeing the particular ways in which their experiences are not only racially and economically determined, but also heavily based upon gendered social dynamics. Providing food for their families, struggling to pay for housing on single incomes, and often facing physical or verbal abuse that leads to separation and divorce are all issues that overwhelmingly affect women. The phrase "feminization of poverty" in many ways encapsulates the type of struggles that many of the women in Halifax County have endured.

Even among evangelical believers or those who profess a "born-again" experience, when God is characterized as a "just" God, or one who exercises justice, this acknowledgment does not translate immediately into acting in just ways or even seeking justice. While such an acknowledgment sets a standard for what justice is, it does not necessarily result in one's manifesting just actions. In the most narrow sense, the implementation of God's justice can be seen as simply an eschatological moment, a point in time when Jesus returns to reward saints and bring sinners to a final judgment. At this point, those who are saved escape eternal damnation, whereas those who are not are immediately subjected to God's judgment. In this view Divinity is seen as exercising justice at some seemingly distant moment. Most important is God's treatment of the unrepentant in relationship to the repentant. When Yvette and Juanita Cleveland reflected upon Jesus' sacrifice, this is the justice to which they were referring. While Ms. Cleveland has entered a life of public activism, her salvation experience was not the sole catalyst for this choice.

These expressions of gratitude are in some ways reminiscent of Cornel West's call for "hope" in the midst of nihilism. "The major enemy of black survival in America," West argues, "has been and is neither oppression nor exploitation but rather the nihilistic threat—that is, loss of hope and absence of meaning."[5] Critics of West point out that "hope" does not bring about the type of material changes that signal "progressive change." While West consistently points out the problems of late capitalism, to these critics his appeal seems disconnected from the material reality of laborers, women, blacks, and others dramatically impacted by the pressures of late capitalism. The more because he is a socialist, his suggestions seemed askew. "Hope" does not necessarily bring substantial change in people's material reality. It does not force political or economic change, just as gratitude does not necessarily result in large-scale change for the common good. What hope and gratitude do produce, however, is endurance and therefore the possibility of change in the midst of adversity.

Understanding Empathy

Women expressed not only tremendous feelings of gratitude, but also empathy. Empathy has been described by anthropologist Tanya Luhrmann as an attitude that rests on a type of "local mapping."[6] In other words, "empathy is the name for the local process through which people come to understand one another as persons with hopes and needs that are meaningful and worthy of respect in their community."[7] From Luhrmann's research among Catholic, Jewish, and new age faith communities in California, she concludes that "the way you learn to experience God, and to have a relationship with God, can have a profound effect on the way in which you experience empathy and, in turn, an effect upon the way you experience people."[8] This description of empathy corresponds to women's faith experiences in Halifax County.

Empathy was not only an expression of their relationship with God; it also grew out of the lived experience of diversity. Because people tend to live on "family land" and remain in the area, different classes of people live along the same rural road. It is not uncommon to see an elaborate ranch-style home on the same road as a condemned wooden home. Although there are certainly sections of towns that are classified by race or class, the country region is far more amorphous. The rural areas do not permit a distance from poverty, or a sectioning of the elderly from the younger generation. Not only are living conditions less partitioned; so are faith communities. Because most people attend "family churches," a range of experiences can often be found in one church.

There are countless occasions for people to develop a cross section of relationships—youth and seniors, middle class and poor, teachers and farm workers and factory workers. Such relationships reflect the commitments of the women I interviewed.

Their ability to demonstrate empathy comes from their experiences as lifetime residents of the county as well as their experience as return migrants.[9] As caregivers to the elderly, parents, and employees, the women demonstrate in their lives an ongoing concern for those in the community. When I asked Ms. Moore about the type of community work in which she engages, she immediately spoke about the elderly. Because of the mass exodus of young adults to places like Virginia and Roanoke Rapids, Tillery has one of the highest unbalanced ratios of elderly to young people in the state. The decline in small family farms and their profitability has led young people to move to the larger cities of Roanoke Rapids, Rocky Mount, or Raleigh where jobs are more readily available. People return to Tillery mostly to retire. This imbalance of older residents creates an immediate need for caregivers of seniors on fixed incomes. "When you consider the kind of community I live in," Ms. Moore explains, "I live in a very small, rural, poor community." Such a community, she states, causes her to "become more alert, more concerned about the people," especially the elderly. "I like to be around elderly people," says Ms. Moore because they give her an appreciation for life and its latter season. Witnessing their vulnerabilities in the mundane tasks of cleaning house and taking medication, she is encouraged to appreciate the health and freedom that she enjoys now in her fifties.

> There's a couple that I think a lot of and the husband has since died . . . And all of their children are away in far cities like California or wherever. And I went down to see them one day and I noticed the house was just dirty. It was just dirty, but she couldn't. She was just getting around with the walker, the little walker thing for what little bit of getting around she did. So, I went back one day and I carried my vacuum cleaner, my bucket, my scrub mop and all that kind of stuff and started trying to clean her house. I asked her did she mind and she said "no." And so I tried to, I went in the part of the house that company, visitors see, you know I tried to help do that. And I took her curtains down to wash her curtains and they had been to the windows so long [chuckles] that when I washed them they tore up in the washing machine . . . So, we managed to get them back together.

There is at least one other elderly lady that Ms. Moore monitors as a part of her daily or weekly routine. This woman's son is on kidney dialysis and is unable to help around the house. Although she manages by herself, she, like the widow, is unable to continue with strenuous household chores. Ms. Moore told me:

> I call her every night and she doesn't go to sleep until I call her to see if she's gotten in bed okay. And "Are you in? Tucked in?" And she says, "yes." And she says, "I'll turn over now." She doesn't turn over, because it takes her so long to turn back over, you know she's ailing. But she doesn't turn over until I call her. So, I call her every night and I wash her hair. I wash her hair once a month. She likes her nails. So, I do her nails and that kind of thing, change her hats around. She wants this over here and that kind of thing. You know. And those kinds of things I enjoy doing. I really enjoy doing. And I don't enjoy them because, I don't tell about it or anything. But, these people just look at you and in their eyes they're just saying "Thank you." You can tell that they wanted it done, but these are proud old people who don't want to ask you.

Ms. Moore's care of the elderly reflects her relationship with God. "It's my spirituality," she explains, "when my heart goes out to somebody for something . . . or when I remember someone who maybe needs a call or something, who's not feeling well or maybe is going through some problem or something." Her schedule as a teacher and director of a local gospel choir is often demanding, and time does not permit many exceptions. She believes, however, that assisting this select group of elderly is what she is called to do. Caring for the elderly allows her to demonstrate appreciation for what she believes to be God's favor toward her.

Much like Ms. Moore, Ms. Sylvia contributes a significant portion of her time to the care of seniors. Although her work with CCT is in an official capacity, the care with which she handles seniors signals a deeper level of commitment, a depth not seen clearly unless one spends time with her on the mundane issues, such as getting seniors to and from the center. Now in her nineties, Cousin Ellie (as everyone calls her) is one such senior.

Cousin Ellie walks funny. Her demeanor is strange to a visitor. When she first makes her way across the room at a meeting of the Open Minded Seniors, the CCT group for the elderly, a new visitor looks on her with pity and a bit of personal discomfort. Unable to stand up straight because of the loss of calcium in her bones, Cousin Ellie walks with a severe hunch in her back. Her five-foot frame bends almost in two as she leans against her cane, slowly making her way across the floor to the ladies' room, the only place she ventures to during the two-hour meeting. Most people would write her off as an invalid, an elderly person without social capital, but not Ms. Sylvia. She picks Cousin Ellie up and drops her off every week before and after the meeting, or she secures a ride for her. I had an opportunity to be this ride one week. I rode with Ms. Sylvia the week before so that I would know exactly what to do and where to go in her absence. She took me down the dirt road that leads to the new seniors' complex. We walked with Cousin Ellie into her first-floor apartment, comfortable enough for one to sleep.

The walk from the car to the apartment was enough for me to gain appreciation for the unrecognized work that Ms. Sylvia performs. I walked on one side of Cousin Ellie; Ms. Sylvia the other. For every step we took, she would take five or six tiny steps. We talked and waited while Cousin Ellie, never saying a word, caught up with our progression. When we finally reached the inside of her apartment, Ms. Sylvia instructed me to get a cold glass of water for Cousin Ellie so that she could have it beside her bed and would not have to make her way to the kitchen. I went to the refrigerator and found inside the lone jug of water alongside a pitcher of tea. A Styrofoam container with leftover food sat on the second shelf and a few condiments in the refrigerator door. It was obvious that Cousin Ellie no longer cooks and has few, if any, visitors. We dressed her for the day, taking off her meeting clothes and putting on a cool house dress for her to lounge. Ms. Sylvia gave her some instructions about who would be coming over later to bring her dinner and what she needed to do in the meantime. We soon left, Ms. Sylvia taking her key and locking the door behind us.

As we left the area, Ms. Sylvia drove me around the neighborhood that surrounds the seniors' complex. Most of the homes on the dirt road are fairly unattractive wooden structures with worn-away paint and feeble porches. She pointed out where another one of the seniors who attends the OMS meetings lives. Ms. Blake, like several other members of this small African American community, is without running water and must either use the outhouse in the back of her home or walk a few blocks to use the facilities at the county courthouse. In 1997 Halifax County had the highest number of outside privies of all one hundred counties in the state. My first experience ever walking into a home without a sink in the kitchen and without an inside restroom was during my field research. The family I visited drew water from a faucet outside their backdoor while their privy was another twenty feet away. Other neighbors who have running water sometimes wrestle with faulty septic systems that erupt and leave sewage around the fringes of their yards. The municipality closest to them refuses to extend its borders, which would give everyone access to the city's water supply, because they do not want to compromise the value of their homes or have to assume tax responsibility for the low-income neighborhood should they not be able to meet the financial cost of switching water systems. As it stands now, the community is within the county's jurisdiction.

I started to ask Ms. Sylvia why it is so important to her that she pick up Cousin Ellie every week and bring her to the Seniors' meeting, but I knew the answer. I had been attending the meetings for months by this time. Not only are the weekly meeting issues relevant to the seniors, but their time of fellowship is also important to them. They catch up on news about what has occurred during the past week. They talk about solutions to sewage problems, economic development issues, local and national politics, the black farmers' crisis, and a host of other issues which they deem important. Most significant, however, they talk with one another about their families, church activities, trips they have recently taken, or friends that have come to visit. The time together is an opportunity to extend one's bragging rights.

Within the group, Cousin Ellie, slow to speak, is highly favored, as is Mother Emmaline. The two of them, well into their nineties, are the eldest OMS members. Their presence is a badge of honor. When visitors come, the first people that they are introduced to are the "elders," Mother Emmaline and Cousin Ellie.

The respect that CCT bestows upon seniors is a small token of tremendous value to the aging men and women who attend the meetings. Many visitors have told the CCT organizers that they add years to seniors' lives because of the dignity and respect with which they treat them. The attention given the seniors, not only through words but also through direct physical care, is what invigorates the Tillery community.

Places like Tillery are easily erased from the public imagination. They are associated with rural life and lack the flare of urbanity. Within Tillery's vast expanse of farmland and forest, houses are spread acres apart. Urgency is not the norm of the day, and tempers do not flare as the result of "road rage." The atmosphere is nice and easy-going, but people are often forgotten.

Ms. Sylvia's participation with the Open Minded Seniors group did not come by chance. She learned of CCT while living up north raising her family. Members of the OMS actively cared for her ailing grandmother and kept Ms. Sylvia abreast of pertinent news back home. Her debt of gratitude, as she explains, is enormous. Yet, when she came to work in this community, she began to serve the seniors for other reasons, namely God's "blessings." "I just feel that [when] I do volunteer work for a community organization, I'm giving back to my community because I've been blessed to come back home to Halifax County at an age when I am still energetic, healthy, and willing to give back because this is where I came from, you know."

She learned at an early age after being reprimanded by her grandmother for laughing at a crippled woman that "but for the grace of God, so go I." This idea of God's grace intervening and giving her the ability to live a full life immediately affects her ability to empathize with others who may not be as fortunate. Returning to the area after an extended period up North has given her tremendous appreciation for the people who remained, worked the land, and secured a home for others. When I asked how she feels about moving back to Halifax County, she explained:

> Thankful! That most of the time, I say, there but by the grace of God go I. And on a daily basis I thank God for opportunity to leave Halifax County. That has been truly one of my blessings. Even though I encountered racism and prejudice up north, at least there were jobs. When I first went there, I worked in minimum wage jobs. At that time it was a dollar an hour. And at least I had the opportunity to work. But, living in Halifax County, if you're not a teacher. . . . I have a saying, "You either teach or preach." There really isn't very much to do in Halifax County. And the people that stayed and attended the farms, what do they have? . . . So coming back to an economically depressed area like Halifax County truly gives me a real sense of spirituality to say thank God I left and thank God I was able to do better for myself.

While Ms. Sylvia's work places her in immediate contact with the elderly in Halifax County, Gloria's work places her in contact with pregnant teenagers. She is a field agent for the department of social services. Although her job does not require her to stay in contact with clients after a certain point, she likes to assist them as long as possible, especially if they have grown attached to her. Much of her personal income is spent purchasing clothing items for babies or food for the families. When I asked Gloria about her involvement in the community, she immediately pointed to the work she does as a field agent, where the daily stress of the job places her in depressing situations continuously. "I don't think I could do the job that I do," she said, "if it wasn't for God."

> I work with high-risk pregnant teens and pregnant women. I work in Scotland Neck, Tillery, Enfield, Hollister, Roanoke Rapids, and Weldon. All of Halifax County, so I travel a lot. I see a lot of things and when I first got the job I was shocked to see people still live the way they live, right here . . . No running water, outside toilets, and people you walk in their house, you can

see the ground . . . One instance I had when I first started. This girl, I went to visit her. I'm petrified of mice and rats, living or dead, I just can't deal with those rodents. And I had gone to her house and I could never catch her home. So, when I finally caught her at home, I went in and I talked with her and her mother, you know, about different things that she needed to do about her prenatal care and stuff like that and things that's gonna happen to her . . . And there was a window on this side [motioning to her left] and I kept hearing something, and I kept wondering because I thought it was the wind . . . and then all of a sudden I saw this little mouse run across . . . Well, to make a long story short, I think the mother picked up on what happened there, so the next visit she was telling me about different things; about the mice and the rats. And that . . . the upstairs was closed off because there was bats up there. And that she was cleaning her fire place out and there were snakes. Well, this was all I needed to hear. I got mad. I said something needs to be done about this. "You all need to be out of this house, because she can't have this baby in this house." So, when I got back to the office, I called housing authority. I called the building inspectors. I called CADA [Choanoke Area Development Association]. Nobody could help me. So, one night I went to a church service and I saw the commissioner that lives in Scotland Neck and I approached him and I told him what I had experienced.[10] And I said, "That is your home town. You should know the house I'm talking about," and I said, "it doesn't make any sense for somebody to have to live like that. Something needs to be done."

After going back and forth with CADA and with the commissioner, Gloria was finally able to secure the family another home and have their present one condemned. According to her, the investment needed to ensure that outcome was great and her strength to accomplish it was solely from God. "To me, had I not been into the WORD, doing God's work, doing the things He say to do, I don't think I could have done it. I don't think I would have cared." While her job description was simply to give prenatal consultation, Gloria insisted her relationship with God and understanding of Scripture gave her the compassion to go beyond the call of duty in seeing that the family moved.

But by being a born-again Christian, God has really anointed me through my heart, through my caring and my giving. Because I know that I have something there that I can work with. And had I not done that, I don't think that I could continue to do the job that I do. Because it's a special job. Some of them, they're teenagers and they're just hard-headed and they don't want to listen, but you still stick with them and you try to do what you can to go through the volunteer program.

On another occasion Gloria again pointed to the centrality of scripture in guiding her relationship with others. "There is a scripture that says if they're hungry, you're suppose to feed 'em. If they're thirsty give 'em water. If they're without clothes, clothe 'em." While she acknowl-

edges, "I don't know what book it is in," the concept of self-sacrifice for
the sake of others is a part of her religious conditioning.

This empathetic self-sacrifice is important to the maintenance of community and community relations. On one level, empathetic activity
meets the basic needs of those people within a particular care circle. In
this way the most tender (in the case of Ms. Sylvia and Ms. Moore caring for elderly women) and the most thorough care (in the case of Gloria securing adequate housing for a teen mother and her family) is guaranteed. God's love and grace are able to flow through individuals and
meet the physical and emotional needs of those in distress. This empathy builds and sustains community.

This element of care is often overlooked in research that points to the
resistance-oriented strategies of black faith. Given the presumed binary
between accommodation and resistance, such caring practices are read
as accommodating structures of oppression because such activity does
not immediately confront injustices that may be readily apparent.
"Band-aids" over "bullet-wounds," especially in the case of aiding pregnant teenagers and the poor, is a common rhetorical critique. Nevertheless, gratitude and empathy are important and even necessary characteristics of community-building. The point of contention, however, is
that such actions do not necessarily lead believers to a sense of "righteous discontent," an overwhelming need to alter the material conditions
of society as a whole through public political engagement and sometimes
confrontation. Gloria's actions brought the concerns of a particular
young person to the attention of a public official. He in turn worked with
her through CADA to rectify this specific problem. Yet overall structural
change in the condition of the masses of poor people in Halifax County
similarly affected did not result.

If gratitude and empathy can cause one to work on behalf of others
creating community and meeting needs, under what conditions do these
expressions translate into public activism whereby the very structures
that oppress people are confronted? In many ways gratitude and empathy if left alone can indeed result in apolitical action that forms a type of
hegemonic replication of distressed circumstances, accommodating dys-
functional or oppressive systems. Idealizing narrow roles such as caregiver or grateful believer as the epitome of one's faith experience can unintentionally reinforce norms of "place" and one's need to *stay* in one's
place. One acknowledges the need to assist with social distress without
confronting systems that perpetuate such distress. In instances where

"righteous discontent" develops concerning the lack of progress and ongoing social distress, how is this discontent maintained? What threatens its existence? What role might the black public sphere play in nurturing and guiding this discontent so that it results in formidable change in society's structures?

READING CHURCH HISTORY

"You could hear a pin drop," Beverly recalled. Throughout the church there was silence. Although moments before, the crowd had erupted into loud applause in affirmation of the speakers' messages, the tone of the rally was now somber. The euphoria heard earlier was the sound of resolve among blacks in Halifax County, determined that they would no longer allow white dominance to penetrate the fabric of their social, economic, and political life. Change was long overdue. The silence testified to the ensuing fear. "You could see the fear in the church. And the reluctance to go up," recalled Beverly. This was in the mid-1980s, and local leaders had initiated a class-action lawsuit against the county.

For Beverly, remembering an event that took place over fifteen years ago is still a significant and moving experience. The entire rally had been organized by the Black Caucus and the NAACP of Halifax County. They had decided to make Shiloh Baptist Church the designated place from which to launch the lawsuit. The church was not only free to them, but also free of surveillance and free of intimidation. Within the church, members controlled the money, the lights, the dialogue, the confrontation, the selection of speakers, and, most important, the entrance and exit of people. This precaution ensured the safety of all gathered. Everyone knew that the stakes were high. Never before had the community filed a lawsuit against the county, not in such a small, rural, and seemingly isolated place where white dominance was the order of the day. The current county commission chairperson was *after all* rumored to be the grand dragon of the Ku Klux Klan.

Beverly sat alongside the others waiting for the first person to walk up and sign the petition. The speakers had just finished delivering fiery sermons about how the time had come and how change was inevitable. Everyone knew that the petitions represented not only the possibility of black representation on the county commission, but also the possibility of retaliation and the loss of jobs if (or when) the names of the plaintiffs were made public. Beverly sat thinking of her children. Single and raising two boys on her own, she could not afford to lose her job. Others were certainly thinking along similar lines. She waited for someone else to move, but no one did. People only waited. Someone had to move. Beverly hesitated, knowing that she had responsibilities and that whites in the county were not sympathetic to black protest and confrontation with the status quo. Everyone had her place and was expected to stay in it. Nevertheless, everyone knew the time had come.

Although the success of the Civil Rights Movement ensured the right to full participation in the electoral process, Halifax County had never elected a black county commissioner. Certainly by the 1980s, folks thought, the county could have elected at least one African American county commissioner, but the cards were stacked against blacks. At-large elections in a place where only the majority of whites were conditioned and free of intimidation to participate as active, voting citizens kept at bay the possibility of ever electing an African American. The only way to resolve the tension, reasoned the leadership of the younger and more radical Caucus, was to organize a formal lawsuit against the county for not allowing minority districts.

The men and women around Beverly sat in the church waiting, maybe praying for the courage that the speakers had just talked about, maybe hoping for insight that would move them beyond fear of the present. Their prayers had certainly not gone unheard. Their petitions for wisdom and strength and guidance were certainly not ignored. After all, they knew their history and they knew that they were a *part of* history. They knew that blacks for years had met in churches just like Shiloh Baptist, praying for the same types of changes that they prayed for, preaching about the same evil of racism that they had just preached about, testifying about the same horrid run-ins with injustice that they had just expressed. Certainly they understood their place in history.

Beverly's recollection was poignant. As she waited, listening to the silence, she reasoned that if she was not willing to move, why should she expect another to? She had determined even before the meeting that she would not be fearful. When the time came, and her contemplation was complete, she was one of the first to leave her seat. Although, like the rest of those gathered that day, she pondered the consequences of signing her name to the formal document, she eventually walked forward, along with ministers and entrepreneurs—those not dependent upon white employers—to take another step toward progress.

Beverly's resolve mirrors the resolve of countless women, who in their struggle for justice and rightness, have hoped against hope for change, lending their souls and bodies to the cause of freedom and equality. Distinct in this history of African American women's activism is often women's spiritual commitments, their reliance upon God to help them on their journey toward freedom. Spirituality serves for them as not only a motivating factor, but also a sustaining balance through difficult times. Though we know little about everyday women like Beverly, we do know about the faith of more public women. Volumes could be written about the faith of women like Ida B. Wells, who in her campaign against lynchings made her reliance upon God a central theme in her journals; or Sojourner Truth, whose real name was Isabella Baumfree, but who proclaimed that she was called by God to *sojourn* across the land spreading the *truth;* or Harriet Tubman, who having escaped slavery, headed back across the Mason Dixon Line at least fifteen additional times in order to rescue those who were still held in bondage. Sojourner Truth and Harriet Tubman fought against the institutions of capital and money to argue for the release of those whose free labor built the economy of the South. Coming between God and mammon, these women called upon the rightness of faith to bring liberation. Volumes more could be written about women like Jarena Lee, Julia A. Foote, and Zilpha Elaw, who stood up to not only the racist practices of society, but also the sexist assumptions of church theologies that ignored their calling and rendered their voices silent. Preaching anyway, they carried the message of the gospel to thousands of people. Time would not fail to tell of Fannie Lou Hamer, Mary McLeod Bethune, Anna J. H. Cooper, Maria W. Stewart, Septima Clark, Shirley Chisholm, Nannie Helen Burroughs, Mary Church Terrell, Rosa Parks, Coretta S. King, and many other women whose faith marked their commitment to the liberation of men, women, and children.

These women's faith in countless ways has been shaped by their experiences in black churches. That the Halifax County Black Caucus chose a sanctuary, a *black* sanctuary, as their meeting place is not coincidental. The walls of the church provided the haven necessary to launch their campaign. Although the history of black churches is complicated and sometimes even seems to go against the movement toward political and economic liberation, the black churches that have participated in these struggles have been central to the liberation efforts of black people in the United States.

BLACK CHURCHES: A HISTORY OF ACTIVISM

Mainline black Protestant churches emerged in the context of a hostile white society and from that point established much of their political and theological positions, which mediated between the spiritual world and the world of the slaveholders. While some black churches grew as a result of segregation from previously mixed congregations, others "arose independently from the start."[1] Although little is known about the form and substance of these early church meetings, historian Mechal Sobel suggests that their existence has been discounted because of their insignificance in the eyes of white slave owners who kept more mainstream records of church activity.[2]

The first independent black church, organized in Silver Bluff, South Carolina, came into being between 1773 and 1775. Blacks who founded black churches were not looking only for a space where they could worship their God in a form acceptable to them, but also for a space where freed slaves could be treated as humans and the issues of their pending freedom could be openly engaged. These independent black churches were the first formal "black public spheres" developed in the United States. Peter Paris notes: "The growth of the black churches is both significant and inspirational. In its history lie the stories of countless men and women, often slaves and runaway slaves, frequently freed men of humble economic stature, completely lacking in social status. Under paralyzing conditions, both during and after slavery, a multiplicity of black churches emerged, some on the plantations, others in segregated urban centers, many along the back roads in rural areas. In each case the black church was the primary community institution owned and controlled by blacks themselves."[3]

When more formal institutions were founded, taking on the identity of major denominations, they were often Baptist or Methodist. Noting the development of black Baptist churches, Sobel explains, "Black Baptist churches began to be established in the pre–Revolutionary War period and continued to grow throughout the antebellum era. At least ten formal black churches were established prior to 1800 (all in the South), and by 1864 some 205 formal churches can be documented—75 in the North and 130 in the slave South."[4] Simultaneous with the growth of these churches was the institutionalization of the African Methodist Episcopal Church by Richard Allen and Absolam Jones in the late 1700s.

Although black churches in the South did not always carve out overtly rebellious agendas in the midst of slavery, they did create spaces where slaves could come together to express their spiritual selves and their longings for freedom.[5] Radical deviations from the more survivalist orientations of these churches are of course represented by churches and religious leaders that actually orchestrated slave revolts and escape plans. Most noted among the slave revolts are those led by Nat Turner in 1831 in Southampton County, Virginia, Denmark Vesey in 1822 in Charleston, South Carolina, and "General" Gabriel Prosser in 1800 in Virginia.[6] These revolts were led by men who believed themselves inspired by God to seek freedom for their enslaved brothers and sisters. By and large, however, antislavery efforts were instigated by black churches in the North who often worked alongside white Methodist, Quaker, and Northern Baptist denominations. According to Sobel, "in the North, black churches became open abolitionist platforms, and blacks cited Christian morality as the basis for their antislavery statements in petitions and public papers. Slavery was a painful subject for Northern black Christians, particularly for Northern black Baptists, an increasing percentage of whom were 'up from slavery.'"[7]

Following the Civil War, the church, according to E. Franklin Frazier, became central to the reestablishment of the Negro community. While scholars have rigorously criticized Frazier's argument that the end of slavery destroyed antebellum black family networks, few dispute the significance his work ascribes to the African American church in the postbellum years. This church, different from the antebellum church, became the institution primarily responsible for addressing many of the day-to-day "functioning" issues of newly freed slaves. The "Negro church" served as a "nation within a nation," a means of social control, a site for economic cooperation in the attainment of education, houses, and land, and, finally, a site for entrance into the political arena.[8] Given that Southern states contributed few resources to the establishment of Negro schools after emancipation, black churches in the North and South (along with white churches of the North) played a major role in establishing schools for freed slaves. Colleges and universities were also a major outgrowth of black churches in the postbellum years.[9] In the arena of political life, potential candidates for office most often came from among the numbers of black preachers, who gained much of their support from their congregants and members of supportive churches in their communities. Following the lead of the AME Church, which was institutionalized on the national level before the war, Baptists and Pentecostals began to form national organizations during the Reconstruction years, beginning with the founding of the National Baptist Convention, U.S.A., in September 1895.[10]

The work of these congregations and their leaders was often focused specifically along the lines of racial uplift, with many of the leaders of churches and organizations like the NAACP and Women's Clubs at the time gaining the titles "race man" or "race woman." Among some of the most notable leaders are W. E. B. Du Bois (NAACP), Booker T. Washington (Tuskegee Institute; Urban League), Ida B. Wells-Barnett (*Free Speech*, Alpha Suffrage Club), Mary Church Terrell (Colored Women's League), and Anna Julia Cooper (Women's Christian Temperance Union). With both a critical approach to white racism and a sense of God's justice, these leaders often sought through the auspices of the black church to bring about substantial change in the condition of African American people.

The second quarter of the twentieth century witnessed what Gayraud Wilmore has called the "deradicalization of the black church."[11] This period between 1925 and 1950, according to Wilmore, was marked by a triumph of Booker T. Washington's notions of gradualism.[12] Given the rigidity of Jim Crow and the heinousness of white crimes against black communities, the "Negro church" made few attempts at integration. Instead, during this period, it found within itself resources for the ongoing education of its communities and the affirmation of dignity and respect too long denied by the larger society. The emphasis upon self-help with a retreat from protest-oriented struggle marked the tradition of the Negro church.

According to Lincoln, with the rise of the Civil Rights Movement and the Black Power Movement, the "Negro church" died, giving birth to a philosophically different church, the "Black church." This church took theoretical cues from these two movements and began to refashion itself as an institution whose mission was more radical than the benevolent and often survival-oriented practices of the Negro church. "The Black Church had been born of the travail of slavery and oppression. Its very existence was the concrete evidence of the determination of Black Christians to separate themselves from the white Christians, whose cultural style and spiritual understanding made no provision for racial inclusiveness at a level acceptable to Black people."[13]

As the black church engaged in efforts to sustain the community against a hostile white society, its priestly elements remained stable. Emphasis upon salvation, life after death, and the eschatological hope of the church's rapture remained central to the church's teaching. Faith and the spreading of the gospel still formed the cornerstone of its message. It was, however, the tension between this calling and the more prophetic call to seek social justice that split one of the largest denominations. In the mid-1950s the call of several ministers to engage in the Civil Rights Movement immediately aroused the sensibilities of the National Baptist Convention under the leadership of Dr. Joseph H. Jackson. Dr. Martin Luther King, Jr., Rev. Dr. Gardner C. Taylor, Martin Luther King, Sr., Ralph Abernathy, Benjamin Mays, and others opposed Jackson's conservative approach to social issues.[14] "Under his slogan 'from protest to production' he [Jackson] located himself in the patriotic, law and order, anticommunist, procapitalist, school of gradualism."[15] Taylor, King, and others saw the need for immediate protest against the oppressive social and economic order in the South and created a contingency called the "Taylor team" in order to oust Jackson from office. Although they were organized and had a large following, their efforts were unsuccessful. Several churches later joined with Drs. King and Taylor in the formation of the Progressive National Baptist Convention, Inc. This historic split signals not only the type of tension that has existed historically between the black church's priestly and prophetic acts of engagement, but also the diversity within the black church.

These historical tensions frame perceptions of black church activism and how people think about their faith in relationship to the social and economic needs of their communities. For some, church and the promise of eternal salvation provide the solution; for others, the church is both a place of personal salvation and a vehicle through which progressive social actions should be taken on behalf of those less fortunate.

THE CHURCH IN HALIFAX COUNTY

Because of this history, it is difficult to talk in contemporary terms about a monolithic black church. The vast experiences of blacks in Christian communities today span far beyond the practices of what Lincoln and

Mamiya describe as the "black church." Black presence in majority black, yet white-pastored churches, participation in multicultural communities of faith, and the growing numbers of black churches in white denominations complicate any narrow definition of "the black church"—not to mention that the mythic "black church" has adopted an assortment of political positions and theological doctrines which work both with and against what some may identify as traditional black political and social missions. Nevertheless, there is a common history of liberation within black communities of faith. This history has been one of struggle in the midst of a racist and sexist society. The churches, and the women who struggle for freedom in Halifax, emerge from this tradition.

In Halifax County there are no megachurches, few if any black churches in white denominations, and far fewer multicultural worship services than are found in major metropolitan areas. Aside from the Catholic church, the Seventh Day Adventist, and one nondenominational church that I visited in Roanoke Rapids, integrated churches are few and far between. In this rural setting, churches where African Americans meet fall largely into the category of "black churches" described by Lincoln and Mamiya—most associated with historically black denominations and most wrestling with the priorities of their priestly and prophetic calls for ministry in the community. The faith of the women who attend these churches reflects this history of struggle between the personal and political relevance of faith.

Evident in Beverly's story, black churches in Halifax County have played a significant role in civil rights struggles. These churches in many ways have undergirded the political and economic goals of black residents in the county for decades. Yet they are not necessarily the standard, nor do they even necessarily represent the majority of black churches in the area. There is a noticeable tension between churches that actively engage in public debate and those that do not. Often this tension exists between those who believe that their central mission is to preach the gospel of eternal salvation and those who believe that part of the gospel of eternal salvation mandates a discussion of present-day social and economic justice. It is not uncommon to hear more socially engaged pastors and lay people lamenting the inactivity of churches focused exclusively on the souls of their members. Among the women I interviewed, this critique was directed toward churches seen as disengaged from the everyday material struggles of their people.

Ms. Moore suggested that the material gains of the church have affected the church's ability to engage larger social concerns.

You know, we're little country churches and [we used to have] a little pump and outside toilet and all that kind of thing . . . I think we got brick churches and air conditioning and inside toilets and all of that and we thought, "Hey, I'm just on my way to heaven now. And this is just all fine. And so I don't have to worry about my fellow man now, because he's okay." And I think some degree of what some may call economic progress has caused people to look at the church differently in terms of the role it should play. And at the same time I think there are large numbers of people who *need* the support that the church can give in so many ways.

Contentment with a degree of progress, Ms. Moore contends, has caused some to retreat from greater concern with the social well-being of others. Ms. Sylvia gave a different explanation. By recalling her conversation with one of the more politically active pastors in the county, she expressed her vision of the problem. "One minister used to say and I kind of agree with him, 'You just stay down on your knees praying, old black folks, and them white folks gonna steal you blind.'" Though she laughed at his imagery, she affirmed the value of both spiritual and physical activity. "I think prayer is the way. I think there is power in prayer. But, I also know that you need to get up off your knees and get out and do something for yourself, with your prayer and your spiritual belief." Sylvia Jones's and Carmen Moore's ideas reflect their concern about the kind of activity various churches in the county engage in. Although they each consider their own church rather active, they believe that some churches do not encourage their parishioners to think critically about their political and economic plight. These types of churches reach across denominational lines. In Halifax County, however, the prevailing denominations include Baptist, Methodist, Pentecostal, and Seventh Day Adventist.

While black Baptist and Pentecostal churches in Halifax County far outnumber Methodist and Presbyterian churches, there are a host of "nondenominational" churches, which self-govern and do not affiliate themselves with a larger body. Among the Methodist, there is one African Methodist Episcopal church (AME) in the county, located in the town of Weldon, along with other United Methodist churches which have a few African American parishioners.[16] The Seventh Day Adventist church in Roanoke Rapids also has an interracial congregation, though the African American families there are relatively few in number.[17] Both the Catholic church and the Kingdom Hall of the Jehovah's Witnesses have their sole locations in Roanoke Rapids.

While the women are free to attend any of these churches and on occasion participate in choir concerts, revivals, or other special services at
nearby churches, most are committed to Baptist churches in the area.
Four of the women attend churches that meet every Sunday, while the
others attend churches which meet on alternating Sundays, either first
and third, or second and fourth.[18] These congregations are central to
their faith experience. As Baptists and those steeped in the African American church tradition, they are led by their tradition to pursue acts of
faith that are both highly public and highly personal, all with the aim of
improving life for themselves and their communities.

RIGHTEOUS DISCONTENT

While I was growing up my parents always warned me about small towns, speed limits, and being black. "You shouldn't speed in small towns . . . The police *will* stop you." It is not as though other people do not get stopped in small towns, but certain people are more likely than others to be stopped. My parents wanted me to know that I fall into the "more likely" category.

It seems that Halifax County, like areas of the country my parents have experienced, has the same problem with small towns, speed limits, and black people. One of the reasons the city council members boycotted the city council meetings in Enfield in 1997–1998 was because the chief of police refused to address the many citizens' complaints about police harassment. When I asked one black former police officer about the problem, he confirmed the reports. In his eighteen years on the force, a portion of which he served as lieutenant, many of the grievances he filed with the chief came from his observation of his fellow officers.

> I had officers that would write tickets to a certain group . . . blacks. And would not write whites tickets. I've made personal observations of white motorists violating the law, and my officers would not, being white, would not write them a violation, would not give them a ticket. I have noticed them give black senior citizens tickets for inspection sticker, for expired tags and I have had a lot of concern. I had a lot of issues. I fought a lot for that . . . letting them know that I wasn't going to tolerate it. When you see an officer standing in an area of a city and somebody, one of the farmer's daughters, rides down through there in a Mercedes

Benz, running 65 mph in a 25 mph zone and he just waves and smiles. . . . Then you see a black come through there with an expired inspection sticker and he hops from that corner to his patrol car and burns rubber to stop them and give them a ticket. . . .

He cut his sentence short, knowing that I could reach the logical conclusion myself. . . . *There is a problem.*

The day that I was stopped by the police in Enfield was my first experience with police harassment. I had never been yelled at or insulted by an officer until the day that I helped pass out flyers for CCT's boycott of Dolphyn's grocery store. George Givens, the director, asked me to pass out flyers at the apartment complex behind the grocery store. As I left the store in my car, the police car that had been monitoring the boycott also began to leave. I paid his movement little attention until I noticed that he had turned left to follow me behind the grocery store. When we were finally at a distance beyond sight of the protest line, he put his lights on and pulled me over.

He came to my window demanding to see my driver's license and registration. When I asked why, he stated that I had passed a school bus with its stop sign out. I politely told him I had not. I knew that he had seen the driver waiting to display her sign and waving for me to continue in the left lane. When I stated, "Officer, you obviously did not see what happened," he only yelled louder, "Driver's license and registration!" I finally retrieved them and handed them over. As he walked away with them, I stepped out of the car to reason with him about why I had been stopped. "Back in the car!" he shouted. Furious and alone, with no one present to validate my experience, I pulled out a piece of paper and began to record what was happening. I could not believe it. I knew that his stopping me had everything to do with my participation in the protest line. Although I was there mainly as a researcher, taking notes and talking with those protesting, I was a part of the protest. I had even agreed to distribute flyers at the apartment complex behind the grocery store.

As the time passed, five minutes, then ten, then fifteen, I noticed that he made no effort to get out of his patrol car and come back to my window. Eventually, another patrol car arrived with lights, no sirens. Both officers got out of their cars and talked for a few minutes, and then the other officer, a woman, returned to her car. The officer who stopped me came to my window, told me that he would give me the "benefit of the doubt" concerning the stop sign, and then issued me a warning. If I did not have my tags renewed within five days, he insisted, he would mail a ticket to my home. (They were not due for another month.)

When I told George the story, he was angry. His sister, Lynn, said that the female officer must have been the new chief of police. The only reason I did not receive a ticket, in Lynn's opinion, was because the Enfield police department did not want CCT to begin a campaign against them. They were having enough problems.

My experience that day in Enfield made readily apparent the barriers to public engagement that some face. To protest, to get involved, to speak out, to run for office, each carries a certain level of risk. African American women who take on the challenges of public life, including those who become elected officials, enter a difficult, sometimes hostile, and often unfamiliar space. Yet, for the women that I interviewed, the ability to channel righteous discontent at prevailing systems of injustice into vibrant black public spheres has made the difference between engagement and disengagement. In these instances their faith has allowed them to express not only gratitude and empathy, which work to build community and sustain relationships, but a righteous discontent that disrupts the status quo, challenging the very social and economic structures that cause their distress.

When channeled into viable public spheres, righteous discontent creates opportunities for the venting and resolving of community concerns. How women utilize such alternative spheres is determined by their interpretation of the challenges facing their communities. Some focus explicitly upon structural problems that impede progress and render African Americans second-class citizens. Ms. Sylvia and Diane's organizing efforts with CCT reflect this type of response. Other women, like Juanita Cleveland and Marie Carter, focus their work much less on challenging outside systems of oppression than on building intraracial solutions to the educational and economic issues facing African American communities. For these women, the legal advances of the Civil Rights Movement have paved a way for African Americans to move more swiftly into the American mainstream; therefore, they concentrate more on internal systems of development.

Righteous discontent challenges the conditions that give rise to poor education, poor quality health services, and poor living conditions. "Discontent" in this scenario means dissatisfaction with the very genesis of the conditions. Such discontent translates into active community-building as well as open confrontation with systems of oppression.

HISTORICAL PERSPECTIVE

Historically situated within the intersecting narratives of Christian activism and American social activism, African American women's public activism is seen in broad-based movements such as the Abolitionist Movement, Women's Suffrage Movement, Anti-Lynching Movement and the Civil Rights Movement. All of these campaigns reflect black women's historic critiques of American systems that perpetuate injustice. These movements, often articulated through various religious discourses, appealed for the creation of a just U.S. society. Rallies, marches, sit-ins, and boycotts all call to mind the public and the hyper-organized forms of such protest efforts.

Although women have been written out of much of this history, scholars have recently drawn attention to the central role of women in protest efforts. In *Words of Fire,* an anthology chronicling the history of black women's activism from slavery to the present, Beverly Guy-Sheftall, presents the speeches, petitions, letters, and resolutions of women who organized for "racial uplift" and the advancement of women. Paula Giddings, in another seminal text on black women's activism, chronicles the role of black women in the fight for integration into the American mainstream. Her title, *When and Where I Enter,* echoes the words of the educator and activist Anna Julia Cooper, who declared in a public address advocating women's rights, "When and where I enter, in the quiet, undisputed dignity of my womanhood, without violence and without special patronage, then and there the whole negro race enters with me." These anthologies and histories resonate with the memoirs of women like Anne Moody, Pauli Murray, Melba Pattilo Beals, Elaine Brown, Angela Davis, and Assata Shakur, who document their own histories within various social movements.[1] Each of these memoirs points to the centrality of women in the struggle for justice in the United States. During the Civil Rights Movement, not only were women "major leaders," but they were "organizers and strategists who helped to mold and shape the direction the movement would take."[2] Even where women's involvement was not consistently public, their work within the movement was invaluable because of the networks they created. "Certain women operated as network centers, mobilizing existing social networks around the organizing goals, mediating conflicts, conveying information, coordinating activity, in short, 'creating and sustaining good relations and solidarity among co-workers.'"[3] Without these systems large masses of people would not have joined the movement, or remained committed to its cause.

In studying women's activism, some scholars have examined how gender constraints specifically affected women's participation in the public sphere.[4] Other scholars have focused on how the dual oppressions of racism and sexism have impacted women's movement participation.[5] Focus upon women's activism, however, has not given adequate attention to the significance of women's faith in their work for change. Scholars who assume that religion causes people to become less involved in activism have missed one of activism's many determining factors. "Faith in the Lord," historian Charles Payne argues, "made it easier to have faith in the possibility of social change."[6] The dearth of literature on this topic, however, cannot be attributed to a dearth of experience.

Judith Weisenfeld's *African American Women and Christian Activism: New York's Black YWCA, 1905–1945* and Marcia Riggs's anthology *Can I Get a Witness? Prophetic Religious Voices of African American Women* make amply clear that women's faith in the context of black public spheres has stood central to activist efforts of the late nineteenth and early twentieth centuries. These spheres allowed for the expression of "righteous discontent" by African Americans outraged by the lack of justice in U.S. society and perplexed by the seeming stagnation of Negro education. Churches created alternative spheres in which to address these concerns. "The church itself," argues Evelyn Brooks Higginbotham, "became the domain for the expression, celebration, and pursuit of a black collective will and identity."[7] It is "a public distinct from and in conflict with the dominant white society and its racist institutional structures. The church-sponsored press played an instrumental role in the dissemination of a black oppositional discourse and in the creation of a black collective will."[8] Given that the black church was central to women's articulation of righteous discontent at the turn of the last century, is this same type of space necessary today for the articulation of women's discontent?

In a special issue of *Public Culture* dedicated to the study of the black public sphere, Steven Gregory argues that over the past thirty years there has been a steady shift in the African American public sphere. This shift, he argues, results largely from the rise of federalism and the intervention of the state in public affairs. Based on his study of an activist group in Queens, New York, he challenges the general assumption that the exodus of the African American middle class from urban centers caused a decline in activism in black communities. Instead, he suggests that the restructuring of a specifically black public sphere has resulted in a shift in activism, particularly as it relates to race-based activism. "This depoliticizing of race in local activism," Gregory argues, "can be viewed in part as the result of a harnessing of the public sphere of African American neighborhood life to state-sponsored mechanisms of political participation, established in the wake of civil rights era activism and urban unrest."[9] Additionally, some argue that since the movement era of the sixties, increased individualism has led to a decline of concern about the public good and, subsequently, a decrease in activism.[10] Others, however, point to new forms of activism that have developed with the legal eradication of government-sanctioned discrimination and the growth of nonprofit, tax-exempt organizations.[11] These new activists often work within government-established regulations to promote their desired (and now federally funded) goals. In addition, the passing of the Voting Rights Act of 1965 and the creation of minority/majority voting districts have allowed the election of a considerable number of black officials. Ideally, these officials advocate from a position of power within the government to bring about needed change in their communities. As city and county officials, school board members, and state and national representatives, they notify communities of pending issues and push for the fair resolution of matters that affect African American communities. These shifts in activism have resulted in a shift in the dynamics of what scholars consider the black public sphere. If the black public sphere, as Higginbotham describes, has been central to the manifestation of activism among African American women, what are the consequences for women today in light of Gregory's observation of its restructuring? Has this public sphere *actually* been restructured in rural areas like Halifax County?

In this chapter I discuss how four women channel their frustration at oppressive structures into organizational spaces that allow them to combine their spirituality and activism in ways that bring about substantial change. On the basis of their activity I suggest that, contrary to Gregory's observation, a specifically "black" public sphere in Halifax County has not been drastically restructured. Massive intervention may have taken place in the North, but federal agencies have not en masse located in rural areas of the South to address issues of fairness and discrimination. Furthermore, the historic tensions that exist between black and white residents in some rural areas have not been as severely disrupted by the influx of industry and various minority populations. In many ways historic black/white tensions continue to dominate local politics. The reality of present-day racial problems in Halifax County allows for women to channel their righteous discontent into organizational spaces prepared to address concerns of black residents.

For some it seems naïve and overstated to talk about restrictions on public involvement at the turn of the twenty-first century when the assumption at least among conservative thinkers is that "race" no longer matters and "gender" bias is rarely an issue. Yet the women's experiences that I describe speak of a different reality. Race and gender do matter, and women's participation in the public sphere is mediated largely by the existence of a predominantly black public sphere. Whether evidenced in the need to fight for disadvantaged youth in their predominantly black school district or the need to fight against hog farms in their predominantly black rural community, one of the central organizing principles has been race.

Entering into the public sphere to address these concerns has been a great struggle for African American women, particularly in areas like Halifax County where white and male dominance has been the established order of the day.[12] Public engagement requires an inordinate amount of determination to overcome initial fears of retaliation and failure. Self-doubt, resulting from sheer inexperience, stands as another gender-specific issue with which they must contend. Such deterrents all have their roots in black women's historic estrangement from the public sphere and discussions about the public good. Decisions about school funding, debates about voting districts, and the allocation of local taxes are all decisions that have been made historically without the critical insight and approval of women of color. In Halifax County, where there has never been a black (or white) female county commissioner and where the county has only recently hired and retained a black female head of a county department, the emergence of women into the public sphere is critical.

Women who have entered the public sphere have often done so through various civic and religious organizations. Ms. Cleveland was catapulted into it by the NAACP during the Civil Rights Movement and later by her home church; Marie Carter was aided by the collective strength of her church in her decision to run for public office; the efforts of a community group, CCT, gave Sylvia Jones and Diane Little the opportunity to express their concerns. Without the influence of these "public spheres" and the reality of a *black* public sphere, the righteous discontent they all felt would not have been sufficiently channeled to result in social change.

Most of the women I interviewed expressed some level of discontent with the treatment of African Americans, the poor, the elderly, or young people in the county. Along with their emphasis upon "personal responsibility," a conservative trademark of black Christianity, there is also a strong recognition among the women I interviewed that issues of injustice must be confronted. When asked the question, "are there issues in your community that concern you?" each spoke of a combination of poor schooling, poor living conditions, on-the-job racism, and the lack of care for the elderly. While these women have managed to carve out productive and loving lives, there is still great concern for the plight of many of the county's less fortunate residents.

These four women's lives reflect a different path from those of some of the other women I interviewed. While all expressed deep concern about the practice of injustice, not all channeled this concern into public action. In many instances they dealt with their discontent over a situation, whether work-related racism or some other experience, outside of the public sphere. They found other ways of coping, either by confronting a boss or reasoning out alternative solutions.

Gloria, for example, while believing that people should speak out against injustice, also indicated that since the sixties "things have changed and made it better for a lot of us." These changes require a different type of engagement, particularly in the case of work-related racism. Instead of protesting or making an issue of the discrimination one should learn to "play the game." "I tell my kids, don't hate the white person. You pray for them, but you can beat them at their own game too and you can also learn from them. Sit back and listen to them. Listen to what they have to say and you can learn some things. And what you learn from them, use it to your advantage." In Gloria's experience race is still a primary indicator for on-the-job discrimination. Faith allows her to simply "pray for" her adversaries. Yet integration on the other hand allows her to sit back and simply listen, "learn from," and then use that knowledge to her own advantage. In Gloria's view she is beating at their own game those who would treat her unfairly.

Yvette, likewise, chose not to enter into public confrontation about racism that she experienced at work. The environment created since the passing of the Civil Rights Act of 1964 has ensured fair treatment of workers in many instances and yet has simultaneously inspired a pretense of fairness among industry leaders trying to avoid litigation. This type of "polite" environment does not lend itself to protest. Despite legislative changes, according to Yvette, there are no African American electricians or maintenance men in the industry where she works. The company, however, gives a public explanation that she immediately rejects. "Electricians work on the electrical stuff that goes wrong in the plant.

Maintenance men . . . they work on the machinery. But, all of those guys are white guys. Those are the higher paid guys . . . They're not going to tell me that every time they interview one [of us for these jobs] his drug test comes up dirty. They're just not going to tell me that." Although this explanation does not satisfy her frustration, her petitions go unheard even in her own struggles for promotion. "Race, racism is still an issue here . . . White people have gotten jobs, they get 'em because they've skipped over blacks. They [white applicants] might be alcoholics. I remember once me and this girl were interviewing for the same job. She had been in rehab twice for alcohol. Both of us applied for the job and she was white. They gave her the job." Yet, although Yvette believes that racism fuels these decisions, she does not know how to address the problem. Frustrated and unable to prove her suspicions, she has resolved to continue her work without filing complaints that may threaten her job.

Some women, however, have taken opportunities like these to locate others who are likewise frustrated. These outreaches create alternative public spheres for the venting of such frustrations. In my research I focus on two alternative public spheres that have supported women's moves into public discourse, the church and CCT. While not all African American churches in the area directly address the issues of discrimination and racism in the county, there are some that do. In addition to churches, grassroots organizations like CCT have worked to encourage women's protests against their mistreatment in society. In the space created by CCT, women, African Americans, and senior citizens are all repeatedly encouraged to feel comfortable voicing their discontent.

SHIFTING GEARS AND MAKING THE CONNECTION: JUANITA CLEVELAND'S ACTIVISM

When she was active in the Civil Rights Movement, much of Ms. Cleveland's work involved participation in the church. Though she continues to volunteer through her church, her activism today does not necessarily center as it once did on a critique of the political system in Halifax County. Instead, it focuses more specifically on the intraracial work of training and educating youth. She is the director of Christian education and, according to the church bulletin, chairperson of the annual Homecoming Committee and director of the theatrical production for Easter Sunday.[13] When I asked about her community involvement, these are the kinds of activities she mentioned. The shift in her type of engagement is linked to both a change in her family structure and a change in her church's leadership.

During the sixties, as field secretary for the Halifax County NAACP, Ms. Cleveland was responsible for the development and maintenance of the organization's membership. At that time there were well over one thousand members in the local chapter, who participated in both sit-ins and boycotts throughout the state. The experience allowed her not only to meet important leaders such as Martin Luther King Jr. and Thurgood Marshall but also to work alongside them. As she recalls, "I was fortunate to see Martin Luther King, Thurgood Marshall. Sat with him, Roy Wilkins . . . I sat with them and when I say sat with, I'm not talking about just being in the room with them. I worked with the resolutions committee on the national level NAACP. I [also] worked with state level . . . [with] Kelly Alexander out of Charlotte . . . We were instrumental in . . . [the case] where you don't have to read according to the registrar."

Understandably proud of her involvement in North Carolina's landmark civil rights case, she discussed the rigid systems of racial bigotry in Halifax County in the 1960s that not only prevented African Americans from registering to vote, but also prevented those who were already registered from actually voting. Her reflections were reminiscent of discussions I had with other women throughout the county, like Mrs. Griffin and Mrs. Little, who vividly remembered being asked to read the U.S. Constitution as proof of their ability to make an informed electoral decision. These state-imposed reading examinations and other Jim Crow legislation ensured a solid block of white domination in the county.

Confrontation with the Jim Crow South was the aim of organized protest. Ms. Cleveland describes her involvement as a young single mother as both "daring" and "scary." Recently divorced from her high school sweetheart, she found that activity in the Civil Rights Movement posed immediate challenges not only to her job (her only source of income), but also to her physical well-being. White residents of the county were clear about their disdain for blacks. Several interviewees, both white and black, recalled the time "just thirty years ago" when blacks were not allowed in Roanoke Rapids after sundown. Indeed, one white resident told of a sign posted just outside the city limits stating that blacks entering the city after sundown entered at their "own risk." Ms. Cleveland lived then in the adjoining city of Riverside, where she continues to live today.

Her commitment to challenging the prevailing system of injustice was reinforced by her engagement with organizations like the NAACP and

Shiloh Baptist Church, one of the central sites for organizers. Her indignation was nurtured by the support of these organizations, and their collective struggle helped to overcome her fear of physical retaliation. As a young woman, full of energy and hope, she wanted to make a difference in her place of birth, so that her children could be reared in a more just environment. Marrying for the second time, however, led to a shift in her attention to public, movement-centered activism. Marriage created immediate responsibilities which placed greater demands upon her time. Although the movement was thriving, her ability to maintain previous levels of involvement dwindled. She recalls:

> We had a great membership. We had membership of about close to a thousand. And then they broke. North Hampton went to North Hampton. Halifax kept Halifax. So, I worked with Halifax County. And we worked. I worked with the NAACP. But, after I got married and had the baby, I was working over there, working at the flower shop, working with the church and then being married I couldn't handle all of it, so I had to give up some of it. So, now it's mostly church.

While masses of women like Ms. Cleveland participated in the movement doing triple duty, at home, at work, and in the streets protesting, many women of that era found that the demands of home life often forced them to remain outside of public work, even when their passions directed them otherwise. Emphasis upon male leadership outside the home and female governance within the home with little male participation was the status quo. Ms. Cleveland's passions eventually gave way to this standard.

Although she stated with a bit of reluctance that "church work" is her major focus today, much of this work nonetheless revolves around the idea of reestablishing a "black public sphere." It is in the church that she believes change in the school system and society in general must begin. Here is where parents should address problems, students should learn to read and write, and teenagers build self-esteem. Today the church is the central site of her engagement not only because it is familiar to her, but also because she has particularly fond memories of the role of the church in her development as a young person. As she recalls, women in the church dramatically influenced her sense of self-worth, making demands upon her that others would not dare. She only wishes that parents today were as concerned about sending their children to church as parents were when she was younger.

> I know what impact the church played on my life when I was growing up and I know how we had to go to church and be involved, but to see

the uncommitted parents now, don't care whether their children go or not, you know to Sunday school. I mean Baptist Training Union (BTU) is out now, they had to cancel that. And to see how dedicated the children were when we were in school, you know . . .

Women like Barbara Conyers and Bettye Brown were her "real teachers." The Baptist Training Union was the place of education both formal and informal. One practiced reading and writing, but even more one learned the values of self-respect and discipline. Ambivalence toward the church is in her opinion "the problem" with today's youth.[14] There are problems, she admits, with the school system, things that need to change because children are not being treated fairly, but some of these changes are issues that the black church, as a community organization, can and should address. Her idea is for the church to become the type of institution that it was when she was growing up. Children would then, despite the school system, gain what they needed for development. In this instance her idealism about the gains of the Civil Rights Movement has been redirected to include the more insular model of segregated community practices.

In her study of community activism in a northeastern city Cheryl Townsend Gilkes notes that some have viewed the community work of her African American female informants as separatist. "In a society in which 'integration' has become the dominant theme in the politics of race, internal community development can often be very controversial, implying separatism and inter-racial hostility."[15] Gilkes counters this argument by explaining that "what has been labeled a 'retreat from integration' is actually the discovery of the internal development that was sometimes accomplished in disadvantaged, segregated, Southern schools."[16] This type of "internal development" is precisely the kind of work that Ms. Cleveland is attempting to inspire in the youth of her community.

The current focus of the church's new pastor validates many of Ms. Cleveland's assumptions about the role of the church outside the domain of political protest. Instead of emphasizing political protest, most of his efforts toward progress center on building children's self-esteem, their knowledge of scripture, and their sense of respect for themselves and adults. A member of Shiloh Baptist since childhood, Ms. Cleveland has seen it endure dramatic changes in leadership over the past twenty years. At one point Shiloh was the site where blacks held rallies and organized boycotts to protest Jim Crow laws and practices. Just fifteen years ago, it was the site of a rally protesting the absence of minority representation on the county commission. The church, now, however, focuses more on the priestly acts of service or what some would characterize as the more mainstream goals of black churches.[17] It has been the site of few, if any political rallies recently, and although one of its members was a premier candidate in a highly contested bid for a Roanoke Rapids school board seat, the discussion of his candidacy never made it to the pulpit.[18] Much of this distancing from political activity can be traced back to the leadership of the new pastor. While the pastor does not completely dictate the actions of the church, his leadership sets the tone for its involvement in community activities. One frequent visitor to the church told me that Rev. McCants is an incredible preacher. Although, according to her, he does not do much in terms of social activism and getting folks involved in protest, he can "preach you right up to the pearly gates." She explained what she meant by not involved in social activism by pointing to the fact that he doesn't allow candidates for political office to speak during service; he does not speak out publicly against the injustice of the school systems, and he does not preach about general social justice concerns. His message to many, however, is timely in that it addresses the urgent desire of people to know God and to live holy lives. His devotion to the more "priestly" versus "prophetic" acts of ministry causes his church more generally to move away from engagement in traditional protest-oriented politics.

While her pastor represents a more priestly model for the black church, Ms. Cleveland herself understands the church as an institution for social change as well as spiritual growth. As she talked about her part in dismantling unjust systems, there seemed little tension in her articulation of the church as both a site for working within the Civil Rights Movement and a site for spiritual renewal. Her views reflect her commitment to the church's ongoing development.

After hearing her explain her vision of the church as a primary site for youth development, I asked if there are school system concerns that the church should address. To this she responded:

> Yes. I think the church should wake up, but you can't wake up if you don't have the parents. You know. The parents got to be involved with it too. Now we don't even have the parents that are even dedicated to even sending, making sure that the kids get the education. You know, religion's out of school, but you do have it in church. The different Bible studies that we have at Shiloh, you know different things that Shiloh Baptist affords, if you can't get the parents interested in what the church

has to afford that will help the child. . . . You know, you can't put it all
on the public school, because the church plays a major role in the development of the child. If you can get the parents committed, if you can
[just] get the parents committed. . . .

Careful not to place the onus of the problem on the school system,
Ms. Cleveland again insisted that the site of change is the church where
she was educated early on and where she is rooted now. In this instance
she rejects the idea that activism is something which should take place
merely in the sphere of the general public. It is within the sacred space,
within the alternative public sphere of the church, that children should
learn to read, write, and develop socially.

In her opinion, though a portion of the problem lies squarely in the
hands of the school system, more important is the question of what the
churches are doing about children's education. Again, this is the model
that was set for her as a child. It is a model that she believes works and
one that she is attempting to recreate. This type of involvement, she in-
timated, demonstrates the connection between her spirituality and her
commitment to community. As director of Christian education, she
works with dozens of children, many of whose parents do not attend
church. She went on to explain that the connection between one's spirituality and one's commitment to community is measured by the impact
that "you have in the church, upon your neighbor, and people that you
come in contact with . . ." Community is not limited to a notion of an
isolated group of people who live next door or around the block or who
are members of a church. Instead, community consists of the people that
she meets in a variety of places—at work, in church, in the neighborhood, throughout the day, at the store, or in the mall. These are the
people that she wants to influence through her work at Shiloh.

MAKING EDUCATION WORK:
MARIE CARTER'S ACTIVISM

Like Ms. Cleveland, Marie Carter locates an alternative public sphere in
her church community. The church members not only inspired her toward political life, they also assisted her in the campaigning process by
posting signs, making door-to-door solicitations, and giving word-of-
mouth endorsements. Many of her constituents have been unhappy with
the lack of concern shown for black school children by the predomi-

nantly white school board. By supporting Marie Carter, they hoped to encourage much-needed change.

I first met Marie upon the insistence of a mutual friend who informed me that she was one of the first African American women elected, in 1992, to the Halifax County school board. As a board member, she attends countless meetings where questions are raised about the quality of education provided for the youth of Halifax County. Contrary to an outsider's view that merger of the school systems is best for the county, residents both black and white are torn over this decision. For some African Americans merging means masses of African Americans losing their jobs and their political influence in the county. For whites it means that their isolated oasis becomes invaded by poor students with below-average test scores, most of whom are African American, an outcome many in Roanoke Rapids have organized against.

As stated earlier, Halifax County has three public school systems: one in Roanoke Rapids, which is over 80 percent white, another in Weldon, which is approximately 95 percent African American, and the county school system, which is at least 90 percent African American. The school systems have been racially polarized since the era of school desegregation and have changed more in law than in practice. High tax brackets and the lack of living wages prevent poorer people, often African Americans, from moving into the more developed Roanoke Rapids. Only in recent years with the abandonment of old homes by former textile workers who turn them into rental properties has there been a significant increase in the number of minorities in Roanoke Rapids.

In the Halifax County school system, the issue of race has always been a pressing one, with whites sitting as the majority on the school board until the 1980s. During this period, all of the superintendents were white along with the majority of principals and school administrators. When African Americans organized to have a more fair representation on the board, their initiatives resulted in the presence of African American male members. The first two African American women were elected to the board over a decade later, in 1992. Their presence has been a source of great pride for members of the community and has changed the racial composition of the school board to one where African Americans sit in the majority. When I asked Marie about her decision to run for the school board, she referenced a combination of divine appointment, family support, church support, and a simple desire to meet the needs of the children of the community, needs too long neglected by standing members of the board.

For over three years residents of her community and members of her church diligently petitioned her to run for the school board. Awed by her stately presence and her evident commitment to youth, neighbors, friends, and other parents urged her to consider running. They believed that her election would place someone in office who genuinely cared about the education and leadership of their children. Although careful not to speak in racialized terminology, she explained that the community wanted the "right people" to speak for their children as opposed to "people who sent their children to private schools." "One of the major issues at that time was the concern of the community that we did not have the right people representing our children. Well, the right people representing the welfare of our children. We had some board members that had children in private facilities. Private schools . . . We say that it's where your heart is. If your heart is in a private school it's kind of hard to really have your heart in both places."

The labels "people concerned about our children" and "people with children in private schools" are euphemisms used to bring attention to the racial imbalance of the school systems. Residents know that private academies are all white by choice. Only in the last three years have any of them made an attempt to integrate, this history of racial separation yielding much bitter fruit today.[19] Residents support Marie Carter because they believe she can counter some of this long-standing racism and help facilitate needed structural change in the county system.

In considering their petition, however, Marie had to wrestle with her own historical exclusion from this level of public engagement. As an African American in Halifax County, she was historically excluded by legal filter and white privilege; as a woman she had a role securely anchored in motherhood and the care of her family; and as one without a college degree, she had not stepped into the class bracket in which African American leaders typically stand. As she told me, motherhood did not necessarily prepare her for political discussions nor did it introduce her to the type of information she would need to know as a school board member. "A lot of people I'm in contact with, we're just mothers, just regular old mothers and regular old mothers don't sit around and talk about politics all the time. You know, all we want is the safety of our children and we want them to get a good education. You know. That's what most moms . . . that's what we talk about. Not about who's in the Senate, who's on the county commission. We didn't talk about [that]. We just didn't do it." Her social class standing also prevented her from immediately identifying herself as one who could engage the broader pub-

lic in such an official capacity. As she states, she never considered herself
the school board "type."

> You know, there's a concept that's always been in the back of my mind
> that the school board members were always, umm [pauses to choose her
> words] I would say . . . This is just my own personal thinking. They
> were always people that were rich or highly educated and somewhat
> snobs. But, I didn't want to fit in that category. I wanted to be myself. I
> didn't want it to change me from the person that I was. So, I didn't want
> to get involved in it where I would be a member of this clique or that
> clique. I wanted any parent of any child—I don't care whether you were
> on this side of the street or that side of the street, 'cause I love all kids—I
> didn't want them to feel like they could not come to me because they felt
> intimidated because of the fact that I was a school board member.

Initially, public sphere work was intimidating to Marie. The conno-
tations alone were enough to make her shun consideration of public office. Yet the desire to change the learning conditions for students and the
opportunity to get more parents involved in the process nurtured her desire to contribute. Mothers, she explained, were not necessarily involved
in the political process because they did not participate enough to understand the details. Elites, both white and black, led the school board.
White elites sent their children to white-only private schools in the
county, yet sat on the county's school board to manage the resources that
flowed through the public school system. Although their children attended private academies, they along with other whites still paid county
taxes, and thus they wanted a say in how the county spent the money.

Ironically motherhood and the influence of her church family made
the final difference in her decision to run. Instead of seeing motherhood
as something that should exclude her from politics, she decided that having children in the school system provided the ideal reason for her service on the school board. "Having two children in the county, naturally
I had a personal concern about what was going on so what better way
to actually find out what's going on than to get out there and get into it?
I didn't really think, I mean I thought I had a chance of winning, but I
was really surprised myself when I did, the first time around." According to Gilkes, Marie's motivation is not uncommon. Gilkes's research
showed that women who became involved in community work often did
so as a result of their "roles" in the family. "As these women talked
about the ways in which they became involved in community work and
the different kinds of organizations and activities in which they participated, I learned about the very intricate and diverse ways in which

people make social change . . . Their family roles made them acutely conscious not only of their own deprivations but also of the suffering of their children and the men in their lives. Their insightful and enterprising responses to these many kinds of suffering led to their prominence in the community."[20]

While motherhood gave Marie the motivation to enter the race, the consistent support of her church family gave her the courage. "Everybody prayed . . . I had friends and I had my church family . . . I had the support of my pastor and my church family and the community and just so many people that were helping me. And I felt really good about that. And I felt whether [I got elected or not] . . . I had already won anyway because they really believed in me." Now engaged in public office, she sees her position on the school board as her "missionary work." She is not only able to advocate for kids whose voices are not heard, but she is also able to broaden the public sphere for the inclusion of more parents, who, like herself, have seen themselves excluded from the political process. This concern with access to the public sphere echoes Habermas's contention that in order for the public to be truly democratic there must be extended participation among society's members. As Marie understands the process of engaging the school board, she shares it with others who then share it with others, facilitating greater participation from those formerly excluded. The support of one public, her church community, helps make possible her participation in the larger public, the county school board, and by extension the community's participation with the school board.

MAKING HEALTH MATTER: DIANE LITTLE'S ACTIVISM

While women like Juanita Cleveland and Marie Carter find the strongest encouragement for their work from the church community, other women are inspired to activism by their involvement in institutions like the NAACP and the Halifax County Black Caucus, or grassroots organizations like CCT, which work to bring about systematic change in the structures of government and public institutions. Though not directly affiliated with specific churches or denominations, these institutions historically affirm women's faith commitments.

Although some of the women I interviewed were not active in the Civil Rights Movement, others are engaged in post–civil rights work. They moved from the margins of activity to the center during the shift from racial domination to racial hegemony.[21] Hegemony, however, did not necessarily camouflage the effects of racism. In many ways, particularly for rural North Carolinians, the process of change to a period of racial hegemony illuminates the issues of race. This illumination provokes many, like Diane, to action.

Though the Civil Rights Movement is seen as bringing an end to that period of racial domination that climaxed during the sixties, the local fallout from the passing of desegregation laws and the Voting Rights Act continued well into the seventies, eighties, and nineties. Particular to these fallouts were decisions about school openings and closings, new administrations, and busing. According to David Cecelski's 1994 study of desegregation in North Carolina, the desegregation process completely devastated black educational leadership and black communities, particularly in rural areas: "From 1963 to 1970, the number of black principals in the state's elementary schools plunged from 620 to only 170. Even more striking, 209 black principals headed secondary schools in 1963, but less than 10 still held that crucial job in 1970. By 1973, only three had survived this wholesale displacement. . . . By decade's end, when black children represented 30 percent of the state's 1.2 million public school students, not one of the 145 school districts had a black superintendent, and 60 percent of those districts did not employ any black administrators." Not only did blacks lose important positions of leadership, but "Blacks lost important symbols of their educational heritage in this process. When black schools closed, their names, mascots, mottoes, holidays and traditions were sacrificed with them, while the students were transferred to historically white schools that retained those markers of cultural and racial identity."[22] Schools in predominantly black communities were often closed in order to prevent the busing of white children into black neighborhoods. Some of these former schools were later turned into factories, offering low wages and often unstable jobs. In addition, private all-white "Christian" academies began to consistently appear throughout the South. Residents of Halifax believe that these academies were developed for two reasons: first, to prevent integration and, second, to rebel against what was seen by some as the secularization of the public school system.

Diane said in our interview that the fallout from desegregation is precisely what inspired her toward organized public activism. Although she considers herself to have been "involved ever since I can remember, with anything, whether it was concerning citizens, or church, or community activities," she states that she was "not always active [at the present level]. But when I did decide to join it was in 1981." The Tillery school closing infuriated her and ushered her immediately into the realm of public "activist." Seen as the center of the community, the Tillery school housed not only weekly school meetings, but also community-wide events and family reunions for residents of the area. When the county school board announced that the school would be closing, a group of Tillery residents organized and walked miles in a protest march to the school board offices. "It [the beginning of her activist work] was in 1981, if I'm not mistaken, and it was when I saw people walking from Tillery to Halifax to fight against the closing of our local elementary school. That's when I first thought about getting involved with local issues. Because we knew that if our school closed, that the school *was* . . . the community at that time."

Although her father was one of the founding members of the organization leading the protest, she and her sisters did not assume major leadership positions in the organization until more recent years. Her activity centered around work, church, and home. An employee of the local sewing factory, she was not one to become heavily involved in protest efforts. Entrance into an alternative public sphere such as CCT would jeopardize her employment. However, the struggle to maintain her community for the sake of her daughter changed her outlook.

According to Cecelski, communities throughout the United States were organizing to confront the engines of power that threatened their way of life. The Tillery school was only one in a host of predominately black schools closed after desegregation, the building remaining abandoned for several years before a sewing factory renovated its shell. Such trends were common throughout the rural South—factories and the development of cheap labor taking the place of education and the development of minds.

After the initial school protest march, residents realized the need for ongoing advocacy for people of the region and thus formalized their protest into a community organization, the Concerned Citizens of Tillery. The creation of this alternative public sphere allowed for the expression of Tillery residents' discontent not only with the prevailing school system, but also eventually with the poor treatment of black farmers by the USDA, the lack of adequate health care for the elderly, industrial threats to the community's well water, and a host of other issues. While Diane's initial concern about the school system led her to channel her discontent into CCT, current frustration over elderly health care has led her to not only participate, but also organize the community's health clinic.

CCT has at least seven major divisions, which address seniors, young adults, and youth and cover topics related to black land loss, economic development, personal health and wellness, and environmental protection. Diane serves as coordinator both for the community youth program and for CCT's health facility. Although she originally had limited experience with organizing, the need for both a youth coordinator and a health center forced her to assume positions she initially thought herself minimally qualified to hold. One position allows her to instill in youth the value of participating in a black public sphere through which to vent concerns, while the other allows her to actively engage in changing health care practices among the men, women, and children in her community.

As youth coordinator she plans activities, both traditional and non-traditional. While the youth program organizes forums on sex education, study skills, and applying to college, it also sponsors a host of non-traditional activities which sharpen young people's abilities to see themselves as connected to the issues and concerns of other African American youth. In 1998 the students made two trips, one to Washington D.C. and one to Philadelphia. The trip to Philadelphia was for the One Million Youth Rally. This, Diane believes, is what education is really about, gaining a critical perspective on the world and on how national and international policies affect you. The Million Youth Rally, organized by the Nation of Islam and other African American groups, drew attention to issues of education, racial profiling, police brutality, and other issues facing African American youth. The day-long summit resonated with the Million Man March, which had occurred just three years before.

In addition to attending the Million Youth Rally, the young people participated in the Black Farmers and Agriculturists boycott of the USDA in Washington. In the cold and drizzling rain, they stood along with over one hundred others with signs protesting the government's poor treatment of African American and other small farmers. Their signs read, "I'm a Future Black Farmer," "USDA: The Last Plantation," and "Racism: Alive and Well in the USDA." Never daunted by the weather or the length of the conference, the dozen or so high school students participated with full attention. During the legislative hearing students sat together, listening intently to the testimonies of black farmers who had lost much of their farmland or their farm equipment due to poor handling of their cases by USDA officials.[23] At one point one of the black farmers asked that the youth stand so that the legislators could see the future black farmers. Understanding their connection to this struggle, the students stood with pride and conviction, later holding conversations outside the legislative hearing about how surprised they were by the appeal. This was, for many, their first time participating in an event covered by C-SPAN. Although most of their parents and relatives no longer farm, opportunities for this type of engagement make young people aware of not only their family history of farming and sharecropping, but also their role in creating a different future.

The youth group competes for Diane's time and attention with the health clinic. In 1988 the community health clinic was formed in order to meet the needs of the growing elderly population. Unable to make it to town, or too poor to pay for consistent transportation into the city, many of the elderly were left without the option of seeing a health care provider. Through a partnership with two state universities, the community center that Diane works with has been able to help meet the needs of these seniors. Since quitting her job at the sewing factory and deciding against a home-based sewing business, Diane has been working full time at the community center. She finds this work rewarding because it allows her to give back. On any given day she could be involved in a local protest, or off to Washington for a rally in front of the legislative offices, or picking up a group of seniors to bring them to their community center.

The health clinic provides a host of services including blood pressure screening, diabetes testing, pregnancy tests for younger participants, and Pap smears and breast examinations for all of the women. It also offers workshops on healthy eating, proper exercise, and prevention and other health related topics. Managing the clinic not only allows Diane to become involved with resolving individuals' health concerns, but it also gives her space for working with the community to protect against larger environmental threats. Ground water pollution, air pollution, and septic tank sanitation standards are all issues that are engaged through CCT's health clinic.

While directing the youth group and coordinating events for the health clinic allow Diane to address community concerns, she understands that one of the key factors in public discussion is the willingness of community members to actually engage the issues. Not *all* issues related to health are seen as open for public discussion. Domestic violence is one such issue that is met with great reservation and many fears. When

I asked if there were other issues of concern to her in the county, without hesitation Diane stated:

> Yes. It's called abuse. Now that may not be publicly discussed, but I would like to have . . . spousal abuse, child abuse, mental abuse, and these are some issues that I hope that our grown folks can address. . . . And in addressing it, I know it's going to be, it's going to be slow going because everybody don't like to stand up and say "This happened to me" or "That happened to me." But if we could get it so that we know that we are definitely supporting each other and we can bond, then these are some issues that we could face together and make some big results happen. For instance, like a rapping session, or a speak-out session. Those are some things that I hope that our grown folks can address and have going.

Women and children's abuse at the hands of husbands and fathers is often not viewed as a public health issue. Nevertheless, violence against women and children remains a leading concern among health care workers. The silencing of the abused serves as a means of control. Diane's statement demonstrates that righteous discontent and the existence of a public sphere alone are sometimes not enough to address issues. There must be a willingness on the part of participants in this alternative sphere to engage the discussion. While Diane is actively involved in a public sphere that tirelessly brings attention to structures of oppression facing African Americans communities—USDA policy against black farmers, police brutality, ground water contamination—the efficacy of this public is only as strong as individuals' willingness to give serious critical voice to these concerns. On issues of race and racism, black public spheres have been forthright and outspoken. On issues of sexism and violence against women, as Diane attests, these same spheres are still struggling against silence. Their silence keeps many women and children unnecessarily in abusive relationships.

MAKING ELDERLY LIVES:
SYLVIA JONES'S ACTIVISM

I came to understand Ms. Sylvia's commitment to public work during my eleven months volunteering at the Concerned Citizens of Tillery, the same grassroots organization in which Diane works. One of Ms. Sylvia's main responsibilities is organizing the Open Minded Seniors—assisting with the group's overall mission of advocacy.

Though raised in the South, she has spent much of her adult life in

Philadelphia. Upon returning to her hometown, she noticed the drastic changes that had taken place over the past three decades. Her small hometown had been transformed into a more tolerant place. No longer was she isolated to the "other side" of the railroad tracks; in fact, she bought a home in the formerly whites-only section of town *and* on the main street no less. She visits shopping centers at will and is able to afford the assortment of amenities in downtown stores. Although as a teenager she was frustrated with the complete lack of job opportunities in the county (that did not entail picking cotton or shucking peanuts), Ms. Sylvia is pleased that today teenagers have work opportunities beyond the farm, even if only bagging groceries or clerking in the local five-and-dime. She gives tremendous thanks to God for allowing her to return to her hometown in relatively good health and enabling her to meet her financial responsibilities in retirement. In the midst of these changes, however, she still believes that the circumstances of the day call for organized protest.

Progress has benefited some, but still not enough. For the few who are able to take advantage of changes, things have improved. For the masses, however, major shortcomings remain. Privileged access to resources, she explains, does not translate into justice. There are a number of people in Halifax County, whom she calls "heroes" and "sheroes," who still do not have access to the basic necessities of life, not to mention its luxuries. These are the people who in her eyes have maintained a home to which she can return.

> They are the true heroes, because they stayed and worked *very* hard. Not me, who went away and came back, but people who stayed here and attended to the crops and maintained this community . . . And I always say, if it were not for these people there would be nothing to come back to. But, they're the people that's at the bottom of the totem pole, economically speaking . . . I mean they have absolutely no resources. I mean they *absolutely* have no resources. Most of them now are aged and they're living on $490 a month.

These are the people with whom she works, the seniors of the community. Within CCT, the OMS is the most publicly involved group. Informed by their positioning in a county overly burdened with unemployment and underemployment, the women who participate in the Seniors' group bear concerns that reflect their locale. Not only their lives but the lives of people in their community are mediated by their raced, classed, and gendered experiences. They boycott grocery stores that have mistreated their employees, lobby at the state capitol for environmental justice, write letters to congresspersons when they believe they have been treated unfairly and letters to the editor to express their thoughts on local issues.

This public space has given Ms. Sylvia the opportunity to voice her discontent with the failure of progress in her hometown. Having lived outside of Halifax County for much of her adult life, she has a different yardstick by which to measure progress and, to her, Halifax falls short. During one school term she worked with the OMS members to protest Dolphyn's, a local grocery store they believe falsely accused one of its employees of stealing. The youth, an excellent scholar and standout on his high school basketball team, was charged by the manager with shoplifting. When the boy denied that he was shoplifting, only discarding the spoiled meat from the previous day, the manager fired him and filed a report with the police.

Outraged by this action, the seniors used their own public space at CCT as a place to debate the issue. During their meetings they discussed the premature judgment of the store owner, the promising future of the basketball star, the district attorney's insistence on prosecuting, and the general failure of the court system to treat African American youth with the same consideration given white youth. Their meetings turned into an organized rally around the college-bound student as they attended each court session with him and his parents. If it had been a white youth, they argued, the manager would have either believed his story and permitted him to continue working or simply released him from his job without filing charges.[24] The OMS members were certain that the case was fueled by racism. Because so few African American students in the rural high schools make it to college, they were outraged that this academic and athletic star faced the possibility of losing all that he had worked for because of the testimony of one man under questionable circumstances.

Early in the morning the Seniors group gathered at the courthouse to encourage the parents and let the judge know that his ruling would not go unnoticed. When the judge decided not to dismiss the case, they protested. There was no evidence, only the manager's word against the student's. Eventually the youth's court-appointed attorney convinced him to plead guilty and receive a fine and community service, which would still leave a criminal record. Fearful of the possibilities of trial, the youth agreed. Early the following week, refusing to allow the manager and the store to come out of the incident unblemished, the OMS organized a boycott of Dolphyn's. With signs reading "Racism—Alive and

Well at Dolphyn's," "Community Fighting Back to Stop Dolphyn's Attack on Our Youth," and "Boycott Today" they marched along the side-
walk in front of Dolphyn's. Although their efforts appeared to have little effect in a community almost completely reliant upon this one grocery
store, the Seniors' use of terms like "racism" and "our youth" codified
a particular public and a cohesiveness within that public aimed at protecting black youth. Organizing a boycott and employing the terminology of "racism" in their flyers brought an uncomfortable attention to
racism at the same time community and business leaders were attempting to classify Halifax County among the more progressive areas of the
state. Additionally, phraseology such as "*our* youth" places the Seniors
group in solidarity with a black public sphere that ideally recognizes a
common threat. The creation of this public sphere depends on a conscious acknowledgment of this shared threat.

Strategic essentialisms, like the reference to a common "racism" and
an acknowledgment of "our youth," are generalizations that call for the
creation of a black counter public sphere. In problematizing such an approach Paul Gilroy points out that there is a legacy within black political discourse that "conditions the continuing aspiration to acquire a supposedly authentic, natural, and stable 'rooted' identity."[25] This legacy,
affirmed by theorists such as Manning Marable, bell hooks, and Cornel
West, does not, according to Gilroy, acknowledge the "need to speak of
racism(s) in the plural rather than one racism singular, unchanging and
final."[26] Gilroy's insights, while problematizing modernity's creation of
bounded and uncontested racial categories as well as uncontested acts of
racism, do not permit the sustaining of a black public sphere. Or, more
accurately, they call into question the cohesiveness of black political language at a time when activists and community members alike are seeing
little difference in consequence between the overt racism of thirty years
ago and the hegemonic racism of today.

The Dolphyn incident is only one in a long list of protests in which
race has been the central unifying point for the Seniors. While Sylvia's indignation over the treatment of this youth found its voice in the public
space created by the OMS, the same space also allows for the venting of
issues concerning the treatment of black farmers and the pollution of
rural land by international industries. For nearly a decade community
members have campaigned against lax environmental regulations set for
the corporate hog industry.

The idea that "hogs, Hogs, and More HOGS" is a major concern for
residents of Tillery signals a shift in economic development over the past

twenty years. From small independent farmers who raise several hundred sows on their family farms to vertically integrated operations that raise into the hundreds of thousands of sows per year, the industry has shifted dramatically in size and proportion. With this shift has come growing community concern. In December 1992, Halifax County residents learned, as one organizer put it, that "the corporate hog world was planning to enter Halifax County as economic development." Although the hog industry eventually located in the county, the organized Seniors group forced county commissioners to pass the first moratorium in the state on hog production until further research could be developed and stricter regulations implemented.

With over $1 billion in sales receipts in North Carolina alone, the growth in jobs and revenue has been a major selling point for the hog industry. The state in fact leads the nation in two important statistics: it has the fastest growing hog industry and the fastest declining number of hog farmers. These seemingly contradictory shifts tell a sordid story of production, land concentration, and profits in North Carolina. When it comes to hogs, neoliberal rhetorics of business profitability tend to dominate public debate as evidenced by the state's ongoing support of the industry.[27] Yet for people who live near the facilities, a different story unfolds.

According to statistics, North Carolina, since the 1990s, has rapidly grown in swine production and has been a national leader in vertically integrated, industrially structured hog farming.[28] Well over 90 percent of the industry today is found in former black belt counties, like Halifax, with histories rooted in cotton and tobacco farming.[29] This shift in economic development for the state is part of a major shift in farmland ownership and operation over the last several decades. According to sociologists Bob Edwards and Anthony Ladd, "The data suggests that the early growth of hog operations in North Carolina from 1982–87 is related to the decline of farmers who derive their principal income from farming."[30] This decline has disproportionately affected African American farmers, who have lost over 907,000 farms over the past seventy years: from "925,000, 14 percent of all farms in 1920, to only 18,000, 1 percent of all farms in 1992."[31]

Residents and environmentalists consistently raise concerns over the health and environmental risks that swine produced in intensive operations create: decline in quality of life, contamination of local water supply, dissolution of community autonomy. Families have canceled reunions, residents have become ill, and many in rural areas continue to argue of the threat to their well water.[32] In response to citizens' outcry, the state has established various committees to investigate the pork industry's role in water and air pollution, as well as what actions can be taken to lessen pollution. Furthermore, grassroots organizers in North Carolina, including CCT, organized a "Hog Summit" in order to bring together citizens, hog industry representatives, environmentalists, and state officials to talk about effecting positive change in the regulation of the pork industry.

The drastic shifts in land ownership and economic development raise serious questions of democracy and how it is experienced in eastern North Carolina. "Is it fair," one resident asked, "that the activities of some are allowed to have enormous impacts on the quality of life of their neighbors, and damaging and irreparable consequences for our environment?" This resident's concerns were echoed by another OMS member who described his experience walking outside of his home. "I can go out in the morning time when it's damp and the wind's blowing this way, and . . . boy, you can't hardly stand it out there, it smells so bad . . . And they're trying to put them right in your backyard, and I tell you the truth, it's a shame, I tell you. They won't put them in their backyards." The question of location is the obvious and predominating question.

African Americans and those too poor to move into the city are the ones who are most immediately affected by industrial hog operations. For Ms. Sylvia the treatment of her community by such operations stands as another indication of the need to create a public sphere that deals with issues of racial inequality. Because of the significant decline in black land ownership, less autonomy exists within communities for determining how land will be used and by whom. When spills occur, even if industries pay for the clean-up, communities suffer the immediate consequences of not having clean water for themselves, their children, and their livestock. Furthermore, hog industries place on rural communities greater demand for city or county water as opposed to well water. The costs for these changes are costs that the community assumes, not the industry. The stress on public resources is then exaggerated because of the needs that often already exist in these communities.

Reflecting these concerns, members of the Seniors group wrote this letter to their state representatives:

Dear Senator:
I am a resident of Halifax County, North Carolina. I live in a rural area of the county where we are still mainly dependent on individual wells for our water supply. I am a senior citizen and have worked hard all my life. I am very much concerned with the protection of the groundwater and aquifers that

stand a high probability of being contaminated from polluting industries, including industrial hog farms. Already, the stench from these industrial size farms has caused me to have to modify my life style because of the odor problem. However, of more concern for me right now is the threat to my drinking water supply. I would appreciate you supporting the current pending legislation proposed in House Bill 515 which will offer protection to others in my community, myself and for the state of North Carolina. Thank you for your support of helping to keep North Carolina a good place to live.[33]

The ability to simply "switch" to county or city water is not an immediate option for most county residents because the resources are not present. So, while industries may assume the costs of moving into an area, they do not have to assume the cost of the adjustments that residents must make because of their presence. Seniors' meetings center around a critique of the hog industry's agenda and its effect upon them. Having a public space in which to discuss these issues has made a significant difference, not only because their protests resulted in the state's first-ever moratorium on hog industry development, but also because the discussions allow them to see their shared problems and struggles.

As Ms. Sylvia expressed her reasons for involvement with the OMS, she consistently deemed it her "spiritual responsibility" to get involved.

> I think a lot of people don't see it as a part of their Christian responsibility, but I do because of what I said earlier about anything that affects the lives of people is a part of my Christian responsibility, not just my civic responsibility or community response . . . Most churches or ministers are concerned . . . at which they should be, with our souls in the hereafter. But, and I am too, but I think we've got to get there. I gotta live here before I die. I won't go to heaven until I die. Until I die, I've got to survive right here.

This understanding of the need to survive "here" before the eschatological moment of redemption with Christ is the reason for women's engagement with the struggles of their community. Faith is then a central element in maintaining consistency in activism in the presence of great challenge. As the women are faced with the day-to-day challenges of living in a community encumbered with racism, classism, and sexism, they engage these concerns with varying levels of gratitude for God's benevolence in the midst of trial, empathy with those who are unyieldingly oppressed, and righteous discontent over the degree of injustice perpetuated.

While the literature has often characterized the religion of women like Sylvia Jones, Juanita Cleveland, Diane Little, and Marie Carter as merely assuaging the emotional and physical wounds of living in an unjust society, this characterization fails to recognize the life and passion for people and justice that spirituality instills. Gratitude, empathy, and righteous discontent shape women's various levels of engagement. As gratitude and empathy work to create loving and supportive communities, they also instill in people a sense of hope regarding the future. This hope alone, however, does not result in radical transformation of a flawed social system. A focus upon the expressions of gratitude and empathy, thus, without a similar focus on the expression of righteous discontent can result in the perpetuation of systems that oppress. In this way agents can become unintentional conduits in processes of power replication.[34] For women actively engaged in public work, the availability of an alternative public gives them a space through which to channel their discontent with prevailing social systems. Such spaces I believe are available in organizations like CCT and Shiloh Baptist Church.

This alternative space offers not only a forum in which to vent frustrations, but also a place for organizing and supporting others in efforts to engender change. The longevity of these spaces is something that Steven Gregory argues is challenged by the creation of federal agencies in the post–civil rights era that are set up to address issues of inequality. This period of racial hegemony, however, as evidenced by the issues that women face, has not led to a decline in race problems. In fact, some argue that racially motivated acts of discrimination and hatred have risen, changing only in quality, not quantity, because of the greater access of people of color to spaces of privilege once set aside exclusively for whites.

The reality of these ongoing racial tensions, coupled with issues of gender and class specific to poor black women, creates the need for an alternative public that can force issues onto a broader public stage. The sustainability of this public within the black church is the subject of "Thursday". As black church discourse is met with the competing and correlating messages of a growing televangelist circuit, I ask whether the discourse of racial uplift shifts. If these TV ministries preach a more "priestly" than "prophetic" gospel, do these messages lead to activism in the more narrow sense of individual transformation?

"ARE WE A CHURCH OR A SOCIAL CHANGE ORGANIZATION?"

When I arrived at the Seniors' meeting everyone was already in line for lunch. Ms. Sylvia and other members of the kitchen staff prepared chicken, beans, potatoes, and fried bread to celebrate this month's birthdays. Mr. Green, the most cantankerous of the group, is 80 years old this month! He gives commentary on everything from how to raise children to how not to trust white folks. Whenever we would talk about my education and finishing the degree, he would warn me with great fatherly passion, "A wise man once said, [meaning him] 'keep your mind open and your legs closed!'" He's ever concerned with young women being led astray from their careers and educational goals because of "no good" men. While his rantings to me can be taken in stride, his criticisms of local churches are often met with great hostility from the faith-filled group of Open Minded Seniors. His ongoing proclamations that there are too many "pimps in the pulpit" receive unrelenting criticism from the members. To celebrate his milestone, his wife purchased a huge cake for everyone to enjoy.

During the meal I sat with Ms. Sylvia's mother and two other members of the group. After lunch, the meeting began. Mr. Alexander, the OMS president, called one of the visitors up to lead a song. A minister at one of the local Pentecostal churches, she gave everyone instructions on how to sing the song. She gave a line and we repeated it. "Fast!" she exclaimed, "like you really mean it!" The song began, "Where will you be when you hear that first trumpet sound?" Everyone joined in—some stood up, while others sat clapping and singing. After she finished the song, several people were still in the spirit of worship. As the minister walked back to her seat, one of the OMS members began to walk around praising God. Several others continued in thanksgiving. Looking a bit bewildered, Mr. Alexander, a practicing Catholic and the newly elected president of the Seniors group, began to ring the tiny bell on his stand as if to bring the room to order. The minister started with another verse of the song. The people joined in. Realizing that his efforts were futile, the president began to sing along. After the verse, very out of character, Mr. Alexander shouted "Hallelujah" to show his solidarity with the movement of the people. I was tickled.

While the Open Minded Seniors are made up of people primarily from the rural area of Halifax County, they represent different churches, denominations, and worship styles. Like Mr. and Mrs. Alexander, Mr. and Mrs. Lincoln seemed a bit removed from the worship service. They attend a fairly middle-class black Baptist church in the city that holds to a more mainstream, subdued order of worship. Mrs. Lincoln looked anxious for the "excitement" to subside. Nevertheless, it continued. The Pentecostals and the not-so-reserved Baptists had taken over the meeting. Mr. Alexander looked to George Givens for direction, but George just shrugged his shoulders, smiled, and continued writing his notes. Making a last-ditch effort to calm the group, Mr. Alexander spoke into the microphone, "All right, all right." To no avail, Mr. Alexander rang and spoke into the microphone. Alas, when the people decided the time had come, the meeting was restored to order.

The first order of business for the day was to discuss the recent trip to Washington to protest the USDA's treatment of black farmers. Everyone had an opportunity to voice her or his experience at the rally. Mrs. Lincoln spoke first. "I was so proud," she recounted. "It's good when you can walk into the halls of Congress and see your brothers and sisters representing you. And they're doing such a good job. I really think that we ought to send Maxine Waters a letter of congratulations. She's doing such a wonderful job." Maxine Waters had given two impassioned speeches, one prior to the congressional hearing outside in the cold with the farmers, and the other during the hearings. Having traveled with the Seniors to Washington, I knew firsthand the events to which Mrs. Lincoln referred. Outside, Maxine Waters's words were simple. I took notes feverishly as she spoke.

> First I owe you an apology. I must apologize for the US government and for the USDA. I need to apologize for the years of discrimination not only against you, but your mothers, fathers and grandfathers have suffered. I need to apologize for all the land you've lost. I need to apologize

for all the loans you did not receive. . . . But, we're here now. The Congressional Black Caucus is here now. And you didn't send us here to be the traditional voices.

Vowing her support and the support of the Congressional Black Caucus, Congresswoman Waters said emphatically, "The plight of the black farmer is at the top of the agenda of the CBC!" Waters encouraged the crowd to talk to, inform, empower, and instruct the CBC on how they should respond to the issue. She stated that although representatives from different regions have different concerns (i.e., there are black urban concerns and black rural concerns) there are general concerns that most blacks hold in common. The plight of the black farmer is a concern that ALL of the members of the CBC should hold strongly.

In closing, Congresswoman Waters thanked the organizing committee for inviting her and told the crowd that it was time that everyone heard the concerns of black farmers. Secretary of Agriculture Dan Glickman would be present at the one o'clock hearing at the Capitol as well as C-SPAN. In telling their stories, Congresswoman Waters instructed the farmers to be themselves, not to feel as though they had to perform for anyone. "Do it the way that it comes. . . . It's time for the world to hear from those who have been dropped off the American agenda."

When his opportunity to speak came, George gave the congressional committee and the USDA a history lesson. "There were over 300 farms in Tillery. There are no black farmers there today . . ." He went on to tell of Roosevelt's resettlement plan and how Tillery was a part of the project. Speaking of the government's treatment of him and his family, George stated, "They treat us like fourth-class citizens who have no right to participate in democracy . . . it is so good to see our black people stand up and say Enough is Enough." He went on to tell the stories of his father and brother, who were both farmers. He and his father have been fighting for his father's land for over twenty-one years. As he concluded he remarked, "I would like to have my father's case solved before he dies."

Another farmer told of losing his wife and children as a result of the stress put on his family. White farmers called and said that he was growing "too big." Soon after, his barn burned to the ground killing 150 sows. He then got into trouble with debt as a result of loans taken out with the Farm Service Agency (FSA), formerly the FmHA (Farmers' Home Administration). After years of living under this stress, his wife told him that "I can't live like this anymore" and left with their five children. For him the issues brought before the USDA affect not only the farmers, but their "families, communities, and the people that we work with."

Following the testimonies, Congressman John Conyers told those gathered that he had "never heard such wrenching testimony about racism in a federal agency in my life! This is a historic meeting." He then urged everyone to place his or her name and address on the pads that were being circulated. Glickman vowed to put "full moral suasion" behind the efforts of the farmers.

Lawrence Lucas, president of the Minority Employees of the USDA, then spoke. He insisted that "intimidation and reprisal have been a process going against the small farmer for years when we speak up." Looking at Glickman's panel, he stated, "And some of the people who are guilty are here today. . . . What we need is a cleaning of the house. . . . Put the Farm Service in receivership. The problem being brought to you is not a black farmer's problem, it's an American problem."

"We can sit here all day long," the attorney for the black farmers commented, "but unless the secretary of agriculture and the beloved president of the U.S. get involved, these farmers will go home and get treated the same way they've been treated for the last fifty years." He told the gathering "there are over $300 million dollars that the secretary can spend TODAY. The secretary needs to put his money where his mouth is." When asked by one of the members of Glickman's team how much he thought it would take to settle the cases of black farmers, the attorney responded, "I think the problem of black farmers is bigger than the Savings and Loan bail out." Finally commenting on the task force that Glickman has initiated, the attorney said, "Glickman has set them up for failure if he does not provide the funds."

As the congressional hearing drew to a close, Maxine Waters told farmers and those rallied in support, "The Congressional Black Caucus will work to ensure your success as you tackle this job." Then assuring the USDA staff that they will be an aggressive force in making sure that the USDA lives up to its responsibilities to the farmers, Waters told the staff members, "We [the Congressional Black Caucus] are not Johnny Come Lately in the game of politics." Turning again to the audience the congresswoman concluded "Trust us."

As the OMS members recounted their assorted memories of the Washington experience, they spoke with pride at the representation they had received from the people they sent to office. They also spoke of their need to continue lobbying Congress until the black farmers' issue is judiciously settled. George lightheartedly recalled a story from just a few years back when, after a rally, one of the members came up to him and said, "I didn't know you could speak to white folks like that!" Too long humbled by the experience of sharecropping, she had gained a certain understanding of how she could and could not engage whites. The group laughed, realizing that this indeed has been a part of their history, but one that they are in the process of reshaping every time they travel and take a stand against an unfair government policy.

As the meeting continued, the time came for the group to make decisions about the T-shirt design for their anniversary in a few months. A new debate ensued. Some wanted a white T-shirt with the picture of an open Bible to demonstrate the fact that God has indeed been their strength. They wanted others to know that they were actively engaged in God's work, not just political work. A few others wanted the picture of a hand, much like CCT's overall logo. This hand is a symbol of unity for the community. All of the organizations of CCT—the young adult group, the Nubian Youth, the Land Loss Fund, the Economic Development Committee (EDC), the environmental protection group (HELP), the health clinic and the Open Minded Seniors—work together to make CCT a success. Armed with their individual reasons, seniors one after the other voiced their support or dissent. Out of the crowd, Mr. Green stood and rebutted rather loudly, "Are we a church or a social change organization?!" It was obvious to him that the shirts should reflect not the Bible, but the extended hand. The Bible, after all, symbolizes the church, the hand symbolizes the community.

The reactions to Mr. Green's proclamation were various. Given the prior discussion of their lobbying efforts in Washington, Mr. Green's assessment seemed true—they are a social change organization. Yet, given the meeting's opening with prayer, songs, and thanksgiving to God, they seem to be a church. The simultaneity of these expressions may appear to some, even to Mr. Green, a paradox—his words ringing with the need to resolve the dialectic. The idea that "social change" and "church" could be seen as oppositional or at best noncomplementary ideals is an irony when one considers the history of black church activism.

Mr. Green's proclamation assumes the relative absence of social activism in the church and the relative absence of faith in social change organizations. The reality, however, is that the two have been interdependent. The black church and social change, given the trappings of a racist society, have had to go hand in hand.

In the final analysis the group decided upon the symbol of an open Bible—however, not just any open Bible. Their open Bible is elegantly adorned with a colorful kente stole. The stole communicates that their activity is not simply limited to the Bible's promise of achieving spiritual liberation; it is also connected to their quest for liberation in the material world—a struggle all too often sparked by the exclusion of people of color.

PRIESTLY
TRANSFORMATION

TELEVANGELISM (AND SHIFTING DISCOURSES OF PROGRESS)

"[A televangelist] every now and then will hit on something about civil rights, but not that often."

Interview with Ms. Cleveland

"All you do is sit here and watch those ministers!" "I do not," Gloria retorted, partially reclined on her Lazy Boy with the lower half of her body snuggled comfortably under her throw. I was growing a bit uncomfortable with the couple's debate, but it seemed like one in which they engaged at least once a week. Their lines and rebuttals seemed rote. He knew she would insist that she does not compulsively watch televangelists, and he would insist that she does. "Ever since you've been ill, you come in here and watch those folks and you believe every word they say." "I do not." Gloria stated her case seemingly for the second or third time that week. "Your problem," she continued with a slight air of spiritual superiority, "is that you don't listen to any of them. You should at least watch *one* of the ministers. You might learn something."

I had only stopped by to visit because I heard that she was ill. Always uncomfortable when married couples squabble in my presence, I sat and listened to both sides of the debate hoping not to be pulled in. Yet while Gloria and her husband were serious about their positions, they managed to sustain a fairly even and light-hearted tone. They never once seriously raised their voices, and Gloria did chuckle in between her defense of televangelists and her petition for her husband to watch. She did not say which minister might offer her husband the best trial run, she only insisted that her husband's participation was important. She believed that he could gain something, but exactly what seemed to me uncertain. I knew that he would not gain a radical, biblical, protest-oriented message of liberation for black people—or a lesson likening the exploitation of laborers, the contamination of drinking water, or the unjust judicial system to the "moral" bankruptcy of the nation. Such messages do not represent the prevailing genre of televangelism. Instead, he might hear a message that would benefit his *own* spiritual growth, at least according to his wife. For Gloria, her husband, though a student of the Bible, questions too many "biblical truths." She believes that he could have some of his questions answered if only he would listen.

Her husband's criticisms, though seemingly ungrounded because he has never watched the televangelists, hinge on an assumption that television preachers are all after money. To him these ministers do not have their listeners' best interest at heart; instead, they master gimmicks like fake healings and floor dramatics to win the attention and financial support of viewers. His criticisms, however, do not hinder Gloria from watching. After all, she maintains some criticisms that cause her to discriminate among televangelists as well.

Gloria's spontaneous debate with her husband is an example of the types of debates taking place throughout the country between those who believe television ministers and those who listen with a skeptic's mindset. These discussions are important because of the rapid growth in television ministries in recent decades. From its humble beginnings on Easter Sunday 1940 in New York, religious television, the "offspring" of religious radio, has mushroomed into a public icon. Originally dominated by mainline religious organizations, today religious television is dominated by evangelical and charismatic religious groups.[1] In the past twenty years, 24-hour Christian programming has multiplied in airtime and its viewership has skyrocketed. The Christian Broadcasting Network (CBN) founded by Pat Robertson and the Trinity Broadcasting Network (TBN) of Paul and Jan Crouch have become world-famous, transmitted everywhere by satellite.[2] In addition, the Inspirational Channel (INSP) and Black Entertainment Television (BET) have been host to a number of ministers who seek to use technology as a means of sharing the gospel with the world. Television ministers maintain followings across the globe in places like South America, Africa, and Europe as well as the United States. Their international appeal implies the universality of their message.

The influence of television ministries on the African American church, however, is a story yet unfolding. While a few scholars have begun to study the influence of this medium on American culture in general, there have not been any thorough studies concerning its effects on the African American church community specifically. One typical study of the general effect of televangelism on the church points out that "a growing number of churches and denominations today are struggling with controversial new liturgies, differing views of social activism, divisive personality cults, disagreements over religiously inspired entrepreneurship and feuds over the appropriateness of popular God talk—all adding credence to the indications that as goes televangelism, so goes American Christendom."[3]

During my research time in Halifax County, INSP was added as the one 24-hour Christian channel in the northeastern region of North Carolina. While county residents have been able to watch television ministers on stations such as BET on Sunday mornings and evenings for years, INSP was the first all-day Gospel channel of its kind in the region. INSP and CBN, both 24-hour Christian channels, are spreading to cities across the country and throughout the world. The long-term impact that these ministries will have on the public sphere of Christianity in general and African American Christianity in particular is as complex and diverse as the communities they enter.

The extent to which televangelists' messages are adopted and acted upon in everyday life is a subject that has yet to be fully examined. In what ways do ministries provide a welcome source of spiritual encouragement for those who listen while at the same time complicating needed discussions of social justice in places like Halifax? Do televangelists encourage people to engage society or do they merely encourage listeners to contribute to their individual social and spiritual advancement? With televangelists coming from various social and denominational backgrounds, what influence is such a medium having on the particular faith experience of black parishioners given the black church's historic (even if overly idealized) role as a place of both spiritual and social uplift?

The everyday concern of women in Halifax County with issues of environmental degradation, inequitable schooling, and political estrangement forces them into debate within larger public spheres. These spaces have been race-specific because the community has been polarized in dramatic ways along racial lines. Given Halifax County's history of racial division, community concerns have often been addressed in black churches or black-operated civil and political organizations like the Halifax County Black Caucus, the Halifax County NAACP, the Coalition for Progress (a racially exclusive though much less radical organization than the Black Caucus), and the Concerned Citizens of Tillery. These spaces significantly contribute to the discourse about what is required for progress, what is required to "make things better" in Halifax County. Television ministries, while not creating for their viewers a tangible public space, also contribute information on how to "make things better." From marital relationships and financial problems to health and race issues, these television ministers offer a variety of solutions to individuals' everyday problems. Some scholars suggest that this counseling discourse in television ministries is one of the reasons for their significant rise over the last several decades. Like the self-help industry, which is also increasing, television ministries are marketed along the lines of providing assistance to the individual looking for motivation to change his or her life circumstances.[4]

Televangelists' ability to market their ministry as a place where the "word of God" is preached in order to relieve a multitude of personal problems gives them a level of authority that other self-help advisers do not have. They offer practical no-nonsense "Bible-based" solutions to people's questions. An emphasis upon Scripture and a direct application of certain forms of scriptural interpretations to one's daily life are what brings about changes. As women listen, however, they also create a set of criticisms that counter the assumption that they are merely passive audiences for authoritative television personalities. Their criticisms offer some insight into the ways in which people adapt television messages into their own lives. In addition, their responses give insight into the difference between notions of progress offered by televangelists and the discourses of progress and social uplift historically located in mainline Protestant black churches. Exploration of these discourses and women's responses to them is the substance of this chapter.

LISTENING WITH AN ATTENTIVE EAR

Gloria's insistence that her husband *at least* watch one of the television ministers suggests that Gloria herself has gained something from watching television ministries. When I stopped by her home to visit, she was reading a devotional, recently given to her as a gift, written by T. D. Jakes, a popular black televangelist based in Dallas. Gloria's conviction is not unlike that of some of the other women I interviewed. For most it is the clarity of the televangelist's message that sustains their attention. Television ministers "teach" with charismatic authority, and the women want to grow in their faith pursuits. This emphasis upon teaching has been helpful for a number of the women in dealing with personal issues.

Yvette, whose son was recently placed under protective custody after witnessing a shooting in a nearby county, explained that one of the benefits of watching ministers on television is that they really teach about family and how to raise children. She particularly likes Rod Parsley, a white televangelist based in Columbus, Ohio. "I listen to a lot of Rod Parsley who was doing a series on reclaiming our kids." For her Parsley makes things clear. "I have understood things that maybe I read once and said, 'Hmm. I see what it means now.' I might not have even given it a thought, but listening to him I could get something else from the same message." For her Parsley's messages struck a chord not only because of the challenges that she has faced raising her two sons as a single parent, but also because of the challenges she sees other parents facing. Parsley's messages give her practical wisdom to share with other women in the community, especially those with whom she works and worships.

When asked who her favorite ministers are and what inspires her about their messages, like Yvette, Gloria emphasized the evangelists' ability to teach from Scripture. She explained that she likes T. D. Jakes and Creflo Dollar because, "they teach more than preach. Creflo Dollar does a lot of teaching and in his teaching, he breaks it down so that I can get a full understanding of what he says." This simplicity makes it easier for her to adopt his message into her daily practice. One incident in particular made her reassess her financial situation. Instead of always looking at the negative side of her finances, she now concentrates on the positive. During one message Dollar challenged the congregation to believe that "you will never be broke again in your life." She said that she received his prophetic word, and "from that day to this, whether it's five dollars or ten dollars, or one dollar, I always have money in my pocket." This testimony in itself keeps her from worrying constantly about bills and the possibility of ever being broke. She simply trusts God to provide when funds are insufficient. Although she and her husband are now financially stable and paying for her youngest to complete college, Gloria has long had a tendency to worry about money, especially after she left her first husband and began raising their children on her own. Dollar's teachings about financial prosperity in the believer's life has at the very least encouraged her not to worry about financial matters. This sense of peace and security, she explains, is leaps and bounds above where she used to be.

Vivian similarly commends the "teaching" of television ministers as her primary reason for listening. While she watches Kenneth Copeland, a white faith and prosperity teacher, she particularly enjoys the ministry of John Cherry, a black AME Zion pastor from Maryland. "That man," Vivian explains, "he teaches. I mean I was sitting there listening to his program taking notes because he was teaching about Daniel. Daniel, Shadrach, Meshach and Abednego." Cherry was teaching on the importance of faith in the midst of opposition. Point by point, Vivian recalled for me the significance of the Old Testament message. As a political prisoner, Daniel refused to eat the King's food and drink the King's wine. Instead he relied upon the diet of vegetables and water from God, proving in the end that God's plan is best. Daniel's triumph of faith at the end of the story was an indication to Vivian that if she too has that type of faith, certainly she could have that type of victory, regardless of the circumstances. Cherry's ability to communicate this message through his authoritative and orderly teaching style is what most inspired Vivian. "He teaches. He breaks it down. He's preaching the whole while, but he also has the subtitles. And he goes into the subtitles and then he has little titles under them . . . And he gives you the verses . . . and you're flipping through [the Bible] and you know what he's saying is right there. And I really, I really enjoy him."

This emphasis upon teaching versus preaching is a differentiation that causes television ministers to stand out in the women's minds. Their ability to appropriate the message into their daily lives and attempts at faith makes televangelism a viable source of spiritual encouragement for most of those I interviewed. Yet, the women do not indiscriminately watch ministers. Upon the basis of personal preference and their own agreement with the pastor's presentation, they choose among the ministries that they support and those that they do not. "I like some of the TV ministries," explained Ms. Cleveland. "I like Jakes and some of the others . . . I like *some* of them. I don't like them all." Distinguishing between those ministries Ms. Cleveland likes and those she does not like requires not so much an understanding of the preachers' denominational affiliations, because women cross denominational boundaries at whim when listening to television ministries. Rather, it requires an exploration of the women's own denominational affiliations and their personal understanding of this type of faith in their lives.

While the women I interviewed visit various churches and on occasion participate in choir concerts, revivals, or other special services at nearby churches, each is a member of a mainline Baptist church. The rural traditions that they come from, however, do not hinder them from participating in the advances that are taking place in ministries around the globe. Living in Halifax County by no means hinders women from lis-

tening to a minister in California, or praying for healing from a minister
in Miami, or sending money to a minister in Dallas who has a foreign
mission project in Mozambique. The explosion of television ministries
connects worshippers with not only the "word" from around the globe,
but also the philosophical ideas of preachers who garner their fame from
a particular type of ministry. Whether Benny Hinn with his healing cru-
sades, or Creflo Dollar with his ministry of prosperity, Rod Parsley with
his Covenant Breakthrough Partners, Joyce Meyers with her down-to-
earth, practical "life in the word" teachings, or T. D. Jakes with his mission to wounded women, television ministries carry with them an attractive message that suggests some form of assistance or liberation for
the listener.

As women discriminate among ministries, the influence of their own
mainline Baptist traditions becomes evident. The worship style of television personalities is the first indicator for women that they must
make choices. When I asked each of them their reservations about television ministries, without exception their very first line of critique was
based upon the performance of faith. The "laying on of hands,"
"falling out," "speaking in tongues" were all initial indicators for
them that they needed to sift through the message and determine for
themselves what they agree with and what they differ with. This initial disconnect from many of the televangelists' presentations was
spurred by their affiliation with historically black Baptist churches
whose doctrines and practices do not reflect these more charismatic
expressions.

When I asked Ms. Cleveland to explain what makes her skeptical
about certain television ministries, she explained that being "slain" in the
spirit, when parishioners purportedly lose conscious under the guidance
of the Holy Spirit, causes her to question the authenticity of the ministry.
She simply does not understand it: "This slain in the spirit and
all . . . some of it I just don't understand. I don't have the knowledge on
being slain. I don't know what that means. Nobody explained it. A lot
of things that they're doing with tongue speaking. I don't believe. Tongue
speaking, I can't handle that because I don't know what you're saying . . . It doesn't edify anybody but yourself . . . A lot of it, I just don't
understand. I don't speak against it. I just don't understand." Similarly,
while talking about what she likes about television ministries, Ms.
Moore immediately points out her reservations regarding charismatic
displays of worship. When people are slain in the spirit, she questions its
authenticity.

I don't want this to sound critical, but there's one televangelist that just looks at people, and I'm not doubting the power of God, maybe I am, but he just looks at people and they all go out . . . Or, he'll look at a whole [section of worshippers] and he'll say "you ready?" and they go *voom*, and they're out. And I'm cynical about that. I don't know why. I believe in the Holy Spirit, and I believe it will come and dwell in you if you are ready and receptive to the Holy Spirit. I don't doubt the Holy Spirit. I doubt the receptiveness of the recipient . . . It's just inconceivable to me that 200 people are standing there and at the very same moment all 200 are receptive to the Holy Spirit to the extent that it carries them out.

Such charismatic displays of worship are for Ms. Moore merely performances. Although she maintains strong belief in the Holy Spirit, she questions the motives of those *receiving* the Holy Spirit. Yvette, too, worries about the authenticity of Spirit displays seen on television. "A couple of them like blowing at somebody and they're falling out; a person just falls out in the Spirit, being slain in the Spirit. God can do it. He can do anything, but I don't know about all of that." Each of the women affirms the power of God to perform anything; however, for each woman the fallibility of the practitioners raises questions when particular faith expressions are unfamiliar or seemingly inauthentic.

Coming from mainline black Baptist denominations means that their worship style, though often energetic, is not generally characterized by great emotionalism or ecstatic dancing, let alone the possibility of being slain in the spirit. Having visited their churches, I know that only one of them has a drum and the most excitement people demonstrate is usually seen in hand clapping, foot tapping, and standing with the choir to sing. Rarely do many parishioners raise their hands in worship or engage in other more outwardly visible forms of praise. While prayer times during worship are often filled with emotional testimonies which may leave a number of people in tears, Baptists generally do not have prayer lines in which a pastor calls people forward to anoint their heads with oil and lay hands on them. This practice, more commonly found in charismatic, Pentecostal, or apostolic churches, often results in a person being "slain in the spirit."

Beyond the women's reluctance to participate fully in various charismatic practices, several voiced concern about the material extravagance seen on television. Elaborate edifices, dress styles, and make-up signal for most a lack of authenticity or at the very least a complete disconnect from the communities in which the women live. These concerns raise the more sociological questions regarding the efficacy of television ministries. The idea that women are listening to "teachers" who are able to instruct through the exposition of Scripture raises questions about what they are learning and, more important, what they are not learning. What is being taught and what is being rejected? How might these discourses deviate from traditional discourses in mainline African American churches?

Scholars like Hans Baer and Merrill Singer have attempted to enunciate the various spiritualist versus materialist traditions within black church experience. That women point out extravagant materialism as a *problem* in the ministries of televangelists points to their own acculturation to a particular denominational understanding of wealth and materialism. Whereas in some traditions extravagant adornment is a sign of God's blessing and favor, for the women such presentations of wealth are excessive.

The mainline Baptist church traditions from which these women emerge do not historically emphasize material extravagance as an indicator of spiritual favor. Nevertheless, there are traditions whose creeds do encourage this type of rationale. The variances between such religious beliefs Baer and Singer characterize as the difference between thaumaturgical sects, conversionist sects, mainstream denominations/established sects, and messianic-nationalist sects.[5] Looking intently at the degree to which churches reject capitalism as a positive economic enterprise, Baer and Singer in their materialist analysis suggest that black churches can be characterized according to their strategies for social action. Thaumaturgical sects are seen as some of the least politically radical because of their belief that "the most direct way to achieve socially desired ends—such as financial prosperity, prestige, love, and health—is by engaging in various magico-religious rituals or by acquiring esoteric knowledge that provides individuals with spiritual power over themselves and others."[6] Though such sects purportedly deemphasize the need for political involvement, Baer and Singer see some element of protest in their rejection of what is considered "pie-in-the-sky religion," or a refusal to wait for one's reward in "some nebulous afterlife." Conversionist sects, with their emphasis upon sanctification and holiness, according to their study, often remain "apolitical" in their posture toward the larger society, relying exclusively upon the individual's transformation to effect change. While this conclusion is debatable, given changes in Pentecostalism, these are the churches described in the model as most historically inclined to preach that believers will receive their rewards in the afterlife. Mainstream churches are "committed, at least in theory, to a reformist strategy of social activism that will enable African Americans to become better integrated into the political, economic, and social institutions of the larger society."7 Mainline Protestant denominations, for example, have historically participated in civil rights concerns and been on the forefront of critiques regarding political and social injustice. They, however, are not like more radical groups, which often completely remove themselves from pursuits within the American mainstream. Lastly, messianic-nationalists in their emphasis upon black nationalism reject, at least "rhetorically . . . both mainstream goals and values."8 Marcus Garvey's Universal Negro Improvement Association, the Nation of Islam, and Albert B. Cleage's Shrine of the Black Madonna all reflect some variation of these types of teachings.

That the women I spoke with, through the medium of television, are able to blend mainstream ideas with charismatic and thaumaturgical teachings speaks to the type of melding of theological and doctrinal concerns that takes place with advances in technology and the globalization of ministry. Nevertheless, such blending also leads to critiques and tensions within newly received discourses. As women stated their initial opposition to certain televangelists based upon their charismatic worship styles, they also criticized various ministers' emphasis upon materialism. These critiques further illuminate the women's commitments of faith and their points of departure. The questions of race, economics, and individualism that women bring to the fore by listening to television ministers are questions that go to the heart of what it means to be engaged in both American culture and Christian culture at the turn of the millennium.

TENSIONS WITHIN NEW
DISCOURSES OF PROGRESS

The women I interviewed had some common television favorites such as T. D. Jakes, an African American pastor of a predominately black megachurch in Dallas; Creflo Dollar, an African American pastor of a predominately black megachurch in Atlanta; Rod Parsley, a white pastor of a multicultural megachurch in Columbus, Ohio; Joyce Meyers, a white female evangelist whose traveling ministry takes her to metropolitan centers across the country; and Frederick K. C. Price, an African American pastor of a predominately black megachurch in Los Angeles. While one definition holds that "African American megachurches are black churches with at least 2000 people attending the weekly Sunday

Service,"⁹ each of the churches listed above, which happen to also maintain large television audiences, claims over 20,000 persons within their membership. Although different in certain theological affirmations, the ministries of these televangelists attract the viewership of a cross section of people. Books by Joyce Meyers and T. D. Jakes were in continuous supply in the local Christian bookstore in Roanoke Rapids. Ironically, the feature newspaper advertisement for the white-owned bookstore in the predominately white central city was a picture of T. D. Jakes and a reminder about the ongoing availability of his latest sermons or books. Although consumers of his products are both black and white, it is not uncommon to walk into the Christian bookstore and see small gatherings of black women talking or sifting through various recently released videos, books, and tapes. Some people, according to one interviewee, are even known to have what they call "T. D. Jakes libraries," a vast collection of his audio and video tapes.

Both television ministries and traditional mainline churches maintain concern over the social and economic progress of African American believers. The discourses television ministers provide around what is required to "make things better," however, contrast in some ways with earlier discourses of progress set forth by mainline black Protestant churches. Included in this historic discourse is a critique of social structures and injustice that is evidently absent in many of televangelists' discourses of progress. If not completely contrasting with this historic discourse, televangelists at the very least expand a conservative strand of this discussion, which focuses primarily on how to progress within America's social and economic system, not on how to oppose it. That television ministers are more prone to align themselves with conservative political agendas is not a phenomenon, however, that has occurred in a vacuum.

This trend in televangelism came about with a move toward religious conservatism in the 1980s, according to scholar Mimi White. "The most visible religious programs that emerged on American television in this context did not represent mainstream Protestant religious practice; instead they featured evangelical Protestantism with a fundamentalist or Pentecostal emphasis. In this sense, the conservative religious doctrine purveyed by the programs embraces a popular, conservative religious subculture."¹⁰

Although some women, like Ms. Sylvia and Diane, who are both heavily involved with the Concerned Citizens of Tillery, maintain critiques of televangelists' ministries that prevent them from being involved

with these ministries, others actively follow their teachings and participate in the national conferences that televangelists sponsor. That television ministries can influence believers' understanding of social problems
and solutions speaks volumes about the type of public spheres that are
being created and dismantled. The historical "black church" is thus
caught between two different traditions. The first tradition, represented
in the previous chapter by organizations like CCT, reflects the church's
more radical history of critiquing political and economic institutions and
systems that repress social and economic progress. The second tradition,
represented in this section by television ministries, reflects the more conservative integrationist approach to social problems, as it encourages
radical changes solely in the individual desiring to advance swiftly in the
American mainstream. Between these two polarities resides a black
church pulled in different directions by its calling to be both prophetic
and priestly in its ministry. In addressing this tension as it relates to the
influence of televangelists, I look exclusively at the television ministers
that women have named their favorites or the most popular.[11] Although
these ministries hold somewhat diverse doctrinal positions based upon
their denominational or nondenominational affiliations, they exhibit
consistencies that together mark a subtle shift in the terms of the debate.

This shift is marked by three distinct characteristics. First, television
ministries' ability to meet the emotional and spiritual needs of individual believers suppresses a need to focus on social ills such as
racism, classism, and sexism. This emphasis upon the individual paves
the way for the advancement of two other discourses, prosperity
teaching and a simplistic multiculturalism. The ministry of prosperity
teaches that the degrees to which one obeys God, prays, and "sows
seeds of faith" (gives financially to the ministry) are the exclusive de-
terminants of one's financial increase. Outside of the individual and
God there are no limitations to amassing wealth. This popular teaching is found in what is commonly referred to as the Faith Movement,
a movement of charismatic leaders whose emphasis upon positive confession is held as the benchmark of faith. Finally, ministries' emphasis
upon multiculturalism without a systematic critique of racism creates
an illusion of racial progress that precludes a discussion of the social
forces which perpetuate race-based discrimination. Again, the degree
to which such media are effective is measured by how women absorb
this alternative discourse and the limitations we place upon an understanding of activism.

Reconstructing the Individual

Much like Gloria's husband, Ms. Sylvia laments the time that her mother spends "watching those folks." Her mother's routine revolves around watching several televangelists throughout the day, causing her to turn the majority of her attention inward on how she can improve her own life. Because she is more confined to the house than her daughter, televangelists provide her with a means of enjoying her time. Instead of mere television watching, she is learning how to build a relationship with God, a pursuit she finds both challenging and rewarding. The method of self-improvement offered by televangelists in this case seems not only a means of entertainment for those confined, but also a means of constructive engagement.

This focus on the individual, some worry, can overwhelmingly influence citizens' social and political engagement as people turn their energies inward and remove themselves from interaction within larger public spheres. Quentin Schultze argues that televangelism creates a new individualistic faith system in that faith "is a matter only of the relationship between the individual believer and God, rarely between the church and God, or even the individual and the church." One pastor from North Carolina with whom I spoke expressed his concern that "television ministries reduce our faith to a process of mental absorption rather than a process of engagement." Instead of emphasizing the need to participate in community, he explained, the Christian faith is reduced to the mere acquisition of biblical knowledge without an arena in which to practice it. The effect of televangelism, intended or not, according to some, is to create a space where such attention is given to the individual that a discussion of how the individual fits into community and is to work on behalf of community is precluded. "In a sense," this minister argues, "it betrays the gospel."[12]

Emphases upon taped sermons and mass conference attendance are key selling tools for television ministries. Highly personal messages such as "How you can overcome your fears," "Five ways that you can tackle your finances," or "Seven steps to a more joy filled you," are examples of the types of messages presented by evangelistic marketers. According to their advertisements, change begins and ends with the individual. If you change, then all the problems in your life will likewise change. There is little emphasis upon a need to critique the social structures that may impede progress.

Joyce Meyers, one of the most popular televangelists, has a ministry that is largely undergirded by the marketing and selling of books and tapes. Instead of having a home-based church, she travels the country, ministering in auditoriums and coliseums to thousands of television fans who travel to nearby locations to hear her speak. Her humorous and straightforward style of offering practical advice on how people can engage their relationship with God has made her a media favorite. Her most recent self-help, Christ-centered books are abundantly present in most Christian bookstores. Her emphasis upon self-help and the individual is reflected in the titles of some of her most recent publications. *Beauty for Ashes: Receiving Emotional Healing* (1994), for example, gives scriptural guidance to help individuals overcome troubling emotional experiences. Similarly, *How to Succeed at Being Yourself: Finding the Confidence to Fulfill Your Destiny* (1999) and *If Not for the Grace of God: Learning to Live Independent of Frustrations and Struggles* (1995) both offer practical, no-nonsense suggestions for living up to one's potential in life. Her work relies heavily upon scriptural references that support the development of the individual. One of her later works, *Eat and Stay Thin: Simple, Spiritual, Satisfying Weight Control* (1999), taps into recent media emphasis upon healthy eating and slenderizing the body—all, however, with a growing emphasis upon the Bible as the authoritative tool for accomplishing the final result.

T. D. Jakes likewise has a ministry largely undergirded by the marketing of books, video tapes, and audio tapes which are projected to heal broken people, particularly women.[13] His messages of encouragement, self-empowerment, and Holy Spirit–living are an attraction to thousands of Christians internationally. His celebrated women's message, "Woman Thou Art Loosed," began as a Bible study in his home church in West Virginia and was given to a national audience in 1992. This message has brought about an enormous revival of women across the globe. In July 1998, over 52,000 women packed the Georgia Dome to listen to the charismatic leader. At the millennium, tickets to the dome event were sold out months in advance, with people registering for participation in the overflow area in a nearby Atlanta arena. While his messages of individual restoration and healing have attracted a largely female following, in 1993 he also initiated a men's movement, ManPower, created to provide "a safe environment for men of all races and backgrounds to receive healing from God."[14] The appeal that such messages have for the restoration of the individual emerged simultaneously with the growth of the self-help industries of the 1980s and '90s.

Televangelism's focus upon the individual, however, is also largely based upon time and the market. Because the medium of television relies upon the quick absorption of an image, television ministers must often convey their messages within a thirty-minute time slot with enough minutes subtracted to sell tapes, announce conferences, and appeal for donations. While the mission and focus of individual televangelists' churches may actually entail a larger outreach to the community, the segment that is presented to the world is focused primarily as an appeal to the individual watching. These brief sermons reflect only a segment of the worship service. Unlike sitcoms, news shows, movies, and documentaries, they are not the product of artificial staging and scripting, produced by people who simply pack up their belongings and go home at the end of the day. What is not seen by viewers is that many members of these large megachurch television ministries are actively involved in community projects that extend far beyond the thirty-minute clip seen on screen.[15] Televangelism presupposes a presentation of real people in real-life (though edited) worship. Nevertheless, what is communicated to the larger public is the thirty-minute, individual-centered clip.

Emphasis upon the individual in this sense can deflect attention from the idea of a common plight and shared grievances with a corrupt or unjust social or political order. In their study of individualism and commitment in American life, sociologist Robert Bellah and his colleagues argue that religion, while largely responsible for fostering community and shared concerns, has also been responsible for the growing individualism in American society.[16] Individualism for them is as Alexis de Tocqueville once described it, "a calm and considered feeling which disposes each citizen to isolate himself from the mass of his fellows and withdraw into the circle of family and friends; with this little society formed to his taste, he gladly leaves the greater society to look after itself."[17] While Bellah and his coauthors do not relate their study to the experience of television ministers, there is a clear connection between the growing individualism in American life that they describe and the simultaneous growth in individualism prescribed, intentionally and unintentionally, by television ministers. As opposed to preaching against the inclinations of American society, ministers reinforce the drive toward individuation.

In many ways the teachings of charismatic television preachers reflect the ideological perspectives of Baer and Singer's thaumaturgical churches. The emphasis upon self-help at this historical moment along with the appeal it draws from large numbers of viewers coincides with the growing conservatism of the American populace in a post–civil rights society. Whereas churches at one time drew the attention of members and sympathizers engaged in social change, many who participate in mass meetings today, whether via satellite or in person, engage in faith rituals which are intended to bring about individual transformation, not necessarily the transformation of society. Individualism in its shrewdest form assures the advancement of particular people who pray (or work) hard without a critique of the systems that work to repress progress for the masses.

Looking to Prosper

Individualism coupled with an insistence upon financial gain, often for materialistic pursuits, forms yet another challenge to historic discourses within mainline Protestant denominations. While some see the emphasis on prosperity as facilitating the creation of an entrepreneurial black middle class, others see such an emphasis as completely disengaged from structural problems in society. While the desire to be solvent is one shared by most of my informants, their absorption of the Faith Movement's claims in this area seems grounded in the experiences of everyday life.

Somewhat different from other forms of evangelicalism and Pentecostalism found on television, the claims of the Faith Movement give attention to passages of Scripture which promise both health and wealth in this life, based upon the believer's positive confession. Creflo Dollar and Frederick K. C. Price are the two most prominent African American leaders in this movement. Ministers like Kenneth Hagin, Kenneth Copeland, John Avanzini, and Robert Tilton are also contemporary leaders and pioneers of the Faith Movement. This belief in the power of faith and positive confession to overcome poverty, sickness, and despair in all forms is reflected in the positive thinking movement of the early 1900s. In his book *The Positive Thinkers: Popular Religious Psychology from Mary Baker Eddy to Norman Vincent Peale and Ronald Reagan*, Donald Meyers argues that part of the outcome for positive thinkers was to move away from viewing the government and political change as the means of acquiring a better life. Instead, emphasis was placed on encouraging dramatic changes in individual thought processes as a means of securing desired objectives, whether peace, security, or economic stability. Napoleon Hill's *Think and Grow Rich* was a highly influential text in the mid-1930s when it arrived on newsstands, setting the stage for further mind-cure prophets. Norman Vincent Peale's *The Power of Positive*

Thinking, published in 1952, forms the backdrop of Frederick Price's work *Name It and Claim It: The Power of Positive Confession*. In the opening of the book Price explains, "Some years ago, there was a book written by Norman Vincent Peale, which was a best-seller all over the world. It was titled *The Power of Positive Thinking*. I submit to you that it is certainly good to think positively. . . ." He goes on to say that while thinking positively is an important first step, there is a second step that one must make. One has to "claim it," claim the promises of God.[18]

While the Faith Movement promises wealth, I only met a few women during my research in Halifax who were wedded to the idea of wealth under these conditions. One beautician that I spoke with explained that God told her that she would become a millionaire. The only way for her to do so, however, was to "walk in it." Therefore, every week she went to the department store and purchased a brand new suit for Sunday church service in order to demonstrate that she believed her financial blessing was on the way. This act of "positive confession," speaking and acting according to profession, was her demonstration of faith in God's promise.

While my interview with this beautician revealed an incredible manifestation of faith in the power of positive confession, few of the women I interviewed expected an extemporaneous improvement in their financial situation or the condition of their communities based upon such acts of faith. In fact they were often critical of the low wages and lack of promotion that they or their family members have received on jobs. Nevertheless, several were still attracted to the teachings of Dollar and Price, who numbered among the women's favorite televangelists.

Discussing her attraction to Dollar's ministry, Carmen Moore explained, "I listen to Creflo Dollar. I have listened to him on more than one occasion and I can sit there and listen to his whole message and the reason I've enjoyed it is that he seems to take the scriptures and break it right down to how can you use this in everyday living? And that's what I like. That's what I need . . ." The simplicity of his message attracts her. That she can continuously listen to his message without criticizing one of the fundamental principles of his theology makes a statement about the degree to which the message of prosperity has become normalized. In fact, none of the women who said that they listen to Dollar's ministry offered an explicit critique of his prosperity theology.

Both Christian communications scholar Quentin J. Schultze and anthropologist Susan Harding note the subtlety of American televangelism. Schultze in his work *Televangelism and American Culture* argues that televangelism in taking on the characteristics of American television culture—its high focus upon individualism, its flare for the dramatic, its quick and easy appeal—gradually merges biblical faith with American culture creating a Christendom uniquely suited to the American Christian and often categorically different from the Christianity of early church leaders. Similarly, Harding in *The Book of Jerry Falwell: Fundamentalist Language and Politics* notes that the fundamentalist dogmatic takeover that she expected to witness in her study of Falwell and the Moral Majority did not take place. Instead of political rallies organized to alter politics, she witnessed a war of words. "Eventually," she notes, "I realized that while I saw little in the way of routine or protest politics in Falwell's Lynchburg community, it was rife with another kind of politics . . . cultural politics."[19] Such cultural politics were aimed at "convert[ing] his people from 'fundamentalists' whose only mission in American society was evangelism, into 'conservative Christians,' who would fight worldly battles and who sought worldly power and influence in the name of 'Christian values.'"[20] These values would largely be defined by Falwell's race- and gender-privileged understanding of and emphasis upon Scripture. This idea of a gradual shift in discourse is likened to the subtle shift that is taking place in the discourse historically located in the black church.

While the women interviewed have not fully subscribed to the teachings of prosperity and in some ways resist its emphasis upon materialism, most have not engaged in a critique of capitalism and its success and failures in Halifax County. Prosperity preaching does not focus upon such critiques either. Ms. Sylvia and Diane, however, as members of CCT are constantly engaged in a critique of the practices and problems of capitalism as they deal with the day-to-day struggles of their community.

Ms. Sylvia makes virtually no exceptions to her dislike of television ministers. By and large all of the ministries are too materialistic. When asked, "Do you listen to ministries of people on television?" she immediately retorted. "No ma'am!" When asked why, she explained, "Because, in my opinion, they are so commercial. I feel that. I'm not saying a person should not be dressed, or have their hair done. But when you have eyelashes on longer than my finger nails, when you have hair four feet tall, and every hair is . . . and the guys, everything is just so perfect and all this glitter . . . It's just too far-fetched for me. Now, my mother watches it without fail . . . I just think it's, for me, it's just too commercial." The commercialization of the ministry, mixed with the "glitter" and the focus on presentation, places Ms. Sylvia at a distinct distance from the ideas of television ministers. It for her is too "far-fetched," something that she is unable to grasp. Such preoccupations with materialism seem to her directly contrary to the nature and calling of God to Christians.

For Carmen Moore this contradiction is clear, but not always readily apparent. One has to "really listen." Although she watches Creflo Dollar, she states, "I don't go out of my way to listen to a lot of them because sometimes if you really listen to some of them, and this is just my opinion, what they're saying has nothing to do with uplifting God." Instead, "It has to do with making themselves look good." To illustrate this she explains the problem she has with the attire of televangelists and the decor of their surroundings. "If you flip on the Bible network right now, on television, there's one right behind the other . . . Oh, there are elaborate suits and sequins and bouffant hair and rings and diamonds and elaborate edifices and flowers and this and that and I'm just cynical about that. You know. One guy has a big pompadour all over here and rings and *Ahhh!* That gets in the way to me." While to her such "glamour and glitz pulls people in," there is a problem: "if you're trying to help me and reach me so that we can be spiritually in tune with each other and I'm sitting there looking at all your diamonds and the outfit you're wearing—some of which are elaborate and that kind of thing—I think that gets in the way." She then contrasts her locale with the larger locale of the television ministry and argues that the size and expanse of the latter dwarf the legitimacy of the work that is taking place in the "country," where she lives.

> I think they're attracted to charisma and glitz and the glamour of the whole thing. I think some are. Now that does not make it right because I think that . . . it gets in the way of MY getting to the message, the meaning of life . . . It gets in MY way and that doesn't mean it's not valid. You know. But I wonder sometimes . . . [For] example, you can take a tiny little country if you will. Doesn't have to be in the country, but a tiny little church family right with a very unassuming, but sincere ministry or leader, with a small congregation whose desire is to help people and so forth, you don't hear of them. Who makes the news? Who has the budgets to get on TV? You know and all that. It's the big ones with all the elaborate everything. And I'm not saying all of them are like this. It's just some I have some problems with.

Ms. Moore is clear about distinguishing between ministries, emphasizing that not all of them create problems for her. As stated earlier, she enjoys the teachings of Creflo Dollar. The idea, however, that she listens to a self-proclaimed prosperity teacher who wears expensive, tailor-made suits and admittedly flies a private jet, *and* at the same time offers a critique of the extravagance of television ministers speaks to the tensions that women wrestle with in attempting to gain messages of faith from ministers. They must actively distinguish between those things they ideologically support and those they oppose. While Ms. Moore struggles with these tensions, Ms. Sylvia makes no exceptions. They are all too commercial for her. There are aspects of certain ministries that disrupt women's spiritual sensibilities simply because of the emphasis upon material possession.

With its emphasis upon material gain, there is little critique of systems that perpetuate poverty. Instead, poverty is at worst seen as a demonic spirit that must be cast off by positive confession. According to prosperity doctrines, financial wealth is a promise of God to all believers. However, wealth is attained not through a reordering of unjust society, but rather through an abundance of faith. "Name it and claim it" prosperity teachings abound, wherein the force of positive affirmation from your lips determines whether or not you will receive this blessing of wealth. Such teachings reflect the immediate triumph of individualism. Those with enough faith will triumph; those without will be left behind. Prosperity ministers do not teach that unjust systems do not exist. Rather, they teach that the believer will "find favor" within the system, advancing by God's intervention through job situations that would inevitably hinder others.

The sign of progress in prosperity is the successful acquisition of things and the display of this wealth to others. Many television ministers who align themselves with this doctrine sport expensive suits, luxury cars, extravagant homes, and elaborate, well-furnished sanctuaries. The subconscious message is that "this pattern has worked for us, it will work for you too." In discussing the problems of prosperity ministries, Schultze argues that their premise is the desire for American cultural norms. "Faith," as he explains the Jim and Tammy Bakker scandal, "was envisioned as a means to personal gain—more money, better clothing, a bigger home, and all of the rest of the trappings of American culture."[21] In a repentant story of things gone wrong with his experience in prosperity theology, Jim Bakker writes in his book *Prosperity and the Coming Apocalypse,* "The more I thought about it, the more I had to admit that I had fallen into that snare. I had allowed the quest for material possessions, the deceitfulness of riches, and the desires for other things to choke the Word of God in my own life, and in the lives of my family members and co-workers."[22] "In a nutshell," he explains, "the prosperity message promises that Christians should expect to achieve health, wealth, success, happiness, and personal fulfillment—not just in heaven to come, but during this life on earth."[23] The absence of such things is assumed to be the result of a lack of faith or the presence of sin in one's life. According to Robert Tilton, one noted prosperity minister, "not only is worrying a sin, but being poor is a sin when God promises prosperity!"[24] This displacement of poverty's causes solely upon the individual is seen by some more mainline religious leaders as the problem with the message of prosperity. The new, reflective Bakker writes that "prosperity teaching emphasizes comfort and ease. There's is little discussion of denying oneself. But real Christianity," he concludes, "involves sacrifice, and Jesus makes it clear that for true followers of Christ, self-denial is a basic ingredient . . . Tragically, too late, I recognized that at PTL I had done just the opposite of Jesus' words by teaching people to fall in love with money. Jesus never equated His blessings with material things, but I had. I laid so much emphasis upon materialism, I subtly encouraged people to put their hearts into things, rather than into Jesus."[25]

In his book *Name It and Claim It,* Price warns the reader that he is explaining "something that will be considered controversial in the traditional church world." With that he lays out his argument for why God wants people to live healthy, wealthy lives and his anger at not knowing it sooner. "When I found out that Jesus not only saved me from sin, but He saved me from sickness, disease, poverty, fear, and any other negative thing that would destroy me and take my life, I got mad! I got righteously indignant!" He goes on to give his interpretation of 1 Corinthians 3:21, "Therefore let no man glory in men. For all things are yours," as God's promise to the congregants. "Underline the words *all things,*" he emphasizes. "It did not say all spirituals. It said, THINGS. Is an automobile a thing? Is furniture a thing? Is jewelry a thing? Are clothes things? Are houses and lands and money things? He said ALL THINGS. ALL means, 'everything without exception, nothing left out.' "[26] Price's emphasis upon the material prosperity of his congregants fits well with contemporary American ideas of materialism and consumption. Amassing things becomes a sign of God's favor and blessing. The emphasis upon positive confession as a means to material wealth, however, distorts the complexities of progress in the twenty-first century. It further hinders a needed critique of classism in the United States. Instead of struggling with the poor against low wages and few if any benefits, emphasis is placed upon the poor pulling themselves out of poverty through faith marked by proper confession. The needed signs of success—cars, houses, and clothes—will follow.

The suits and sanctuaries of prosperity ministries in general suggest the church's arrival at a destination that precludes reality for many in the television-viewing audience. The possibility of progress and material wealth has been stifled for many by the reality of existing in a place weighed down by class exploitation and racism, issues prosperity ministers often fail to address. This movement to see financial wealth as a right of all believers camouflages the need for a serious critique of capitalism and its derivative, materialism. The idea of material accumulation as a sign of God's favor distracts attention from the very real problems of exploitation and exclusion within a free-market society. These systemic problems do not disappear with the mere proclamation of faith.

In his socialist critique of the black church teachings, Cornel West notes that there have been few genuinely socialist black pastors, although some are at least willing to engage in a critique of capitalism and the consequences black communities suffer as a result of its abuses.[27] In the early half of the twentieth century, the rise of industrialization brought immediate critiques from pastors like Junius Caesar Austin, leader of a 5,000-member Baptist church in Chicago. According to historian Randall Burkett, "[Austin] characterizes the United States industrial system of laissez-faire capitalism as 'a relic of 1776,' and declares that the capitalist social order, which 'clings to the moribund platitude that all men have equal opportunities to acquire and achieve' is predicated upon a 'mistaken idea.'"[28] Austin's critique of capitalism resonates with those of countless other ministers who have attempted to engage both an evangelistic and a social gospel. Faith teachings in their focus upon material wealth, contrarily, assume a priori the functionality of the capitalist system and the best ways for maneuvering within it. These types of assumptions leave little room for contemporary critiques of NAFTA, the WTO, or other free-trade agreements or organizations which engage in the random placement and removal of industries into and out of locales like Halifax County.

The response of faith ministers, however, to criticisms that they are too focused on material possessions or that they encourage people to focus on acquiring things is that they at least encourage people to think beyond their current circumstances. If poverty is identified as something negative and bad, even demonic in nature, then people are forced to think beyond the status quo. This, as seen in Price's testimony, was the motivation for his ministry. In mainline churches he had never been told that he could live beyond his circumstances. Now, at least, he believes he holds the key to material wealth.

Worshipping Multiculturally

Ideas about individualism and prosperity also meld with televangelism's approach to multiculturalism. Race is seen not as a systemic problem, but rather as a problem between individual people, a problem of individual prejudices. The tendency of television ministries to focus on multiculturalism to the exclusion of a systematic critique of racism or classism often leads to a facade of racial progress.[29] According to scholars Avery Gordon and Christopher Newfield, "multiculturalism in the 1980s sponsored renewed protests against white racism, and yet it appeared to replace the emphasis on race and racism with an emphasis on cultural diversity."[30] The impact of such shifts within the church is telling. There are discussions of interracial activities and multicultural gatherings and yet few discussions of race, racism, or racist behavior. While the drive of much of black Christianity has focused historically upon recognizing the equality of all people-kind, this insistence was often historically met with hostility from the vast majority in white American culture. In an attempt to reconstruct this history and present a united front, white and black television ministers strongly encourage interracial activity.

In a sermon, T. D. Jakes gave voice to a common understanding among Christians. During the dedication of his church's Dallas-based Metroplex Economic Development Corporation (MEDC),[31] in the presence of then Governor George Bush, the mayor, other guests, and his congregation, Jakes proclaimed, "This is not a black gospel. This is not a white gospel. This is not a Japanese gospel. It's not a Mexican gospel . . . I don't have to change the message according to the color of skin. For there is one Lord, one faith and one baptism. One God, above you all, in you all and through you all. His name is Jesus!" Unlike some who tend to ignore the impact of race on the experience of believers, Jakes is prone to discussing the complexities of race. Both his ManPower conference and his Woman Thou Art Loosed conference are overwhelmingly supported by African Americans. When he preaches to these audiences, he makes clear the struggles specific to African American men and women whether related to jobs, family, or incarceration rates. During one Manpower conference, the backdrop of the meeting showed a collage of African American leaders from Frederick Douglass to W. E. B. Du Bois and Booker T. Washington to Martin Luther King Jr. At the same time, Jakes strongly encourages a multicultural agenda. As he continued his message of unity during the dedication, he proclaimed, "More and more we are seeing the walls breaking down. And when the world gets tired of trying to legislate morality and make people love one another and figure out how they're going to deal with bigotry and hatred, wouldn't it be wonderful if they looked in the church and saw black men and white men and brown men, males and females, young and old, Jew and Gentile holding hands and singing songs [worshipping together]?" The universality of the gospel message, as indicated in Jakes's sermon, is both the goal and the appeal of Christianity. Because of its outreach to all people, it *ideally* creates unity among those who profess belief. Such Christian proclamations attempt to live up to the Scripture's command that there be no more "Male or female, Jew or Greek, bond or free in Christ."

Rod Parsley's "World Harvest Church" in Columbus is a prime example of this interracial ideal. Viewers are able to commend the common fellowship of thousands of people of different backgrounds. From the couch or kitchen in North Carolina, Georgia, California, Minnesota, or New York, Christians are able to witness the "ideal" in practice. When asked what the church should look like, one of my informants explained that the church should look like Parsley's church.

The idea that worshipping together resolves the deep tensions of a racist past is a common theme among television ministers who prescribe solutions to a history of racism. "Reconciliation" through shared worship, shared praise, and shared sanctuaries is the balm that resolves years of degradation. That women in Halifax County point to the ideal on television as the way worship should exist illumines the complexity of the message. Without a rigorous critique of systemic problems, however, there is little reconciliation. For men and women to worship together on Sunday morning does not mean that they have shared convictions about the death penalty, affirmative action, the justice system, workers' rights, living wage laws, the erosion of minority-majority voting districts, or a host of other issues that influence racialized divisions in U.S. society.

Several African American pastors' rejection of the Promise Keepers' prayer vigil on the Mall in Washington, D.C., in 1997, indicates the complexity of discussing a multicultural faith agenda without substantial critiques of race. For black ministers who did not support the march and who either aggressively or quietly dissuaded their congregants from attending, the issue dealt with race and its omission as a critical point of concern. For them, the idea of worshipping with white preachers and congregants on the Mall camouflaged the deep-seated tensions that still exist. They did not want to merely "hold hands and cry" with white men over the atrocities of racism and exchange apologies without the promise of tangible changes in legislation and the approach of whites toward blacks in business, education, and politics. Carl Ellis, a black evangelical scholar, was quoted in *Christianity Today* stating that he credits Promise Keepers for making race a central theme in their meetings. He then adds, "Tears and hugs and saying I'm sorry is a good first step, but for me, the question is not one of changing the hearts of individuals as [much as] it is dealing with the systems and structures that are devastating African-American people."[32] It seems that the numbers of African American pastors who did not participate in the march hold similar concerns.

Race, as countless anthropologists have noted, should not be seen as a mere issue of skin color, but rather as a much larger and more complex issue of power and economics. To conflate race with ethnicity (or multiculturalism), anthropologist Lee Baker argues, is to "blur racial disparities" and accomplish little if anything for poor people of color.[33] "Although disregarding race is logically accurate and theoretically sound in terms of biological categories, it is historically, socially, and politically problematic. It disregards the complex processes of racial formation and evades racism."[34] To the extent that televangelism groups together all people under the universal, ethnic-inclusive banner of "Christianity" without attending to ongoing racial tensions, it camouflages the need for a serious critique of systemic problems that reproduce racialized inequality.

In the early '90s this issue metastasized for televangelist Fred Price. In a January 1999 interview with *Emerge* Magazine, the pastor of the 17,500-member Crenshaw Christian Center in Los Angeles stated, "I assumed that when you are at a certain spiritual level, that things like the color of skin wouldn't matter." His recent fall-out with former mentor and friend Kenneth Hagin Jr., however, had proved him wrong. "I operated on that principle until I was rudely awakened." After hearing Hagin's teachings on interracial marriages, Price began a boycott of the multimillion-dollar Hagin ministry. During the exclusive interview, Price revealed, "In the taped sermon, he [Hagin] tells the Black and White parents of his congregation that if they don't want their children to marry interracially, they must begin training them early. He explains how he talked with his own child about drawing the line: 'We're friends. We play. We go together as a group, but we don't date one another . . . I don't think we ought to mix any of the races.'"[35]

Because he was unwilling to acknowledge the fallacy of his statement and his father, also a pioneer in the Faith Movement, was unwilling to force him to recant, Hagin's words drove a wedge between him and the famous African American pastor. Price, after doing further research, decided that he needed to pull away from the ministry he had participated in for over twenty years. Known as a "faith teacher" or "prosperity minister," Price learned his theology under the tutelage of the senior Hagin. Both he and Dollar were supporters of the ministry. While Dollar decided to remain with the ministry after becoming aware of Hagin's comments, Price saw the experience as the beginning of his mission from God to teach on race, religion, and racism. Calling the church "one of the most racist institutions on planet earth," Price launched a year-long sermon series in October 1997 addressing the problems of race and the church. Every Sunday morning from his Crenshaw Christian Center in Los Angeles, viewers listened to him critique everything from the racist biblical interpretations of the story of Ham, to the racism he encountered from the city of Los Angeles while trying to lay the infrastructure for his $26 million facility, to the silence about racism in the church which leads young blacks to find spiritual guidance in more racially militant organizations like the Nation of Islam.[36]

This "holy crusade," as he terms it, has received ironical notice from some long-term critics of racism in the church. Cane Hope Felder, a leading theologian at Howard University Divinity School, in the same *Emerge* article that highlighted Price's move, likened Price's awakening to the type of awakening he hopes Supreme Court Justice Clarence Thomas will one day experience.[37] (His criticism is a play on the notion of a black cultural politics. According to this logic, persons who are "truly" black and who supposedly speak to and represent black people would naturally be opposed to the types of conservative—anti–affirmative action, anti-redistricting, pro–death penalty—politics of Clarence Thomas. Furthermore, a truly black preacher would not hesitate to speak out against these types of prejudicial policies when opportunity permits.) That Fred Price has remained silent on these and other race issues for so long and only began to raise criticism when *he* was blatantly offended by a colleague in ministry is the reason for Felder's sarcasm. Although Felder is glad that Price has finally come to see racism in the church, his transformation, according to Felder, has been long in the making.

Criticisms from women in the research study, however, centered around the idea that Price has gone "too far." His year-long sermon series is too extended, and his proclamation to the entire church and viewing audience is too extensive. Convinced also by the idea that the church should be a multicultural place of worship, some women express discontent with Price's tone. According to Yvette, "From what I understand Frederick Price has had a personal experience that he keeps bringing this up and I think it's something that's eating away at him . . . But, he's getting so in depth, that he's just hung up on this racial issue . . . He's taken it a little too far. Instead of preaching love, he's preaching, to me, the opposite." For Yvette, Price's stress on race and racism demonstrates more of a personal experience that he has not been able to resolve. His emphasis, thus, on the history of race and the church and the ongoing challenges of the church as a racist institution seems too much. It brings the issue of race to an institutional level, when to her, his experience of racism is individual. Gloria expresses a similar concern. "Only if the issue arose in that church should it be addressed in the church . . . I feel like it all depends on what went on in your church or your congregation . . . If it was a national thing . . . then I could somewhat see you speaking on it on a national term. But, if it was done directly to you, I don't think it should have been broadcast." In both their views, Price has reduced the discussion of racism to a problem that occurs on an individual basis as opposed to a structural problem that should be resolved on a larger level. Like the subtlety of prosperity teaching, the subtlety of multiculturalism without a critique of racism signals the triumph of individualism. Racism in this scenario becomes an issue of individual prejudice, an unwillingness to treat individuals fairly or an unwillingness to participate in multicultural or interracial settings. Literary scholar Wahneema Lubiano observes that such practices "trivialize" racism, by "turning its attention to individual remedies, to attitude adjustment, to "color-blind" legal adjudication" instead of looking at racism as "the systematic operation of power at work throughout our political economy."[38]

To say that pastors such as Price who have historically encouraged multiculturalism without a serious critique of racism have been most popular among television audiences is not an overstatement. The theology of this type of simple multiculturalism pervades much of what is presented on television, even when churches themselves may be more heavily involved in combating racism. Such silencing (color-blind/race-neutral discourses) can have the effect of reproducing racism if the structural dynamics of racism are not addressed.

The impact of televangelism is a question yet unfolding. The ideas of individualism, prosperity and materialism, and multiculturalism without a critique of racism raise formidable questions for the black church as a public sphere historically engaged with America's systemic racial problems. While one can acknowledge that not all black churches have engaged in critiquing these problems, it is still important to note that historically black churches and black church leaders have been in the forefront of this struggle, creating discourses for dismantling systems of oppression.

While the women of the study listen to televangelists, they are able to discount much of the emphasis upon individualism, maintaining a critique of structural inequalities and commitments to the health of their communities. In several cases, their spirituality is directly connected to and intertwined with the lives of others in their community. For those living in the rural South, however, this may reflect more an experience of locale than a sheer ability to resist the individualist emphasis of televangelism. For example, all the women that I interviewed live in Halifax County because their families originate in the area. They did not move to Halifax because of a large corporate relocation project or another job offer. Instead, their parents, siblings, and other family members form their connection to the county. In this way they automatically inherit responsibility within a larger community of people.

Furthermore, their ability to resist the individualistic thrust of televangelism is connected to their age. Still able to travel and maintain their independence, the women do not rely upon television as their major source of entertainment or spiritual guidance. Even those who do watch television ministries heavily, like Gloria, have close family affiliations as well as work with those economically disadvantaged in the community that keep them from maintaining a completely individualistic focus.

Discourses of individualism obscure connections to and responsibility toward a larger community of believers. Likewise, the emphasis upon prosperity not only encourages one to see wealth as a God-given right, but it also precludes a critique of the very systems that perpetuate poverty. Instead of preaching or teaching about the perpetuation of poverty rates by corporate industry looking for cheap labor, ministries focus on how to acquire wealth through work, faith, and sowing financial seeds. The ability of these women to resist the consistent focus on material gains, however, is connected to their locale. They understand that people are poor not only because of a "lack of faith," but also because of the long history of farming failures, the difficulty of locating steady employment in a depressed area, and the challenges of securing quality education.

Furthermore, the dissociation of racism from ideas of multicultural-ism appeals to viewers' desire to live in a community where race does not matter. In the process, the systems that perpetuate racism go unchecked. The ability of televangelism to conflate race and ethnicity to the point that a systematic critique of racism is precluded is tempting to many. For the black church, called because of the history of racism in the United States, to be both priestly and prophetic in its ministry, the challenges presented by televangelism are complex. While the medium offers min-isters of all racial backgrounds access to communities of people around the world, it carries with it totalizing and reductionist tendencies. These tendencies allow for an easy and immediate articulation and appropria-tion of individualism, materialism, and a simplistic multiculturalism.

While they may be able to render spiritual support and inspiration, television personalities, unlike local pastors, are unable or unwilling to speak to these specific issues. As these ministries offer encouragement and hope to thousands upon thousands of individuals, their assorted messages of individualism, prosperity, and multiculturalism camouflage the need for a critique of society's systemic problems. Popular television ministries, thus, often appeal to the emotional and spiritual needs of in-dividuals without addressing overarching social and economic structures that oppress.

This appeal to the emotional and spiritual needs of the individual, however, begs the question of the type of transformation that the min-istries are providing. Because women listen to the ministries' emphasis upon building family, encouraging greater faith, and promoting a con-servative though focused attention on money, I suggest that another type of change is taking place in their lives. While social scientists have not often measured the degree to which personal transformation can be con-sidered activist, that women are engaging in these more personal demon-strations of faith does signal changes worth examining. In the Friday and Saturday chapters the role of personal transformation in the lives of African American women worshippers will be explored.

"LOOSED WOMEN"

Out of the sea of worshippers, I never expected to see anyone that I knew. According to the news, there were over 50,000 women present. Although mostly African American, the women attending the conference represented various ethnic groups and socioeconomic backgrounds. I came at the invitation of a friend. My research was in a lull, since I had just finished the first eleven months of fieldwork, and I decided to spend a few weeks away from Halifax County in order to regroup and prepare for the final interviews. The 1998 "Woman Thou Art Loosed Conference" fell in that time.

The preaching that morning was charismatic and electrifying. We heard from both Darlene Bishop and Juanita Bynum. Bynum's 1997 message "No More Sheets," given at a singles conference in Dallas, had immediately catapulted her to national prominence in evangelical and charismatic Christian communities. The singles conference, sponsored (like the Woman Thou Art Loosed Conference) by T. D. Jakes's ministries, packed the Dallas Convention Center with women and men aspiring to live Godly lives as single adults. Bynum's message, a mixture of preaching and personal testimony, challenged men and women to resist the temptation to become emotionally dependent upon and physically involved with people other than a God-ordained spouse. Her tearful testimony to promiscuity, shame, and emotional instability, coupled eventually with the healing grace of God, led the group to an ultimate climax in which they repeated after her, "No more sheets! No more sheets! No more sheets!" (a metaphor for premarital sexual relation-ships).

This morning at the Georgia Dome, Bynum's words carried a differ-ent type of message. Instead of intimate relationships, she spoke of re-ceiving an anointing from God. The anointing, a mixture of spiritual blessing and financial breakthrough, seemed to resonate with the desires of the majority of women present. With the promise of material acquisi-tions like Gucci shoes and Versace bags, Bynum commanded those gath-ered to give expeditiously. "Run, you want a blessing? You better run! Don't walk. Run!" She wanted the women to run forward and throw their monetary offerings onto the stage. Taken aback by the usurpation of what I had known to be the traditional impetus for giving, gratitude, I sat amazed at the women running to "sow their seed."

Women from around the country filled the Georgia Dome for this three-day conference. The messages earlier that morning had been so en-couraging, even liberating for the thousands of women who had been, or were still, in abusive relationships. Bynum's midday message seemed to continue in this vein until she began her financial appeal, which marked a slight deviation from what preceded. The conference had been built around the idea of liberating women from the emotional, physical, and spiritual impediments in their lives.

Creating a different type of discourse for church women, Bishop Jakes by founding the "Woman Thou Art Loosed" conferences had ut-tered a clarion call for women to take control of their lives. "If you love *yourself*, you wouldn't allow . . . ," the new discourse insisted. Ideas of complete self-sacrifice for the benefit of the marriage covenant, as some preach, were disrupted this week. Women in abusive and life-threatening relationships were encouraged to leave. Women who had spent their lives caring for everybody else except themselves were en-couraged to reevaluate their commitments. Women with special gifts and talents that they had kept hidden were encouraged to share their gifts with the world. Women who wanted to open businesses of their own, instead of working for somebody else who "doesn't appreciate you anyway," were encouraged to shake the fear and walk in faith. ALL in the name of Jesus!

According to the ceaseless proclamations by platform guests, God had sent this messenger, T. D. Jakes, and had given him a vision to "loose women" from their social, economic, and spiritual chains. Just as Jesus "loosed" the woman who was sick of an infirmity for eighteen years,[1] Jakes proclaimed that God has called him to help deliver women who are

themselves in bondage not only to sin, but also to dissatisfying and oppressive social circumstances. In words reminiscent of one of his earliest
"Woman Thou Art Loosed" sermons, Jakes challenged women in the
personal areas of their lives.

He challenged the idea that everywhere at all times women are expected to be beautiful, fitting into an advertiser's image of beauty—perfect hair, perfect make-up, and a pencil-perfect figure. "At every age of
life," he admonished the women, "you're beautiful. Whether you're little girls running up into daddy's arms, or young women going to the
prom, or walking down the aisle with a wedding gown on. Or, whether
your hair has begun to change like leaves into silver wisps and God dec-
orates your face with time. You're beautiful. At every stage of life. Fem-
ininity has its own fragrance. Never forsake it for masculinity. Feminin-
ity has its own aroma."[2] After affirming their value as women in a
masculinist framework, he admonished women to stop assessing their
life's worth based upon whether they are in a romantic relationship. Contrary to those who preach that women are preordained and biologically
conditioned to desire relationships, Jakes stated that women are "socially conditioned to epitomize relationships" from the time they are
given Barbie and Ken dolls to play with. Men, he contrasted, are given
machine guns and baseball bats. Pointing out the fallacy of this early conditioning, he challenged women to build the areas of their lives that will
make them successful and trust God to bring that person into their life,
"if," he added, it is meant to be.

In the meantime, he exhorted women to pamper themselves. "Anybody been through what you've been through and MADE IT. You've got
a right to be good to yourself. Celebrate YOURSELF! . . . Quit waiting on
somebody to celebrate you. Celebrate yourself. Take yourself out to dinner!" The admonishments to pamper, encourage, love oneself were in-
cessant. God, the argument continued, has loved women enough to make
them unique and special. God has also delivered them from abusive relationships, suicidal moments, depression, divorce, poverty, the list continued. In return women need to realize that God has something else in
store for them. "Why do you think He kept you alive . . . you didn't lose
your mind . . . you didn't go crazy . . . Other women have gone crazy
who have been through what you've been through!"

Space was validated for older women, young women, wealthy
women, poor women to engage in a type of communal healing process.
"Many thousands of women," he concluded, "are going to be loosed
today."

Suicide is going to be loosed today; spirits of depression are going to be loosed from you today; hallelujah, homosexuality is going to be loosed from you today; right women in wrong relationships. You're going to be loosed. Addictive behaviors, where somebody's abusing you, you're going to be loosed today. Loosed today from spirits of bondage, manipulation and control where somebody's trying to control everything you do, want to know where you're going and when you're coming back. Loosed.

Troubled relationships, both sexual and nonsexual, were seen as areas of women's lives that keep them in bondage. His emphasis on such relationships was consistent. Homosexual as well as other forms of extramarital sexual relationships were articulated, according to the evangelical and charismatic traditions of the speakers, as relationships that prevent women from complete freedom. There was little talk of great structures that oppress or jobs that oppress. Instead, the impetus was upon women to free themselves from self-imposed limitations and self-imposed hatred. The only way to do that, Jakes declared, was for women to love themselves as God has loved them.

Juanita Bynum's message continued in this vein until she reached the offering time. Mixed with the appeal for the offering was the promise of an idealized American middle-class consumption pattern. One would gain material accessories, not just necessities, by giving to God. This morning, mixed with the idea of gratitude, the expectation of a major financial blessing was the impetus for giving. "You're lookin' at my Gucci shoes and Versace bags!" she continued. The only way to gain that type of material wealth was through giving, major giving. "The Lord just told me that every woman in this building is suppose to give a $98 seed offering!" Minutes later she exclaimed into the microphone, "God told me that there are twenty people in here that are to give $1,000 offerings. You know who you are!" Women started running forward. I thought for sure there were going to be no takers for the second call. From my seat of skepticism, I doubted whether five people would tramp to the stage. To my surprise, when I looked up the stage was covered with women, all presumably standing there with checks for $1,000. I tried desperately to reassess my understanding of the 50,000 women who filled the Georgia Dome on that hot July morning for a conference committed to "loosing" women. Why were they giving their hard-earned money? What did they expect to gain? What did they *need* to gain?

The woman seated next to me had flown in the evening before from Michigan to attend the conference. As she wrote out her $200 check, she enthusiastically told me of her blessing from the last time she was at "Woman Thou Art Loosed". "I went home and quit my job because I was finally fed up with their treatment . . . A few weeks later I was called to another job and when they told me my salary, I, Praise God, I was making $10,000 more than I made at my last job. God is so good. If you just trust Him . . ." With that abbreviated testimony she began her journey down toward the stage.

Despite her testimony, my questions continued. Would this message of prosperity and material gain be so profoundly compelling to a sea of white men? Would a room full of white middle-class men rush to the stage to sow their seeds of faith in order to gain Gucci and Versace paraphernalia? (In other words, do they do this at Promise Keepers?) Or, is there something particular to these women's experiences or the experiences of their communities that leads them to respond with such enthusiasm to the promise of a new house, a new car, designer clothes/shoes/handbags based upon one individual act of faith? Are women conditioned to follow religious leadership more assiduously than men, and so are more likely to give spontaneously? Or is there a combination of market forces and oppression that led to such enthusiastic giving? My questions did not assume that the imaginary sea of white men would be any less materialistic. In fact, many would already own huge homes, fine cars, and tailormade suits. Yet, their relationship to money is likely different. Their access seems different. White middle-class men are most often the realtors, car dealership owners, store owners, bank loan officers who acquire, purchase, and disseminate money and consumer goods. Or, they are the friends and family of people who do. Although a growing number of black women have this type of access, the vast majority of them do not. Could this be my explanation? Or, is this an age-old manifestation of charismatic religious practice that, regardless of race, gender, or class background, inspires people to respond with such visible and exuberant demonstrations of faith?

During the first break, as soft music played, I went to the foyer to look at the book/music/video tables. The commercialization of the gospel was in full swing, people encouraging you to buy this tape because "it's a blessing" or that one because so and so "really ministers." As I skimmed the tables, I ran into Gloria, one of the women from Shiloh Baptist. We hugged, acknowledged the slim chance of meeting in such a mass of women, and exchanged our impressions so far. Our conversation was brief though informative. She was here with a group of women from Halifax County who had chartered a bus to Atlanta. Several women from her church had come, along with some from surrounding churches. Though she enjoyed the other speakers, Bishop Jakes's message was by far her favorite.

In the time since the conference, I have much pondered the relationship between faith, money, and sexuality. Sex and money were two of the major issues addressed by the conference. Bishop Jakes preached a message about liberating women from intimate relationships that were abusive and self-negating. Juanita Bynum, through a complex fusion of biblical exaltation and appeals to American consumer values, challenged women to give financially, "sowing seeds," so that they could become prosperous.

Liberation had taken on a new tone, decidedly centered on individual transformation. Much as in the growing trend in televangelism, the emphasis for change, for liberation, is placed directly upon the individual. Hope for liberation is met not by transformations in any system, but rather by transformations in the individual. These changes require a degree of faith that will ideally catapult the believer into engaging more fervently in a type of personal activism.

FINANCIAL PRIORITIES

The afternoon homecoming program at Diane's church seemed to go off without a hitch. Diane had worked so hard in helping to organize it, making sure that everyone knew the time and place and what their responsibilities included. I attended in response to the invitation she extended nearly a month before the event. Once the mistress of ceremonies announced that it was offering time, she directed the ushers to begin from the back and march everyone toward the front to lay their offerings on the offering table. People began to file from the back pew first, then the next, then the next, until everyone in the church had an opportunity to walk across the front of the altar and make her contribution. I was seated in the front row in full view of everyone who passed and the gifts they left behind. Dollar bill after dollar bill landed gently at the center of the table.

I sat so close to the front of the church only because Diane insisted. I generally sit closer to the back, toward the center aisle, but today was different. Of all things, Diane wanted me to sing a solo. Though I agreed, I wasn't quite prepared for the merger of my faith and research in such a public forum. I practiced and practiced to make sure that all went well. The small white-framed church was packed today with those returning for the afternoon service. My solo came rather early in the service. I moved to the side podium closest to the choir stand, fumbled a moment with the microphone, and began to sing.

God is truly amazing.
God is truly amazing.
God is truly amazing . . .
He is the sun that brightens up my day . . .
He is a friend in the hour of need . . .
He is the door. Faith is the key. My God is truly amazing . . .

Gospel artist Denise Williams made this song popular in the mid-
'80s, and it immediately became one of my favorites. After the solo
was received, Diane continued the program with the offertory appeal.
While I am not convinced that my solo gave the type of boost that
pastors often like just before the offering, I trusted that members
would give regardless. It is not uncommon, however, to hear a pastor
encourage the musician to "play some giving music," as though the
joy and rhythm of the music will inspire greater contributions. Because the pianist was absent, we marched that day without any background music. Instead, we gave in silence. Maybe the silence was the
reason for the constant flow of one dollar bills, or maybe afternoon
programs do not invite the same type of offerings that morning services do. After making our contributions we stood to ask a blessing
over the gifts, the givers, and those who had a desire to give but were
unable.

If one measured the giving of African American women congregants
based on services such as this, the perception would be skewed. Afternoon services seem indicative only of what people give as a gesture of
goodwill from what they may have left over. Most serious contributions
are made during morning services. These contributions often come in the
form of tithes and offerings. For the women in Halifax County, this commitment to giving is taken quite seriously.

MONEY, FAITH, AND
PERSONAL TRANSFORMATION

As deeply concerned as black faith has been with social and political dynamics, it is still largely a conservative and evangelical faith, concerned
with the experiences of sin and redemption in the believer's life.[1] Turning away from past behaviors and seeking personal restoration are
themes that continuously emanate from the pulpits and pews of most
African American churches. From the preacher's sermon on Sunday
morning to Wednesday night prayer service testimonies, the expressed

desire of most believers is a relationship with God that results in lasting change in the way they manage their everyday lives.

The growth of conservative televangelism, especially in African American communities, coincides with this desire. While televangelism, with its focus on the individual, material gain, and a naive form of multiculturalism, can draw attention away from the need for critiques of political and economic structures that oppress, it simultaneously nurtures the desire for personal transformation found among most believers. This, I believe, is its appeal. Televangelism in many ways meets the need for individual transformation, directly and indirectly dealing with the personal wounds that black women experience in a racist and sexist society, though most televangelists would not use this terminology.

While women engage in forms of activism designed to extend political freedom and challenge unjust social systems, they also engage in other, more personal forms of activism. These acts do not necessarily change institutions or structures, but when taken earnestly they radically alter women's understandings of themselves, their abilities, and their commitments. While such changes in some instances affect a larger community, they are, more often than not, highly personal. These changes are about personal empowerment, not social revolution, per se. I consider them "activism" because women are neither passive, nor are they simply reacting to a set of circumstances. Instead, they are clearly defining new boundaries for themselves and new understandings of the power of their resources. Feminist scholar bell hooks argues that most women, even before they can get to a place of demanding social revolution must undergo a type of personal restoration. "Before many of us can effectively sustain engagement in organized resistance struggle, in the black liberation movement, we need to undergo a process of self-recovery that can heal individual wounds that may prevent us from functioning fully."[2]

In this chapter and the next I discuss two forms of personal activism that women of faith undertake, tithing and redefining intimacy. When considering the relationship between structure and agency, it is important to consider the vast number of ways in which people resist. While women actively engage in the work of social protest to change institutions, the need to become proactive about their own lives is also important. Living within the tension between advocating for structural change and engaging in personal transformation is the everyday work of these women believers.

While not all of the women tithe, the experience of such giving is common. Diane, for instance, instead of paying "tithes," pays "salary," a concept developed in rural churches years ago whereby a certain amount is decided annually for each male participant and each female participant to give. Men's "salary" generally has been slightly higher than women's "salary," because of the apparent contrast in wages under the share-cropping system. To this day Diane's church operates under the practice of salary.

I focus on tithing because it is the practice engaged in by most of the women interviewed. While the act of giving in general is activist, I argue that tithing serves three major purposes, which when taken together are explicit forms of activism. First, tithing fosters a critique of materialism and conspicuous consumption. Second, tithing contributes to institution-building, the development of alternative public spheres. Finally, tithing empowers women with control over their resources. This process illustrates how spirituality encourages women to engage their individual worlds as "private activists." These agentive acts, however, are not without contradiction. The tension between tithing and living in a material-ist world often leads to discrepancies in practice. Furthermore, the practice of tithing when major bills are due forces us to seriously examine the benefits of women's financial gifts in light of the tremendous sacrifices that are made.

THE CASE FOR TITHING

Tithing is a commitment to give at least one-tenth of one's earnings to what is considered by most believers to be God's work. Most often these contributions are made to a local church. While some studies point to more liberal notions of tithing, such as giving a "portion" of one's earn-ings to the work of the church, the women whom I interviewed were ex-tremely clear on the need to give at least one-tenth of their total earnings. In spite of circumstances that seem overwhelming, women insist upon giving their earnings to the church. Regardless of bills that are due and sometimes even despite poor credit, the drive to return to God what they believe God has given remains more powerful than the pressing demands of late payment notices. Such commitments by women of color in de-pressed communities raise profound questions regarding the power of faith. How do women arrive at such radical conclusions about giving? Should their giving be considered irrational in light of their material needs? What do they actually gain by giving?

As scholars note, there is relatively little research on the dynamics of giving in the African American community. Only recently with the research by Calvin O. Pressley and Walter V. Collier has a systematic study been undertaken to explore the dynamics of giving among black churchgoers. Despite its breadth, this study admittedly concentrates on the giving patterns of more urban, middle-class, and affluent black denominations, not emphasizing the dynamics of women's giving in depressed rural communities like Halifax.[3] Given the time and effort dedicated to "raising money," it is important to render scholarly attention to the financial practices of black parishioners and their attitudes toward giving. The financial independence of the black church has been largely the result of the giving practices of its members. Not needing to rely upon the benevolence of white trustees, as many black colleges do, or the generosity of white church institutions, the black church is "the most economically independent institutional sector in the black community."[4]

Women's philanthropy in Halifax County is distinctive not only because of their propensity to give but also because of the conditions under which they give. Their commitments seem to transcend the boundaries of class and locale. It is not just more wealthy, more established members who give 10 percent, but also those whose financial houses are in disarray. Sometimes women in these situations are the most likely to give. While on average black Protestants give about 2.5 percent of their total household earnings to the church, compared to 3 percent given by all conservative Protestants and 2 percent by all mainline Protestants,[5] the women I interviewed give the desired 10 percent. Their commitment to giving often results from a combination of obedience, gratitude, and the expectation of a better financial blessing.

For all of the women interviewed, tithing is a normal and necessary part of their spiritual development. If they were not tithing, women often felt that they were "robbing" God.[6] God is consistently defined as the benevolent giver of all gifts, material and nonmaterial. In obedience then to scripture and in gratitude for the resources God has provided, one willingly gives tithes. According to Yvette Stephens, when one tithes she or he is merely giving back to God that which God has given. "Because God said give Him the first fruits . . . He wants to be first in everything. He wants to be first. He wants to be before your husband. He wants to be before your kids. He wants you to worship Him, not your house, not your cars, not your this and that. And all He asks is that ten percent. He says that's fine. Like I say, it's His already. He gave it to us. So, all He wants is ten percent of it back." In Yvette's view she is merely returning to God that which belongs to God. Seeing her money as God's money is easier, in fact; it makes sense for her to "give back" that which does not belong to her. Apparent in her explanation is also the priority with which God and subsequently God's tithe are esteemed. In her opinion, God wants to be first. As a result, all other relationships and demands must stand a distant second. Husband, family, and material goods are all positioned in subjection to God. This idea radically contradicts social dictums that would assume that her first priority is to her husband and children. In this way, priority is given not to those relationships dictated by society as the norm, but rather to an understanding of God.

Marie expresses a similar commitment to tithing in that it is an obligation, one is "supposed to give" in order to maintain the work and fabric of the church. One keeps up the church as one would keep one's own home. Unlike money given to a charity or to a school building fund, when money is given to the church, particularly over a period of time, a degree of pride in ownership is acknowledged. She explains, "We are, as Christians, supposed to give ten percent to help support our church. I'm saying my church because you have to pay bills, you have to keep, you want to keep your church just like you keep your home, you know. And we're responsible for taking care of our church home." Church for Marie is seen as "home," the place where life and nurture are given, the place that one cares for. Her ownership of this sanctuary requires her contribution. Juanita Cleveland likewise spoke of tithing as an obligation. One "owes" God a tenth. "I know payin' the tithe hurts, but you get it back. You don't pay it because you're going to get it back; you pay it because you owe it to Him [God]. You owe it." In this statement Ms. Cleveland acknowledges that there may be financial strain in giving the entire one-tenth, yet faith and experience tell her that she gets it back. In spite of the "pain," one must give the tithe. She continues, "It's to me like, He's given so much and we owe that to Him. It's not that you can pay Him for anything, because He owns everything, it's just like being obedient to that principle."

The point of giving for each of the women is in recognizing ultimate ownership. The tenth of the income that they give to the church is *not* theirs from the beginning. They are merely *giving back* that which they believe rightfully belongs to God. This is the point upon which all other decisions are based. Acknowledging that all gifts are "blessings" from God causes them to passionately desire to "give back." In discussing her job history, from making $98 per week in the 1950s, to being laid off, to an eventual work transfer, and then finally being able to retire at $800 per week at the age of 54, Ms. Sylvia states that it was simply "God's intervention that helped me to get a decent job." According to her,

I feel that that was directed by the Holy Spirit, I really do. And from that
point on, I just relied on staying in touch with all three of those folks,
the Father, Son and the Holy Ghost . . . Today, I believe firmly in tithing
in my church, because I just feel that had it not been for the blessings
that I received. . . . I was able to retire from my job at 54 years old and
come to North Carolina and live a quality life. I didn't do that by myself,
okay. I just think it was numerous, numerous, numerous blessings.

This acknowledgment of God as the bestower of all gifts causes her both
to stay in the forefront of issues related to social justice and to maintain
a level of personal responsibility for what she deems the "blessings" that
come her way. When I asked what tithing is to her, she reiterated the idea
of God's blessing. "Tithing is, you're supposed to contribute at least 10
percent of your income to your church and before I came here I started
doing that because I knew that it was only by the grace of God that I was
able to get into the employment world and in 25 years go up to a job paying me $800 a week for forty hours."

One study has shown that American Christians in general give out of
a variety of motivations. High family income, high involvement in
church activities, and conservative theology are all strong factors.[7] However, when one considers the religious denomination of the givers, two
other factors, according to the study, influence Baptist givers: the
spouse's commitment to the church and the age of the giver. People between the ages of 40 and 65 tend to give more. While such sociological
circumstances undoubtedly affect the dynamics of women's giving, the
women I interviewed explain their giving more based upon personal experience. Such convictions are consistent with Calvin O. Pressley and
Walter Collier's conclusion that "although social action and community
service are important considerations for African Americans' church giving, they are less important than spiritual and religious considerations."[8]
According to their research,

The highest ranked reason [to give] was "to keep my covenant with
God." The other reasons, in order of their average rank, were giving is a
way of paying back blessings received; feeling that the church has a genuine need for donations; thinking that the programs sponsored by the
church are appropriate; believing that the programs are helpful to the
community; coming from a family that always gave to others in need;
and feeling that giving leads to rewards in life.[9]

The women I interviewed similarly convey a strong sense that God has
blessed them *personally,* that God has given blessings particularly to

them, whether a job, finances to meet needed bills, or daily resources. As a result, they try to honor God by giving back.

WHAT TITHING ACCOMPLISHES

Working against Materialism

For each of the women, tithing presents a fundamental response to the idea of conspicuous consumption. Robert Wuthnow argues that excessive spending influences not only people's finances, but also their faith. "It [materialism] influences our consumer tastes and our preference for high-paying jobs, but it also alters our capacity to pray, the nature of our prayers, and the ways in which religious tutelage instructs our values. It becomes harder for us to hear messages about the suffering of the poor, the need for economic justice, and the desirability of seeing God's handiwork in simple things or in nature."[10]

While living in a rural community ensures boundaries to some degree of excessive spending, the women in my research are still consumers. Access to lavish shopping malls and clothing boutiques is not easy for them. Major shopping trips to cities like Richmond, Petersburg, or Raleigh are often planned in advance. While Roanoke Rapids, NC, is equipped with a mall, the selection of stores is limited.[11] Nevertheless, the temptation to consume is something about which they each express concern. The tension between the desire to spend and the need to tithe leads them to a constant critique of their spending habits, their need to tithe out of obedience to God's command placing restraint on urges to consume.

Marie says that her faith experience has caused her to reorder her priorities regarding consuming. Spending and the accumulation of things began to place her in a type of bondage. "God doesn't want us to be *bound*" and "anything that *binds* you," she explains, is problematic. She goes so far as to label the excessive preoccupation with money "evil." One sacrifices time from church in order to go to work, or worse still, one begins to consume in an effort to provide excess for one's children, only to make them "ungrateful" and "unthankful." Realizing that her propensity to shop was based upon the accumulation of "things," she decided to place greater value upon those things that did not have monetary value per se, such as relationships with others and care for her church membership.

> I used to have to try to get things. I'm not saying to try to make me feel good about myself, or trying to keep up with anybody else. I know God

doesn't want us to be in debt. You see, as you read and you study God's word, He doesn't want you to be bound, because anything that binds you is going to take your focus off of Him. You see God doesn't want us to make money a God. The scripture didn't say "money was the root to all evil." A lot of people get that confused. Money is not the root, but the LOVE of money is the root. So, if I'm so in love with money that I gotta work all the time, never get a chance to go to church on Sunday or if I have to work all the time, so I can make money and make money so I can buy this so I can keep up with the Littles or the Henrys or whomever it is across the street or if I have to work all the time to get my children everything that they want and then they'll probably be so ungrateful and so unthankful. . . .

Marie immediately identifies debt with bondage. The desire to consume and the "love of money" are examples of bondage that she believes God abhors. As a result, she has attempted to reorganize her priorities, to "liberate" her mind from the American tendency to consume. She continues a critique of her past by attempting to strike a balance between the need for and the abuse of money. Under her new system of ordering money, she realizes first that God is the owner of her resources and that she must give to God as God commands. Then she must reevaluate her needs versus her wants.

Being a Christian has allowed me to see that money is good because we need it to get by, but I also recognize that God said that He would supply our every need . . . so I'm not out here trying to get every dime that I can get, where I can't give to God, where it will bind me to the point where I can't give God any of my time or any of HIS money. Because it's not my money anyway or MY time . . . EVERYTHING that I have belongs to God and He's just allowing me to use some of it. So, I try to do what He asks me to do and I try to teach my children to do that, not get so bound in finances and credit cards . . . I have made that mistake . . . You know the first years of marriage or whatever you get so tied up with credit cards that you can't give to the church if you wanted to because you don't have the money to spare . . . He gives us wisdom and wisdom helps you understand your finances and lets you know that "Hey, you know you can't afford that." You know. You do this and [God] will convict you too because you sit in church and you say, "I can't even give any money to God because I was, I just had to have that dress. Didn't need it, but I just had to have it." Being a Christian has taught me . . . put things in a proper order. First things first and God, He has to be at the top. I mean there's no if, ands, or buts about it, some things we [can't] compromise . . .

While Marie has admittedly overspent in the past, she attributes the balance in her spending today to her spiritual development over time. Once having held traditional American values of competition and affluence, she now finds these values challenged by the need to reprioritize her life. This new emphasis releases her from the desires that can lead to financial bondage.

Whereas Marie's spiritual growth has led her to a place where she is able to resist sporadic desires to spend, Gloria's spirituality brings her to acknowledge that she has a "spending problem." In that she names her spending practices a "problem," in light of her need to tithe, she has begun a serious critique of her appropriation of American cultural norms. As scholars such as Julie Schor in *The Overspent American* (1998) have suggested, in the United States spending is encouraged; spending is expected; spending keeps the "economy going;" but spending is also financially detrimental to personal budgets and leads many Americans to financial ruin. When asked if and how her spirituality impacts her finances, Gloria states,

> I'm bad at finances. I have a problem sometimes. And I know I have a problem. I have to. And I always ask God "Please help me with it." I tithe now. I tithe with my tithing every month, you know. I pay my bills that need to be paid. But, I overspend. It's not that I just throw it away. But, I don't know why I have a habit of overspending. I always want to buy things because I'm always giving things away. The type of job that I have allows me to give. And I love helping people. And if I have it and I don't have no use for it, I'm going to give it. And that's when it comes out, when I want something else, I go out there and buy it. But, I need help with my spending habits. I do overspend sometimes. When I look back, [I say] "you didn't need that. You could have done without that." So, I ask God to help me with my spending habits.

Mixed into Gloria's explanation of her spending habits is a clear articulation of a problem that she believes God can help her solve. She tithes, she pays her bills, yet she overspends. While she attributes her overspending to purchasing things for others and needing to replace items that she has given away, she does not absolve herself from the reality of the "problem." That she turns to God in order to remedy her spending habits reflects the priority she gives her spirituality in ordering her financial matters.

As women express their desire to honor God through tithing, their practices remain in tension. Three of the women—Ms. Cleveland, Gloria, and Marie—said that debt is a major problem for them. Both the pull of materialism and the struggle of living in a depressed community are challenges to their financial stability; nevertheless, they each insist upon the priority of tithing.

Institution-Building

While tithing enables a strong critique of materialism, the actual process of tithing contributes significantly to building the church as an institution. Whether money is allocated for the building, payroll for pastors and staff, or the maintenance of church programming, women's tithing practices significantly undergird the institution. Because of such efforts, black churches have aided historically in the establishment of schools, credit unions, senior facilities, low-income housing, and a number of other economic ventures in the African American community.[12] With resources levied from tithes, offerings, pledges, and a host of other resources, they have contributed to scholarship funds and other means of educating youth. While churches in Halifax County in general have not reached the level of establishing credit unions and living facilities, a number have been active in starting building funds, scholarship funds, benevolence funds for people in crisis as well as bereaved families, and other ventures to aid the community. The pastor and congregation of one church that I visited were actively involved in raising funds to establish a seminary in their area, a place where local pastors can attend classes throughout the week in order to enhance their biblical knowledge. Courses were already being offered in mobile homes, and funds were being sought for a permanent building. The women interviewed are in large proportion major contributors to these types of efforts.

During an interview I had with one pastor, he went from room to room of his 400-seat facility to demonstrate the degree to which the church has developed over the past fifteen years. It is an occasion for extreme pride in some of the more rural communities when a church is able to have carpeting or add another restroom or build a small dining hall on to the rear of the edifice. Such additions mark the progress of the church. To some who feel that "pastors are too concerned about the building" the emphasis on the edifice is a reason for ongoing criticism. For others, newly erected or renovated church buildings stand as a mark of pride, "We used to have a wooden structure, now it's bricked in with carpet," reported one church member. Indoor plumbing and air conditioning in smaller, less established churches mean that family reunions and weddings can now be held in comfort.

As a general rule, the financial burden of maintaining a church falls upon a small percentage of the church's members. One study estimates that "75 percent of the money in a typical church is given by 25 percent of the people. Sometimes the ratio is closer to 80:20."[13] This estimate stands regardless of the race or socioeconomic background of the church and its membership. That the women I interviewed are among the primary contributors to the church speaks profoundly of their level of faith and commitment. Pastors interviewed readily remarked on the significance of the women's contributions to the overall development of the church.

Many women deem it their spiritual obligation to give to their churches. In lieu of being able to give directly back to God for all of God's blessings, women see fit to give to "God's house" and "God's work." As Marie explained, one is supposed to tithe in order to keep the "church home" like one keeps one's own home. This giving, however, was not merely for the sake of maintaining a sanctuary. The women interviewed concerned themselves with the overall dispersal of the money. For them the church is supposed to be about community work. As a result, several expressed ambivalence about whether to give if the church was not properly distributing its funds. Both Marie and Ms. Sylvia have at times considered not giving to the church because of suspected misappropriation of funds. "There was a time that I did not give to my church like I should because I felt like, 'they're not using the money like they're suppose to!'" By withholding her resources, Marie was attempting to hold church officials accountable for the management of resources. Ms. Sylvia, likewise, has withheld her giving in attempts to hold church officials accountable. Explaining her tithes, she states, "it says to me that I'm giving back to the church, to God in a sense, but not God because sometimes when you give your money to the church they do what they want with it."

Their withholding of funds, however, was only for a season. Later reasoning convinced them that they must continue to give sometimes "in spite of" for the maintenance of the church and God's work. Marie told me,

> I was looking at it from a human standpoint and not from a spiritual standpoint, because God didn't ask me to see where the money went when I gave it. He said, give it from your heart. In other words, my heart was not in the right place. But now when God blesses me financially, I like to bless. I don't say bless God, because God doesn't need to be blessed. But, I like to bless the church that I belong to to keep God's business running in the church.

Coming to a similar resolution, Ms. Sylvia expressed her convictions: "That's not my responsibility. My responsibility is to be true to my soul,

be true to what I feel. I give it to my church and hope that they will . . .
continue Christ's work . . ." After all, God is first concerned with their
personal sacrifice, and secondly God, it is believed, will hold church officials accountable for any misappropriations.

One gives to the church in hopes that the church's finances are managed efficiently by those in charge. Often in rural churches this authority goes to male pastors and deacons who make business decisions for the
church. In rare instances, most often in Pentecostal churches, there are
female pastors. Thus, the question that scholars raise about women sustaining a patriarchal institution remains. Why would women continue to
give to an institution that does not allow their complete and uncensored
participation?

Ms. Sylvia and Marie demonstrate that for the sake of the "common
good" of the community and out of personal faith commitments, they continue to give money to their church even when the distribution of funds is
questionable. The common good in this sense is the hope that churches will
give back to the community. Ms. Sylvia explains, "Like the church I'm in
now, I feel very good about tithing because they are a church that has outreach and they are a church that's doing things for other people. [It] is a
very progressive church, they do encourage people to vote. They do have
outreach, you know, community and so forth and so on." For Ms. Sylvia,
tithing is about maintaining or attempting to reclaim the church institution
as a space of community outreach. Her church currently offers a senior citizens' class concerning that age group's nutritional needs. Each week the
van picks up seniors in the surrounding area, those who are members and
those who are just interested in the subject, and brings them to the church.
During the sessions, seniors work through a book designed to aid them in
altering their diets to meet their health needs. Ms. Sylvia's mother went
through her book with me with great enthusiasm, pointing out the types
of fruit she should have each day and the book's methods for preparing
food to ensure fewer calories from excess fat and less salt to ward off hy-
pertension. The van also picks her up for senior choir rehearsal, missionary night, and prayer meeting.

While these types of outreaches are what drew Ms. Sylvia to the
church, she is also concerned about her church's involvement in politics.
As she recalls, the church was at one point a vibrant space for the venting of concerns related to African American experiences with the larger
public. The church in essence served as a buffer between a racist society
and home. For her, the Civil Rights Movement stands as a premier example of what the black church should be about today.

Okay, back during the civil rights days, the church was a place where people could come and be ministered to holistically. . . . First of all spiritually. Then, they were dealing with the politics. And what was the politics about, civil rights, that you were not treated fairly. If you needed assistance, for example, you had some hard times and you were laid off . . . You were able to go to the church and say, "I need some help." I'm not talking about abusing any situation. I'm talking about genuinely, needing help . . . How are you going to pay bills if you can't find a job and you can't find a job because you're black. So, in the sixties, fifties and sixties, the church, I feel, ministered to people, not only spiritually but in other ways.

While she carefully articulates the need for the church to be a benevolent institution, this benevolence is a particular expression of care in the midst of a racist society. Ongoing care in today's church is based upon this same premise, that it is often difficult to find work that pays living wages, especially for African Americans in Halifax. To maintain the church as a viable public sphere for this type of engagement requires acknowledgment first of racism. Today, Ms. Sylvia reports, "the minister will stand and will not encourage people to vote." Comparing it to a time when there seemed to be greater urgency, she expressed disdain at the lack of immediacy given to the details of politics.

Black churches create an alternative public space not only for the discussion of issues, but also for carrying out an assortment of public events. In the continued absence of parks and swimming pools in predominantly black communities, activities such as Vacation Bible School, Sunday school, and picnics at the church create spaces for children's recreation. Church facilities also serve as meeting places for the NAACP, community groups, the Black Caucus, and a host of other civic/political organizations that work on behalf of African American citizens. In the absence of financial resources to build more adequate facilities, women's tithes help to maintain church facilities already in existence.

Self-Empowerment

The women interviewed are not "poor" women. While some of them may have limited access to resources, they are nevertheless philanthropists. As Yvette puts it, "If the Lord has blessed me with it, I feel like He's blessing me to bless others." They may not give as much money as others, but often they give proportionally more than some who are rich. They recognize that their contributions to the church are significant not only for the church, but also for the community. Their commitment to this work makes it important for them to manage their own resources. Responsibility for their finances and for their community are not passed along to another, but rather lie squarely on their shoulders.

The type of sacrifice involved in the women's consistent efforts to tithe is for them a mark of spirituality's role in making them financially independent. At one point each expressed preoccupation with materialism or anxiety about financial obligations. Now, their faith brings them a degree of security even in the midst of trial. For Carmen Moore this takes the form of an almost carefree attitude toward her finances, while for Vivian Dawkins it takes the form of meticulous stewardship over her resources. Ms. Moore said, "I can remember when, you know, I worried more about am I going to have a dollar in 2 or 3 weeks, but my experience has taught me that the more I give, the more I get. And I have never been . . . at the point where I just did not know where my next meal was coming from. And my spiritual experiences in terms of financing have taught me that the more I give . . ." Overcome with emotion, she ceased her explanation, only to reiterate the truth of her claim by pointing to the simple manner in which she manages her checkbook. "I can't tell you right now how much is in my checking account because it's probably very very little. But once I've done what I'm suppose to do, then I'm not worried about it any more, 'cause that's all I feel the good Lord promised me, that He would take care of my needs. And that's my belief . . . I don't believe He's worried about me having a whole lot left over to stockpile somewhere. So as long as I'm able to pay my bills and give where I give, I'm done. I'm through with it." While her way of handling her financial situation causes her some concern because she focuses on meeting day-to-day needs seemingly without preparing for the future or laying aside wealth for her family, the freedom that she has now compared to before is a great source of comfort for her. She no longer worries about meeting the necessities of life because she believes that God will ultimately provide.

Ms. Cleveland likewise expresses a freedom from worry that she insists she previously did not enjoy. Her husband taught her the importance of tithing even when it looked as if other bills would not be paid. She would watch him. The light bill would be past due and she would say, "Surely you're not paying your tithes this week," and he would insist upon being faithful.

> My husband was a tither right . . . and I'd be fussing, "You can't. You gave the light bill!" . . . I'm saying, "Boy! The lights are gonna be cut off

Monday morning! [laughter]" And so really, I didn't see it then. I really
didn't see it. I said, I can't see. He said, "You need to tithe. You need to
tithe." I said, "Charles, how can I tithe when I'm paying for this and I'm
paying for that. I don't see." He said, "You're suppose to pay that first."
I said, "I don't see it. I don't see it." And he would take it and he would
tithe every week. He would tithe. I mean he would tithe out of everything he got, he would tithe.

On the occasion of his giving the light bill money for his tithes, that same
day he was unexpectedly given money by a former student as a token of
appreciation. The student gave an amount that far exceeded the cost of
the light bill. This experience, Ms. Cleveland explains, was a turning
point that taught her to trust implicitly in God's provision.

> I pay my tithe. I don't care what bill is due. I pay my tithe when I get my
> check. That's the first check I write. [laughter] I pay my tithe. I pay my
> tithe. I'll tell you what, I'll pay my tithe. My tithe is my 10 percent. I pay
> my tithe. I pay my tithe. I pay my tithe, first! Even on this fixed income, I
> pay my tithe first. And you know what, I don't know about the other
> bills, but somehow or another, the Lord just lets me stretch 'em out . . . I
> don't worry about 'em. I really don't worry about 'em . . . Now, bills
> that have to be paid, you know, on the date, I try to get those on at that
> particular time, at that particular time. You don't pay it [tithe] because
> you're going to get it back, you pay it because you owe it to God. You
> owe it. I tell myself, "Thank you Jesus. I know you're going to take care
> of me, Lord God." [more laughter] I pay my tithe. I pay my tithe. I de-
> clare I have to pay my tithe. It might not be as much as some of the oth-
> ers, but that's not the important thing. The important thing is that you
> pay what you got. What is due Him, ten percent.

Since her husband's death a few years ago, Ms. Cleveland has been
overwhelmed with the responsibility of managing the household finances. His death left her with tremendous medical bills, overextended
credit cards, taxes, and daily household maintenance bills. She told me
during one of our interviews that before I arrived she was in tears, crying out to God for help in figuring out how she was going to pay the
$7,000 in taxes she now owes to the government from when her husband
was ill. "I've never had to worry about bills this much. I never had to
worry about a bill . . . It's rough. I wouldn't advise anybody to be in the
dark, especially if you have a husband. You need to be a part of paying
bills, so you'll know what bills you have due. But, God is going to see
me through those. We didn't know until really his death as to the financial state we really were in. And I found out it was a terrible state." Even
in this desperate state of financial difficulty, Ms. Cleveland insists upon

paying her tithes. The experience has challenged her complete joy in giving, but not her commitment. She still trusts that "God is going to see her through." Tithing is a way for her to demonstrate her trust and also a way of ensuring God's blessing upon her finances. After all, God "gives back" that which has been given.

The challenge of managing money in difficult times has led to Ms. Moore's almost carefree attitude toward her finances and Ms. Cleveland's insistence upon giving. However, when women are married to men who do not understand or appreciate tithing, the issue is not only these individuals' personal management of money but also the organization of the marital hierarchy in which they find themselves.

While speaking at one point about her activity within the church and the kinds of activities she engages in to empower young people, Vivian Dawkins talked of her personal life and the contradictions therein. She is a consistent tither, yet her giving has been challenged by the actions of her husband. In a detailed exchange she indicates the type of tension that exists between her marital relationship and her relationship with God. Recently she and her husband have dealt with financial difficulty intensified by his being laid off from a local factory.

> He was working at Telsco [pseudonym] and, his job he was doing they terminated it. So, he got a permanent layoff and he was what? Shift manager, team leader, I don't know what you want to call it. But, he was getting paid pretty good, so when they cut him back, when they got rid of that job, it was MY income. And my income really wasn't doing that much, you know. We stayed behind, stayed behind and we got really behind, then he got one job and that was about a 2-hour drive there and back home. So. That was up in Virginia. But, the pay is not that much. We're in a financial bind now. And I'm torn because I don't even, I don't tithe the way I should. And I know that God wants me to tithe. I have a spouse who doesn't understand it. God wants me to be submissive to my husband. And see, I'm, I'm torn. I shouldn't be because I know what God wants me to do, but God also wants me to be submissive to my husband.

Her concern was largely that of pleasing God, developing a resolution that in her mind would satisfy the desires of God. Yet this conflict continued as she explained her reason for submission to her husband and how she planned to resolve her dilemma. When I asked, "What to you is submission?" she said:

> Submission. It just says that wives should submit themselves to their husbands and it to me is letting the husband be in charge, letting him be

the man of the house, letting him take charge of things and if he asks you to do something, do it . . . But, the other side of it is right before it says that. It says . . . husband and wife should submit themselves to God. Then the woman should submit herself. So, either way . . . the wives are supposed to submit themselves to their husbands . . . Obeying God and obeying my husband. I submit myself to my husband, but if he asks me to do something against the will of God then, . . . that's where I draw the line . . .

Vivian clearly accepts a conservative theology of spousal submission that deems her actions subject to her husband's approval. Although there are variations on what submission looks like for couples who ascribe to this theology, in Vivian's household this order demands her attention to all domestic duties. Vivian assigns herself the socially constructed gender role of housekeeper, cook, and caregiver on the assumption that her activity is completely sanctioned by the will of God. Yet, knitted within this web of stipulations and mandates is a carefully crafted means of escape: "but if he asks me to do something against the will of God, then, . . . that's where I draw the line."

My question at this point is, who determines? In those silent places where God has yet to speak, or where in Vivian's case it appears there are two conflicting ideals, who determines what God's will is? The obvious answer is that she does, and because she does, within what seems a sealed contract for her unchallenged submission remains the silent and subtle push of resistance. To demonstrate, Vivian explained to me that although her husband has a problem with her tithing, she is keeping a diligent record. Every Sunday she writes down how much she owes God from that week's work. She has been engaging in this practice for several months and when her husband "comes around," as she says, she plans to pay God back for all the weeks that she has missed. She has not given up on tithing, nor has she completely succumbed to her husband's demands. She has woven a space for her spirituality to thrive in the midst of her dilemma.

I am not so bold as to argue that her act of resistance stems in any way from her having a feminist or womanist agenda, but I would submit that *her* beliefs about God, though on one hand they confine her to a very specific role of subordination within her marriage, also provide for her a way of escaping its all-consuming power. She envisions submission as embodying a particular role, one of caregiver, cook, and housekeeper, yet these responsibilities are defined in her mind's eye, according to what she believes God's will to be.

Spirituality is a component of life that has the ability to both confine and liberate, based upon one's vision and understanding of who God is and what God's requirements are. These ideals are often shaped by the race, gender, and class dynamics of society. For African American women in particular, these dynamics and women's responses to the forms of oppression that often accompany them are frequently informed by the way in which women embody spirituality. Their faith empowers them to remain consistent tithers, thus demonstrating resistance to American consumer values, and gives them an ability to reprioritize spending in a way that emphasizes a commitment to community over a commitment to personal, material gain. Tithing also furthers the aims of institution-building, guaranteeing a location and a forum in which community events and dialogues can take place. When public facilities are unavailable or nonexistent, the institution of the church provides an alternative space with resources sufficient to meet the needs of the larger community. Finally, tithing allows women to maintain an ongoing critique of intangibles like anxiety over financial responsibility or tangibles like unsympathetic husbands.

Women's commitment to tithing compels them to give even when the resources to do so are in question. Management of finances then becomes an act of faith alone, and not always an act reflecting the discipline that would come from a strict budget and rigid guidelines. The presence of faith, however, without an active budget and plan for spending can lead to further debt. While not all of the women tithe under these circumstances, it is obvious that some do. History, however, has demonstrated to them that when they tithe, resources for other needs are made available. While it is important to operate from a budget and to plan expenses, as Marie suggests, not tithing as a result of anticipating a shortfall for these women is not an option. To not tithe may or may not alleviate their debt, but it will certainly displease God. In the meantime, they receive contentment from knowing that by tithing they have at least "honored God."

It then becomes imperative that, in receiving the gifts that women like Marie, Ms. Cleveland, Gloria, and Ms. Sylvia make to the church, churches honor the sacrifices that women have made. After all, if it were not for the contributions of women like this, as Cheryl Townsend Gilkes's words echo, *there would be no church*. If black women waited to give until they had the financial resources to spare, there would be no benevolence, tutorial, or senior care ministry, not to mention a pastor's salary. As Ms. Sylvia explained, she will continue to give (as many women will) and leave the leadership of the church accountable for answering to God, for the deeds done with the money. Having seen the sacrifices made by congregants, some churches (particularly in urban areas) have begun to respond to the more immediate needs of their memberships by offering financial management workshops, estate planning seminars, and a host of other outlets for assisting members in managing personal income regardless of how large or small. In rural communities like Halifax such sessions are even more crucial given the significant amount of black-owned land that is lost when senior citizens die without a will and an accurate means of distributing their inheritance.

As women experience the sense of spiritual freedom that comes from the act of tithing, it is also important that they engage in a thorough, though no less faith-filled, stewardship of their resources. Assistance in this area is but one of the gifts the church could return to its faithful supporters.

SEXUAL POLITICS

Significant to the experience of spirituality is the expression of sexuality. According to most mainline churches, maintaining standards of fidelity within marriage, chastity outside of marriage, and respectability in the process is required for the profession of a truly spiritual life. Because sex is seen as both a physical and a spiritual act, "proper sex" influences one's access to God and one's intimacy with God. Women's experiences of sexuality, thus, have been key to their expression of spirituality. Therefore, not only do women make faith decisions that direct the management of their finances, but they also make faith decisions that affect their bodies.

The connection between spirituality and sexuality, as ordained minister and religious scholar Michael Eric Dyson notes, is fundamental to the Christian faith.[1] He explains that while many have accepted the philosopher Descartes's notion of a body-soul split, such a teaching is impractical for the practice of faith. "The link between sexuality and spiritually" is even "hinted at when the Bible talked of the church as Christ's bride, and alternately, as the body of Christ," he adds.[2] This fundamental connection allows for the discussion and practice of sexuality without the stigma of shame and disgust. For women of faith to enter into healing and life-giving discussions of sexuality, it is important for them to understand sexuality as part and parcel of their spirituality.

Women's redefinition of their intimate experiences provides the potential for empowerment in ways that give them more authority over their bodies. Based upon their spiritual transformations, women set boundaries for when and how lovers can engage their bodies. In addition new patterns of communication are opened with spouses and children about not only the physicality of sexual intercourse, but also the emotional and spiritual dynamics of such intimacy.

Redefining intimacy requires an understanding of the assorted histories through which women enter into intimate relationships. These histories reflect both the "pristine" narratives of women molded by expectations of virtue and chastity and the harsh realities of early sexual involvement and unwanted pregnancies. Their sexual histories speak to the commitment of marital coitus, the pain of rape, and physical abuse as well as the fear and uncertainty of teenage pregnancy, all too common among women in the United States.

While white women share this history of rape, teen pregnancy, and physical abuse, black women's experiences of sexuality are shadowed by a history of ownership, exploitation, and forced pregnancy for the sake of profit. Not being able to define who, when, where, and how their bodies would be engaged, black women under antebellum slave law and postbellum Jim Crow engaged in countless struggles to assume authority over their own bodies. These struggles were in large part against a prevailing system of capitalist exploitation, which used their bodies for breeding and their bloodline for the maintenance of racial order.[3] "Ideological exaltation of motherhood—as popular as it was during the nineteenth century—did not extend to slaves. In fact, in the eyes of the slave holders, slave women were not mothers at all; they were simply instruments guaranteeing the growth of the slave labor force. They were 'breeders'—animals, whose monetary value could be precisely calculated in terms of their ability to multiply their numbers."[4] Considering this history, black women's struggle to control their own bodies took on new meaning in the postbellum era. This struggle for ownership was coupled with a struggle for dignity in a cultural space that had created images of jezebel, sapphire, asexual "mammy," or the "work horse" as the archetypical black woman. Literary scholar Gloria Wade-Gayles, in her work on black women's fiction, makes clear how these stereotypes are based upon both black women's race and gendered positioning. "The problem," she writes, "of understanding the anomalous position of black women in America is further complicated by the tendency to interpret their reality exclusively in racial terms. As incredible as it might seem, images that are unmistakable sexual caricatures or that clearly relate to the sexual roles of wife and mother are often presented as interpretations of blackness, not womanhood."[5]

The Mammy figure was seen as the self-sacrificing caregiver of other folks' children. Her soft and gentle spirit brought calm to white women and aided them in keeping their homes in order, even at the expense of her own. The desire of men black and white, the Sapphire, was constituted as the sassy black woman whose direct and aggressive persona made her uncontrollable. The Jezebel with her loose sexual morals was seen as the woman whose body belonged to everyone but herself. Her sexual experiences were always for the benefit of others. Finally, the Workhorse, "the mule of the world" as described by Zora Neale Hurston, worked like a dog, caring for the concerns of white women, white men, and black men. Her labor was expected and the toll on her body taken for granted.[6] These images have not only existed in movies and print media, but they have also informed the way in which black women's concerns have been addressed by the larger society.

Through the mid-twentieth century it was difficult, if not impossible, to prove that black women were ever raped. Their gendered experience, informed by their racial caste, made the evidence of their assault virtually invisible. Legal scholar Kimberle Crenshaw argues that historically in cases of rape where white men assaulted black women, there was no precedent for conceiving of this crime as one of racial terror.

> The singular focus of rape as a manifestation of male power over female sexuality tends to eclipse the use of rape as a weapon of racial terror. When Black women were raped by white males, they were being raped not as women generally, but as Black women specifically: Their femaleness made them sexually vulnerable to racist domination, while their Blackness effectively denied them any protection. This white male power was reinforced by a judicial system in which the successful conviction of a white man for raping a Black woman was virtually unthinkable.[7]

Sustaining the value of black women's bodies and obtaining justice in cases of assault and abuse under prevailing notions of black female promiscuity have been difficult at best.

That women contemporarily engage in a struggle to define the boundaries of their sexuality speaks volumes to the agentive power of spirituality in their lives. In my research it was evident that women at forty and fifty come to decisions about their sexuality differently than women in their twenties. They often come to such personal debates from a history of relationships, marriage, divorce, children, and grandchildren. These experiences dramatically affect how they see themselves and their potential for intimate relationships. Three of the women interviewed are in long-term first marriages, two are divorced, two remarried, and one widowed. Their ideas about sexuality stem from faith as much as experience.

The women interviewed were taught propriety as the standard of sexual engagement by their parents as well as their churches. According to psychiatrist Gail Wyatt, many African American women now in their middle years were early educated by the church that sex is a "sacred act reserved only for marriage."[8] Based on the teachings of home and church, young ladies "didn't," and if they "did" and were "caught with child," then they married the father. While these teachings were meant to ward off premarital sex, the "warnings" were not easily adhered to by inquisitive teenagers eager to explore their sexuality in an environment that promised little opportunity or educational exposure beyond high school. In some instances the unbridled passions of older men were impossible to fight off. One woman was a victim of incest as a child, two were victims of spousal abuse, and three were teenage mothers—the boundaries of their sexuality historically violated. Each of the teenage mothers, Ms. Cleveland (as young as fifteen), Yvette, and Gloria, was forced into an early marriage that eventually ended in divorce. This practice set boundaries not only on their sexuality, but also on their potential to develop a mature understanding of themselves apart from marriage and family responsibilities.

Other women spoke of not engaging in sexual activity because of the fear of what their parents might do. As Ms. Moore explained, "The first thing that came to mind [as a young girl], was not what the Lord said. What came to my mind was what mom said she was going to do." These early ideas of "fear" and marital responsibility are now in many ways inapplicable to how these women engage their sexuality. Pregnancy for most is a nonissue, fear of "what people think" has far less importance, and parental disapproval is a concern that carries far less weight at forty than at twenty. Today, however, the women hold ideas about sexual activity that are sometimes even more rigid than those of their earlier days because of spiritual resolutions they have made. Instead of fearing "mom," they reverence God.

That these women have insisted upon new parameters for engagement with their bodies testifies to the type of transformation their spirituality has inspired. The women interviewed spoke primarily about marital intercourse and their preference for this type of commitment. They see it as a means of honoring God as well as a means of honoring their bodies as "God's temple." For them reclaiming their bodies has meant finding security and joy in the confines of a monogamous heterosexual relationship or in celibacy.

Given this premise, it was easy for me to assume that once women had "born-again" experiences, or rededicated their lives, then they adopted the dictates of Scripture toward chastity and monogamy as an overarching lens through which they redefined their bodies. They refused lovers before marriage and committed to them afterwards. However, this has not been the case explicitly. Women live lives of complexity, constantly defining and redefining their boundaries in light of their faith. Each affirms the value of chastity before marriage and monogamy within marriage, yet their new boundaries reflect both their understanding of their faith and their stated desire for intimacy as women. How they instruct younger women on the lessons of sexual involvement stems from both their biblical understanding and their understanding of current social dilemmas.

PROTECTING SACRED SPACE

Experience has taught women that sex does not equal intimacy and that intimacy is not something one finds in haphazard relationships. Instead, if anything, intimacy is difficult to discover and hard to maintain. "Intimacy," according to Marie, "is a feeling that a man and a woman are going to feel for one another because that is something that was set forth at the beginning of time." This type of predestination manifests itself in love. "Everything," she explains, must be "done out of love."

Women hold to ideas about intimacy in order to guard their own sacred space. This space for them is not limited to their physical body, but also includes their spirit. They are concerned not just about the physical consequences of sexual engagement, but about what their sexual engagement says about their commitment to God and their willingness to submit to God's desires.

Yvette, a self-professed born-again Christian, expressed repulsion toward not staying on the path of purity during her dating years. When she was "in the world," sex was a regular part of her activity, and yet she was not emotionally content. In previous relationships she felt that she had given too much of herself only to receive little if anything in return. Although she indulged the relationships' sexual activity, she would spend a significant portion of time thinking to God "maybe one day, you know, you'll send me somebody." After giving her life to Christ, she completely stopped dating, resolving that "Lord, if you want anybody to be in my life you'll put him in my life. Right now it's just me and you . . ." Her commitment to not dating was for her an attempt at redefining the boundaries of her sexual and emotional involvement.

Once she met her husband, things were different. At forty-five, after several years of developing a relationship with God, she knew that her decision to abstain from extramarital sexual activity was best for her and her fiancé. They adhered to these boundaries all but once. This experience forced her to speak with him about the possibilities of marriage. "We went and spent one weekend out of town and I felt so guilty. The Holy Spirit whipped me so bad. We never did go out [of town again]. Because fornication is just as bad as not tithing. So, I told him, I said, 'This can't work.' And we do not, neither one of us, we do not go out of town and spend another night in a house together no more until after we get married!"

Her clear articulation of the boundaries of their relationship does not necessarily reflect his commitment but rather her personal convictions about how her body should be engaged. To return to her previous form of sexual engagement was to her "like a dog returning to its vomit."[9] She had given up what she deemed detrimental in her life, only to once again return to her previous lifestyle. She further explained that the experience at the beach that weekend was "miserable." "It was really miserable . . . the Lord had come into my life and cleansed me, why am I going back out here and get this old stuff that I was doing before." For her, maintaining chastity was a way of allowing God to cleanse her from the mistakes and pain of her past.

Yvette's view of her sexual activity is highly informed by her consistent, daily reading of Scripture. Reading the Bible as the inerrant word of God has become the guidepost against which most of her decisions are made. Along with prayer, religious historian Marie Griffith notes in her study of evangelical women, "the Bible is another important means through which spirit-filled women seek intimacy with God."[10] While some argue that this type of conservative reading of Scripture can be oppressive and yield continuous feelings of guilt and shame, the type of authority rendered from the reading of Scripture produces for Yvette an intimacy with God that usurps the authority even of her pastor and other preachers.[11] When the time came for her to marry, some raised questions about whether or not she, as a divorcee, should remarry.[12] In response to their cynicism she reminded them of what the Scripture teaches: "once you accept Christ ALL things are new, not some of them." Members of her church wanted to know if she was going to ask the pastor for permission. To their continuing inquiries, she responded, "I don't have to ask the pastor. I have to ask the Lord. That's the only one I have to get it right with . . . He told me that old things are done away with once you've been born again. So, you gonna tell me that He'll forgive me for fornication but He won't forgive me because I made a mistake and got married when I was in the world!" The scriptures not only affirm for her the need to be celibate before marriage and faithful within marriage, but they also determine the politics of her remarriage. Even if the pastor disagrees with her marriage, his authority pales in comparison to her new understanding of Scripture. This type of scriptural authority has liberated her to some extent from the dictates of social custom and allowed her to map with some certainty the parameters of her sexual engagement.

Such authority is also evidenced in Gloria's discussion of her sexuality. Marriage was a necessity if she and her husband were to continue their relationship. As she explained, "I had sex before I got married. And the way things were going, I began to feel uncomfortable. That's why we talked about marriage, because he had wanted to move in with me and well, I've been there. I've done that. I didn't want to do it again. When I rejoined church and became a born-again Christian, I began to adhere to God's Word. That was a sin. I didn't want to do that again. I wanted things to be right."

Like Yvette's, Gloria's desire to adhere to a conservative reading of scriptural dictates of sexuality sparked her desire to redefine her sexual boundaries. Sex was no longer suitable outside of the confines of marriage; instead, marriage was a necessary institution to express mutual desire. For both Gloria and Yvette there is a definitive relationship between sex and marriage. In order to have one, you must have the other. Their decisions to engage in sexual activity in the context of marriage were not, as some scholars suggest, the result of adjusting to a "middle-class" lifestyle or the need to prove acceptability according to social norms. While changing certain relationship patterns may have given them a level of social validation, this was not the impetus for what they did. Their desire to honor God with their bodies formed the basis for their decisions.

Yet, each of the women was willing to concede that marriage alone does not lead to greater intimacy. Marriage did not spark for them a greater sense of passion for their mate, nor did it resolve lingering issues. For some marriage has initiated, instead, other issues. Boundaries not only outside, but also within the confines of marriage need to be established in order to nurture one's relationship with God. As Gloria said,

"God says . . . if you're married, you are to cleave to your husband and a husband cleaves to his wife and the only time that you two should separate in anything is the time that you two go into prayer. I have no problems with that as long as it's my husband. I do have problems with it if I'm trying to study the Word and my husband wants to be intimate with me. That bothers me because that's my time with God. You know. I'm giving my time to Him. I'm trying to learn some things from Him. And he is trying to disturb me and he's getting on my nerves. [laughter] He's getting on my nerves. And I think that he knows that too sometimes." This very tension has been the cause of many disagreements in their marriage. Although she did not go into great detail because her husband eventually entered during the interview, she did ask that I pray for them—a deviation from my "researcher" role—because their marriage is deeply troubled. Yet, Gloria's tension about "when" to be intimate is matched by Vivian's questions of "how" to be intimate and maintain an honorable relationship with God. As women negotiate these boundaries, they are discovering new ways of understanding themselves as Christian women. Their struggle is not outlined in any manual, but is rather an ongoing process between them and God through study of the Bible and prayer.

For Vivian the tension lies in distinguishing between that which is "of the world" and that which is "of God." Unlike Gloria's husband, Vivian's husband is not a believer and does not attend church. Her debate is more complicated in that she is attempting not only to uphold her own standards, but to proceed in such a manner as to win her husband over to the faith. As in her battle over tithing, she wants to honor God without alienating her husband. The dynamics of her body politics become a battle between demonstrating in a "worldly" fashion her passions for her husband and demonstrating what in her mind's eye are Godly expressions of passion.

> My husband and I, we've reached it [oneness] on some things, but we haven't become one, the way God wants us to be one yet. God, I know what God wants me to do. No fornication. No adultery. Fornication is sex before marriage . . . Adultery is sex outside of marriage, outside of your spouse. . . . I've turned away. I used to even, dress in the little teddies . . . and all that. And I even feel funny doing that, even though it is for my husband. I really do. I really do. It [her salvation experience] has really impacted me a lot because I wonder "God, is this pleasing in your eye?" I mean I am so, you know, I get so wrapped up and caught up in trying. I think I try too hard, and see that slowly kills it, you know, for my husband, because he wants me to tell little, just talk to him. And there are just some things that God does not want you to say.

Her husband is convinced that she does not "talk" to him in the same manner, that there are boundaries where there used to be none. When I asked what types of statements she believes are inappropriate, she explained, "I talk to him during the sexual act, before the sexual act. He says it's not the same . . ." Understandably reluctant to reveal the details of their discussion, she stated only that he wants her to use curse words and that as a child of God she should not be using such language.

> There are curse words because, F——— [mouthing only the first syllable] to me is not a word that you would say, not being a child of God, you wouldn't say it . . . I just don't feel right saying it. It's just, you know, and I have said it and I felt so bad afterwards. And he really. He really can't see it. He can't see it. He doesn't understand why I feel the way I feel . . . But, it's [her spirituality] affected it a lot, but then you know I have to look at it and say, "You know. You have to please your mate." But, your mate is not going to give you eternal life. So, you really have to draw the line and put your foot down. And I'm drawing that line, God's will.

Adamant about her position, Vivian engages in a comparison of rewards. Because her husband has only limited influence upon her future while God has ultimate influence, Vivian reasons that to honor God is more important than adhering to the desires of her husband. Such a resolution, however, is not easy. It means there is direct conflict between what she desires and what her husband desires. Her spirituality has led her to interpret even private moments of passion with her husband against a broader, intangible, spiritual reality. Her body is no longer that which is available to simply grant her husband pleasure; it is also that which she should be using to please God. By affirming her position, putting her "foot down" and "drawing that line," she makes clear her boundaries.

While married women negotiate their own set of body politics within the confines of marriage, single and widowed women of faith must also renegotiate the boundaries of their intimate experiences. Their decisions about sexual intimacy often, however, reflect a more liberal interpretation of Scripture than what is preached in their churches. In her work on single women and sexuality Rev. Dr. Susan Newman deconstructs biblical authority as taught in many churches by arguing that the teachings of the church, based on the Old Testament and the Apostle Paul's letters to the early church, do not fit into today's contemporary context. "Women have been robbed of the positive aspects of their sexuality in the Bible. And Christian women today are sexually frustrated because they have tried to literally interpret their lives today based on this ancient biblical text."[13] She further maintains, "We are doing a disservice to our daughters, and ourselves, trying to fit a 2001 peg into a 400 B.C. hole . . . Women in ancient civilizations did not have to deal with sexual abstinence as women do today; girls were betrothed at the age of five and given in marriage between the ages of thirteen and sixteen."[14] Newman's reading of the text requires a far more liberal view of Scripture than is taught in most Baptist churches. Her suggestions lead one to disassume the authority of Scripture and create a set of faith assumptions that operate outside of traditional understandings of the Bible. While her assumptions about scriptural authority will be challenged by the most devout Christians, her articulations of believing women's sexual experiences nevertheless resonate with the decisions to which many of the women I interviewed came.

While the church calls for complete celibacy before marriage, several of the women spoke of a modified type of restraint, which allows for "exceptions" under the right circumstances. They set boundaries for their sexual engagement without affixing a rigidity to their interpretation. From their experiences in marriage, and now as single women, they understand that sexual activity does not necessarily equal intimacy. In fact, many of their responses to celibacy are a direct reflection of their marital histories.

When Ms. Sylvia described the husband that she desires, she spoke in terms directly contrary to the memory of her ex-husband. "I want a husband that wants to take care of me and a husband that has my interest at heart for a change. Now, I've been giving and giving and giving, maybe it's time I received something." She chuckles at the thought of such a person and her seeming selfishness, but she goes on to explain that she left her husband because he was not taking care of household responsibilities. She was the primary provider and care giver. "I gave and gave and gave. And I did not mind giving. I gave because I felt that is what I should have been doing. My children were not responsible for being here and I felt that as a parent, I had to do the best I could." In some sense the expectation placed upon her by her husband was that of the "work horse." Her responsibility in the marriage was to work and provide emotionally and financially for the family, meeting his needs and caring for the children. Unlike the media ideal established for her white and middle-class counterparts, she was black and poor and thus undeserving of love, tenderness, affection, and care. Her job was to labor. Her decision to leave that relationship was in large part a decision to redefine herself over and against the image of the "work horse" created for her. This new space has allowed her to adopt a new vision of romance.

Although she realizes that "it is definitely sinful to be involved sexually at this stage of the game [prior to marriage]," she believes that "everybody needs to be loved, to be cared for." This desire to be loved and cared for allows her to enter into what she would consider less biblically ideal, yet nurturing relationships. In these relationships she determines, based upon past experience, what she needs in a partner—someone who's "not just interested in sex," someone with whom she has "something in common," someone who has an appreciation for "the trinity, the Father, the Son and the Holy Spirit." Once she's met this ideal person, things "just happen." God, after all, "understands human nature and human frailties."

Ms. Sylvia's remaking of the call to celibacy in the single life places her outside of the mainstream of Protestant beliefs, though maybe not outside mainstream practices. She conforms neither to church pressure to remain celibate, nor to social pressure that validates a life of reckless abandonment. She engages celibacy on her own terms. This practice has, however, forced her to hide the details of her relationship from fellow believers and certain family members. We spoke of her lover only by nickname and never in the presence of others.

Juanita Cleveland, a widow for several years, likewise must renegotiate the boundaries of her intimate relationships. This process is difficult because she recalls the joy that sex brought her and her husband, a former pastor. "My husband loved sex. We both loved it. I guess that's why we enjoyed it so much." Their enjoyment of each other was even questioned by a friend who once remarked, "I didn't know ministers had sex!" She laughs at her friend's naiveté, explaining the value of sexual intercourse. "I think it's a gift from God, I really do." This gift, however, is so important that one must share it only with one with whom you share a committed relationship.

> Well, if you're in love and if you have a person that you are intimately involved with, and this is the person and you want to wait until you are married, that's okay. But, I told my pastor, well, my former pastor, about it when me and my husband met. He said, "Wait until you're married to enjoy sex." I told him, I said, "Suppose I find out that we aren't compatible. Because you can't back out!" I said, I'm going to tell you right now, I love sex. I said, I love sex, so if I find out we're not compatible. . . . Now why should I be married to somebody if I'm not going to enjoy or can't you know, like can't function? NO. I said. Shoot! [Much laughter.] No. I want to know before. I guess. I just say it's one of those things. We say, abstain from it, abstain from it. I'm saying well if I'm going to be in-

volved with a person, I want to know that we are at least . . . compatible. And if I like sex and he doesn't like sex, what am I going to do? Marry somebody who doesn't even care for sex, or who's going to frown on it. No. That's no kind of relationship. I love sex. [laughter] The only reason I don't have it now is because I can't. But, if I could I would. I sure would. I would enjoy it just as much as I can. Just as much as this little body would let me enjoy it!

Her freedom of expression is drastically different from what is characteristically understood as the church's silence on issues of sexuality. For Ms. Cleveland, sex is a part of life that God intended people to enjoy. It is something that is even very natural for women to enjoy. They should not be bound to ideals of always pleasing men as a "responsibility," but they should freely enjoy that which God has created. As Ms. Cleveland expresses it, "every woman craves for sex. That's a part of our growing up."

The women's views of sex mark a distinction in some instances between what is believed and what is practiced.[15] While sex is believed to be a passion that one should enjoy within the bounds of matrimony, it is also renegotiated on the basis of one's previous sexual experiences. Not finding love and appreciation in marriage makes it easier to find validity in intimate sexual relationships outside of marriage, even when the relationship stands, according to one's own interpretations, in direct conflict with professed tenets of faith. Nevertheless, the women all maintain that the ideal of sexual intimacy within the covenant of marriage is best. For married and single alike, when conflict arises within relationships, sexual intimacy challenges and reframes faith. Thus while the tenets of faith establish a set of ground rules for intimacy, faith expressions are often challenged by the realities of singleness and the compromises necessary within marriage.

"IF ANYBODY TOUCHES YOU":
A MESSAGE TO YOUNG WOMEN

Women hold certain ideas about sexual engagement, not only to protect their own "sacred space" but also to protect the sacred space of others. Ideas about celibacy and marriage are presented as means of protecting loved ones against high teenage pregnancy rates and sexually transmitted diseases. Within this discourse is a larger discussion about the need for biblical ideals of sexuality in order to facilitate the regeneration of society as a whole, decreasing the numbers of abused and neglected children. In addressing these issues, close relationships between mothers and daughters or grandmothers and granddaughters become powerful points of departure for agency.

Within these relationships silencing is not permitted. While the women spoke of varying degrees of comfort in talking with their children or grandchildren about sex, they all felt that the discussion itself was important. Gone are the days when parents told their children to "be quiet" because they were asking about "nasty" stuff. These very attitudes the women confirm have been detrimental. Two who experienced motherhood as teenagers pointed to this type of silencing as contributing to their early pregnancies. They were curious and learned too early the responsibilities of sexual activity.

Yvette spoke not only of the silencing that left room for her teenage pregnancy, but also of the silencing that perpetuated her sexual abuse. In those days nobody wanted to talk about it. Nobody would talk about it. She thought that her parents knew. She was even certain that they had caught her grandfather fondling her or her sisters, but they did not want to say anything. Thirty-plus years ago, her grandfather had earned a reputation as a respectable black farmer. Status was hard to come by and, once earned, was rarely if ever relinquished. Even when her grandfather passed, the church was filled to capacity with standing room only. People spoke of him as a hard-working man, a good father, a faithful church member, a friend. Yvette wanted so much to blurt out "child molester," but she couldn't. The family wouldn't let her and she wouldn't let herself.[16]

The pain of that experience has been with her since she was a little girl, forced to follow her grandfather out to the horse stables where it happened. Embarrassed, afraid, confused, she did not talk about the experience even with her sisters, who shared the same pain. Only in the past few years have they brought themselves to talk about it. "Never," Yvette insists, will her granddaughters have to live like this. They must always be open to talk with her. To this pledge she commits her energy. "I try to spend a lot of time with them. Let them feel free, maybe so they'll know if anything happen you can come tell grandmama. I don't care what it is." Her experience and her commitment to her granddaughters leaves her cautious even around the man she trusts the most, her husband. She notices them when they are together because she remembers how nobody ever expected something like that to happen in *her* family.

To build a relationship of trust and openness is the greatest gift she believes she can give her granddaughters. The silence is too painful. When I asked if she ever talked to God about the problem, she stated, "not that

I can remember." Her lack of communication with God about the issue, even the lack of resolve that such a process gives today, speaks to the importance of human relationships. Although she sees herself as a committed, born-again Christian who has the freedom to take her problems to God, she is still troubled that she has not been able to speak to her parents about her abuse. As she remembers, "I said, 'They don't care about this happening to me. They don't even ask.' I felt like they didn't care enough to say, 'Is everything all right?' They didn't have a close enough relationship with me where I could just go back over to them and tell them. That hurt. Even to this day," she reminds me, "my parents never really came and sat down and talked with us."

That her parents refuse to talk with her about her abuse and that she and her sisters have only since adulthood been able to acknowledge their shared abuse speaks to the power of silence. In her description of Celie from Alice Walker's *The Color Purple,* literary scholar Karla Holloway speaks of the "abuse, rape and trauma that have become the tenor and tone" of her life.[17] ". . . Celie is told up front, on page one, in the first line and in italics: '*You better not never tell nobody but God.*'" This type of silencing, Holloway explains, creates a fracture within women's "contracted identities." For black women to "speak out" becomes a "dangerously engaged practice."[18] This type of fracturing, according to Charlotte Pierce-Baker, is a "sacrifice of the soul."

> For black women, where rape is concerned, race has preceded issues of
> gender. We are taught that we are first black, then women. Our families
> have taught us this, and society in its harsh racial lessons reinforces it.
> Black women have survived by keeping quiet, not solely out of shame,
> but out of a need to preserve the race and its image. In our attempts to
> preserve racial pride, we black women have often sacrificed our souls.[19]

Yvette's desire to end this cycle of abuse and silence emerges from the emotional pain she has experienced as a result of the physical abuse and her family's refusal to acknowledge it. By protecting the grandfather's reputation as a respectable black farmer and never acknowledging Yvette's wounded childhood, Yvette's family forces her to choose loyalty to family and race over an appreciation of her own wholeness. She endures a fracturing of body and soul that she refuses to allow her grandchildren to experience.

This desire to create a relationship of trust with her granddaughters extends to other children in the community. She nurtures and protects them, letting them know that they too can always talk with her. On numerous occasions she has loaded her car with children to take to the park or vacation Bible school, or some other event. Kids stay at her house. "I worry about the kids," she explains, "because the adults, their morality. They don't have any morals. We had something. You know you just didn't do anything and everything." Her distress over children in the community came across even more as she told about a sister and brother in her husband's Sunday school class who were forced to watch their mother and her boyfriend engage in sexual activity. The kids today are with a foster family and are not allowed back into their mother's custody.

Yvette's care for her grandchildren is much like the care that other women give their daughters. An open space to talk about sex and sexuality is fundamental for them. Not speaking about sexuality is like not giving children ammunition with which to fight as they battle through the maze of today's hyper-sexualized society. In Halifax County the need to address these issues seems more imperative given the exceptionally high incidence of teenage pregnancy.

Marie spends a significant amount of time with her daughter, making certain that she is comfortable talking with her about anything. "I talk about it [sex] with my children like I'm eating ice cream. Anything they want to ask me." Now a junior in high school, her daughter has begun to ask a series of questions regarding her own sexuality.

> She asked me a question, she said, "Mama if I had sex with a boy would you like to know?" You have to stay very calm when you have teen-agers. [chuckle] I told her, well let me tell you like this. Society has put sex on a pedestal that it should not be. I said, now if you REALLY want to have some good sex, wait until you're married . . . and you can have ALL the sex you want! Freely. Because that's how God made it for you to enjoy. And she thought that was funny. I said, GIRRRRL you can have ALLLLL that you want!!!

Attempting to redeem sex from its glorified position in society and place it within a normal, yet desirable context, Marie reminds her daughter that sex is "God made." Affirming these values, she hopes to intercede in any future decisions that her daughter makes about sexual activity. She continues to explain that God "is not pleased" when sex is taken out of its proper context. The growth of pornography and child pornography proves her point. These types of sexual ventures distort for her God's intention when God gave humanity sex. "Everything God made is good. And He made a good thing when He made sex in its right context." Although she realizes that her children may opt for alternatives to celibacy,

she believes that it is important to teach them early the benefits of waiting for sex.

Ms. Moore holds this same philosophy. Although her children are
grown, she believes that society in general should return to the "old teachings." The prevalence of disease and unwanted pregnancies leads her to
believe that society has taken a deviant path in its free sex propaganda.

> The prevalence of AIDS, the prevalence of unwanted pregnancy and the
> prevalence of children who are just dying to have a hug and little chil-
> dren who are not loved and children who are being abused. Moms
> whose lives are turned all around because they're having children so
> young, that they can't grow up themselves. Then they end up growing
> up with the child and then one generation begets another, begets an-
> other, and on down the line. It just perpetuates itself.

Out of frustration with the current state of society Ms. Moore reasons that there is little to debate. Biblical standards of celibacy and marriage provide a necessary answer to many of the problems young people
face. Interestingly, she does not attribute her response to "spirituality"
per se. "I'm not sure it's all spirituality," she says, "but I'm concerned
about that [the list of social problems] and I don't want to be naive
about this [sex]."

The reality of so many social ills stems in her eyes from society's rebellion against biblical models.

> I think if we went back to old teachings, biblical teachings in terms of
> save yourself for your husband, that maybe would eliminate some of
> those problems. So, I guess my answer to you is, I believe we need to go
> back to those old, you know, go to the Bible for instruction. I believe
> that everything we need to live by is in that book. I'm saying that we
> need to go back to the Bible, but not just for spirituality's sake. We need
> to go back to the Bible because I think the Bible will tell us how to take
> care of some of all these, all these other problems that come about be-
> cause of sexuality.

The message of marriage and celibacy is espoused by each of the
women, but for different reasons. For some, celibacy and marriage are
ways of guarding one's spirit; for others it is not only an issue of great spiritual significance, but a pragmatic issue of physical consequences. Premature sex can lead to sexually transmitted diseases and unwanted pregnancies. These lessons of intimacy, taught to daughters and granddaughters,
are tools for empowering them as they begin to define their own body politics. Silencing on these issues, for them, prevents such empowerment.

Returning to the "old teachings" to which Ms. Moore alludes, how-ever, would require reconsidering *how* young people are taught about sex. As Frances E. Woods asserts, many in the church and in the com-munity speak to young women about sex without giving the same type of attention to the education of young men. "What are we to make of the double standard," she asks, "for teenage sexual behavior that allows boys to sow their oats, yet expects girls to keep their panties up and their dresses down? . . . What are we to make of the practice in some churches of shunning pregnant teenage girls, and elevating their male counter-parts to leadership roles?"[20] In addressing the sexual concerns of young people, the church will have to reevaluate the "old teachings" which allow double standards that do not hold all parties responsible for sex-ual involvement. These ideals pass not only formally from the pulpit to the pews, but informally from women to other women and men to other men.

NONCONFORMISTS AND CONFLICTING MESSAGES

For all the ways in which the women I interviewed have been using their faith to analyze and reshape their sexuality, there are also blind spots in their analyses. The most obvious ones involve same-sex relationships. As they explained their commitments to marriage and celibacy, their ex-pressions of sexuality were presupposed. Sex is a godly, heterosexual act. This understanding as I pierced deeper, carried with it assumptions about homosexuality and the language with which one could speak about it. This language, sometimes punitive and negating, works along with the mechanism of silence, to create what some scholars consider a homo-phobic church community.[21]

In her text *Sexuality and the Black Church*, Kelly Brown Douglas ar-gues that black Christians, through their use of what she considers his-torically misinterpreted biblical texts, create homophobic and abusive environments for people who are homosexual. The language of this abuse, argue anthropologists Jenell Williams and Mindy Michels, creates an atmosphere of violence. They are careful to note, however, that "re-searchers have not explicated direct links between anti-lesbian/gay speech and anti-lesbian/gay violence—in fact, speech and violence are not even clearly linked on a theoretical level."[22] Nevertheless, anti-gay/lesbian speech may provide an alternate channel for those who might otherwise act violently toward gays and lesbians.

While the women I interviewed do not intend their language to engender violence, their language does place special moral emphasis upon the sinfulness of homosexuality. This emphasis along with an insistence upon silence and negation reinforces the assumptions and practices of a homophobic society. In my research, homosexuality, when considered a sin, stands apart from other sins. This understanding was clear in the discourse of the women interviewed. There was something special and unique about homosexuality that did not allow it to be grouped with the sins of fornication (sex before marriage) and adultery (sex outside of marriage). This power dynamic places those who practice homosexuality at a clear disadvantage to others in the church who go against the understood biblical standard of heterosexual marriage.

As women teach others about sex, the difference in discourse is seen primarily in the allowances made for heterosexual intercourse versus homosexual intercourse. Without language to sufficiently articulate reasons for disagreement, pronouncements about sexually moral and amoral interactions reflect degrees of homophobia. Referencing their own sexual past and for some their sexual present, women spoke of their improprieties as "bad choices in judgment" or "being naughty," reflecting a degree of lightheartedness in regard to their sexual sins of premarital and even extramarital sex. Yet, the discussion of homosexuality carried with it a high level of imputed disgust. Women responded with tremendous disapproval at the thought of such sexual encounters.

Likewise, the abusive languages of silence and disdain carry with them not only moral judgment but a hierarchical understanding of "sin." Such disdain is rarely expressed for the friend who has an occasional rendezvous with her male partner. Nor is such disdain offered for the family member who has consistently engaged in extramarital affairs.

Ms. Sylvia's experience with premarital sex stands as an example. As discussed earlier, she sees the need for intimacy as a God-created desire. In her singleness she finds that premarital sex has been an excusable option. It is something that "just happens" between two people who hold common values and who care about each other. Not only has her relationship brought her sexual fulfillment, but it has also allowed her to once again see her body as beautiful. Her younger lover affirms for her the value and beauty of her body as complete and satisfying. In talking about her relationship, she uses the language of "exception." "I am not a married person," she explains, "and I realize that it is definitely sinful to be involved sexually at this stage of the game." Acknowledgment of her sexual "sin," nevertheless, leads to an exception. "But," she continues, "I think God understands human nature and human frailties. Everybody needs to be loved, to be cared for. And unfortunately, God didn't give me a mate right now that I can be married to. So, I do . . . I am not frivolous. I will not just go with anybody. . . ." As she continues to explain, things "just happen. They happen. And of course, the Lord will forgive you, I'm sure of that. As I said, that's where I am a little weak." However, in speaking of homosexuality, she uses the language of disgust and negation. After she described for me the "right type" of sexual relationship, I asked her to explain how her faith dictates what she sees as "right or wrong" sexually.

> MF: So, how does your spirituality inform what you think is right or wrong sexually? Like what types of relationships are right? In a sexual context?
>
> Ms. Sylvia: Well, the one I just explained. The wrong one would be somebody I would meet say today. And we would go, maybe go out to dinner, and we would have sex that night, ohh no, no, no, no, no. We have to have something in common and not only just in common, say both of us like to walk in the woods or both of us like to go for drives. No. It's more than that. Both of us have to have some spirituality, pertaining to—as I said before—the trinity. I mean he has to be in touch somewhere.
>
> MF: So . . . What do you think is God's idea of the right type of sexual relationship?
>
> Ms. Sylvia: [It] is to be married to somebody. And of course now, I've been married to somebody already and I'm divorced. So, there too you get into that situation of this . . .
>
> MF: Male, female.
>
> Ms. Sylvia: Hmm?
>
> MF: Male, female marriage. Male, female marriages, because there's . . .
>
> Ms. Sylvia: Pllilllease. You don't mean male to male? and female to female?
>
> MF: Yes.
>
> Ms. Sylvia: No, you don't mean that.
>
> MF: I'm asking you what you think about it.
>
> Ms. Sylvia: Male. Female. Look, X all that other. Forget that. No, I don't believe in males marrying the same. No same-sex marriages. For me I think it was meant to be the opposite.
>
> MF: Even in just sexual relationships?
>
> Ms. Sylvia: Oh, absolutely. Pllilllease.

The notion of "X-ing all that other" is in many ways a form of silencing. Notions of eliminating, deleting, or erasing emerge. If one "X's" something out, then it does not exist. It no longer has to be addressed. Yet, people and their identities cannot easily be removed from the public eye regardless of how different their choices. "Virtual silence," Douglas argues, "beyond moral invectives and self-righteous assertions—has characterized the Black community's consideration of gay and lesbian society."[23]

Attempting to get beyond the question of same-sex marriages, which is almost a separate issue in the minds of many Christians, I asked about "sexual relationships" in general. Her language, however, remained at the same level of disgust. Compared to mistakes she has made about her own sexuality, engaging in same-sex activity is a far worse, even punitive choice. This, however, often comes across as a discursive stance as opposed to an outright rejection of people who self-identify as homosexuals. Friends and family members who identify as gay or lesbian, for example, were discussed with love and care and a reluctance to judge.

Ms. Sylvia's verbal affirmation of the inappropriateness of homosexuality is more complex than her statement gives light to. While she highly disapproves of homosexual relationships, she is known throughout the community for embracing *everybody*. One young woman, Janet, whom Ms. Sylvia befriended is a lesbian who has refused to keep her sexuality hidden despite the close-knit community in which she lives. As they worked together on issues in the community, Ms. Sylvia and Janet developed a friendship that today leads Ms. Sylvia to embrace her as one of her many "children." Their relationship in many ways contradicts her statement of complete negation and highlights the complexity of homophobia in the black community.

During a roundtable discussion with the women about my research findings and write-up, Ms. Cleveland demonstrated concern about my section on homosexuality. Before she could explain, the other women present began to express to her the significance of the research and how we shouldn't treat homosexuals any differently from anybody else. When they finished, Ms. Cleveland completed her thought by saying that she only wanted to make sure that *I* did not write too harshly about gays and lesbians because she has a relative who is gay. The allowances made for friends and family members who are gay, however, come across as "exceptionalism"—the assumption being that most gay people are deviant *except* the ones known personally.

Marie and Vivian applied the punitive language of death and damnation, rather than that of disgust and negation, to the context of homosexual relationships. To Vivian homosexuality is a choice that people willingly make that goes against scriptural mandate. When I asked what she thought of homosexuality, Vivian responded: "It's still wrong. I mean because of Sodom and Gomorrah. Those men were homosexuals and they had lived that lifestyle. God destroyed Sodom and Gomorrah because of the way the men were living. And someone can say that they were born that way. They're lying. Because it's a choice that you make, like I choose to disobey God. That's a choice that I make. . . ." Defining homosexuality as a "choice" as one would choose which shoes one will wear in the morning, Vivian negates the real struggle that many gay and lesbian people experience in coming to terms with their sexuality, especially those who are Christian. In the United States it costs to be gay, lesbian, or bisexual. One loses family, friends, and often jobs over the issue of "coming out." And yet many still maintain that such an experience is an often easy "decision."

Marie, likewise invoking the condemnation story of Sodom and Gomorrah, uses even stronger punitive language. Her list of comparisons conflating homosexuality with sex crimes reflects the distorted view that many hold of gay people.

> God has blessed marriage. And He's going to bless you with your sex life for you to enjoy and to multiply. On the other hand, it's an abomination of God to be a homosexual. This is what God's word says. He didn't make men to have sex with other men or women to have sex with other women, or have sex with children. Or, our sisters and our brothers. In the Bible time, of course there's nothing new that's happening now that's not written in God's word. You see parents having sex with their children and brothers and sisters and God's like "Sodom and Gomorrah you know." It was evil and God hated it and He destroyed it. And sex is something that was meant for a man and a wife.

Unconsciously linking homosexuality to incest, Marie makes a comparison between two consenting adults in a same-sex relationship and the abuse that occurs when a parent enters into an incestuous relationship with his/her child. Homosexuality and abuse are different, yet in the language of disgust the two appear comparable.

Gloria, unwilling to pass judgment, made little reference to the sexual act and more reference to the relationship that forced her to address the issue of homosexuality. When I asked her ideas about homosexuality, she said:

Sex of the same sex? I can't say whether it's a sin, but, Sodom and Gomorrah. I think about that when people always talk about gay people.
I always think about Sodom and Gomorrah. And how so much, or
whatever they were doing that was going on over there, you know.
Even with the animals and stuff, how God felt about that. That's
something. I try to have an open mind. If that's what you want to do,
then that's your business. You know, I can't condone you or condemn
you for what your preference is. If that's your sex preference, then,
fine. I just try to keep an open mind about it. I don't agree to it, you
know. I choose not to go that way, but if that's your choice, that's your
preference, then that's your thing. That's something you and the Lord
have to work out. I'm not going to shun you. I'm not going to stop
talking to you because of your sex preference . . . I have a cousin that's
a lesbian, you know. I don't shun her. Why should I, you know. I don't
stop talking to her because that's what she likes, long as I'm not doing
it.

Gloria's language of negotiation attempts to find a balance between her
disagreement with the lifestyle and her acceptance of people. As she invokes the punitive reference to Sodom and Gomorrah, she simultaneously critiques this language by stating that she "can't condemn or condone" the lifestyle of another. This tension for her becomes evident in the
acknowledgment of her lesbian cousin. To "shun" or to "stop talking to"
her cousin because of her lifestyle seems an unreasonable alternative.
Sexuality, for Gloria, should not be the defining element of her relationship with her cousin and simultaneously should not be the defining element of her relationship with others.

Black Christian heterosexual women and lesbian women have yet to
find a discourse that adequately articulates both their disagreement over
matters of sexuality and yet their common struggle against racism and
sexism. Patterned answers such as "love the sinner, hate the sin" do not
sufficiently explain how love operates when the premise of one's self-
hood is in question. What part of the "sinner" does one love? How does
one negotiate that boundary when another sees her sexuality as integral
to her person?

Furthermore, some scholars suggest that "one important outcome of
the social movements advanced by lesbians, gays, bisexuals, and trans-
gendered individuals, has been the recognition of heterosexism as a system of power . . . Within this logic, heterosexism can be defined as a belief in the inherent superiority of one form of sexual expression over
another and thereby the right to dominate."[24] This assessment, however,
does not adequately describe the conflict around homosexuality felt by

black women in Halifax County. That is, it does not acknowledge the spiritual lives of people who believe that sex and sexuality are acts that have consequences in both the material and the nonmaterial world, people who actively assess their sexual practices according to their belief in God. For these believers a belief in heterosexual marriage is not about dominating another group, but rather about pleasing their God. Nevertheless, labeling "heterosexism" a system of power, and one admittedly perpetuated by the church (the mosque and the synagogue), does force the church to more carefully and consistently examine, express, and live out a sexuality that reflects its own beliefs. For some churches this process has meant leaving denominations that preach heterosexuality as God's only ordained expression of sexuality to form what they believe to be more inclusive worship services. For others, it has meant living more closely to the standards of what they consider biblical Christianity, modeled in monogamous heterosexual unions, in hopes that their lifestyle will inspire others to do likewise.

The language that women engage to discuss alternative lifestyles is a language often filled with complexity based upon their attempt to negotiate between what they believe is morally acceptable and their belief in the humanity of others. Such language, however, often carries with it an overdetermined degree of disgust and punishment. When used in community, this type of language can immediately create cultures of silence and negation that work to suppress the value of another's existence, in turn affirming homophobia. For women who use sexuality as a tool for liberating themselves and their daughters from the pain of abusive relationships, unwanted pregnancy, and sexually transmitted diseases to simultaneously incorporate the language of abuse and negation in their discussion of alternative lifestyles is to validate yet another system of oppression.

Furthermore, the church's treatment of homosexuality, as some in ministry acknowledge, hinders the pressing need to address issues like HIV-AIDS in the community. This disease in many communities of faith still carries a stigma based on its early articulation as a gay-male disease. In Southern communities especially, however, as health studies indicate, it is becoming more and more a disease rapidly affecting black heterosexual women. These current trends mandate a more honest discussion of sexuality, particularly in the church.

In much the same way that women's spirituality causes them to renegotiate their financial dealings, spirituality allows women a space to create new boundaries and expressions for their intimate lives. The changes that they make create liberating spaces for how they engage sexual partners. This space for them is defined in a manner that views their bodies as temples to be loved and intimately known as opposed to abused or neglected. As they redefine their intimate encounters, they also create discourses for explaining to their children and grandchildren the sanctity of their bodies. This open space ends the silences that some have experienced as a result of rape or premature pregnancies. Yet, as they teach young women the benefits of guarding their sexuality against premature relationships, the women that I interviewed often unwittingly create discourses that silence a discussion of alternative lifestyles, in many ways reinforcing homophobia. Women's spirituality in the most radical ways can thus create both an empowering and yet constricted discourse when addressing the private areas of their lives.

CONCLUSION

On Sundays we, as Christian believers, go to church, and we find grace that heals the broken places, hope to enter the coming week, and strength to meet its challenges. Sunday is where we make sense of it all. Monday, Tuesday, Wednesday, Thursday, Friday, and Saturday all come together on Sunday. Renita Weems describes how Sunday was the apogee of the week for her family. "Our working-class hearts," she writes, "ultimately fixed on one thing alone."

> Sunday held out to us the promise that we might enter our tiny rough-hewn sanctuary and find sanctity and blessing from a week of loss and indignities . . . The Sabbath allowed us to mend our tattered lives and restore dignity to our souls . . . After a week of the body toiling away in inane work and the spirit being assaulted with insult and loss, Sunday was set aside to recultivate the soul's appreciation for beauty, truth, love, and eternity.[1]

Whether from the preaching of the word, the inspiration of the choir, or the testimony of the saints, on Sunday opportunities are found and answers are discovered. It is a day of both rejuvenation and repentance. In Halifax County, the axis of community life centers on Sunday. Young women, senior citizens, and the young men who choose to remain in places like Halifax make it to Sunday service. Most have not made the more urban and upscale transformation to "come as you are" services.

Dressing up here is still a matter of demonstrating a desire to give of one's best to God in spirit and in attire. It is a day for high-heeled shoes, pressed dresses, and suits with matching ties.

If testimony service provides inspiration by recounting what God has already done, prayer service encourages a type of humility and boldness about what God needs to do. Prayer service defines for any visitor the type of trials present in any one congregation, any one community. Members stand spontaneously during this portion of service and ask for specific prayer requests.

> *Please pray for my uncle. He was diagnosed with lung cancer.*
>
> *Please pray for my mother. She was diagnosed with cancer.*
>
> *Please pray for my sister. She's suffering from diabetes.*
>
> *Saints, pray for my brother. He's back in jail.*
>
> *Those of you, who know the words of prayer, please pray for me. I just lost my job.*
>
> *Please pray for Brother Deacon. He's back in the hospital.*

In this setting family members ask prayer for other family members; congregants ask prayer for co-workers; deacons ask prayer for members in their care circle; and choir members solicit prayers for friends in other states. No one has to be present to receive prayer. Prayers are simply offered. It is a way of communicating individual and collective struggles from the week's events. It is also a way of soliciting supernatural intervention into seemingly impossible situations.

One day after prayer service, a visiting minister took the microphone and began singing. His words were soft and slow at first, but his intensity increased as the choir and the congregation began to give voice to the meaning. Struggling with a deteriorating bone disease, he seemed to embody the very words of the song:

I'm still here. I'm still here.
I made it through, so have you.
I've come through the fire
and I've been through the flood,
but I'm still here, kept by His blood.

As the choir continued the chorus, many wept, most worshipped with hands raised, eyes set toward heaven, or heads bowed in humble awareness of uncertain mortality. At that moment prayer service became a time for worship and celebration of God's intervention throughout the week.

Next week may be different (or not); difficulties may still arise, some new, some old. Nevertheless, when next Sunday comes, the testimony will remain the same. "I've come through the fire / and I've been through the flood, / but I'm still here, kept by His blood."

If nothing else, Sunday is a testimony of God's ability to sustain life in the midst of trial. If Sunday provides us with the opportunity to reflect upon the week's activities and inspire vision for the future, then let us not make this Sunday any different. This "Sunday" chapter aims to shed light on this "week's" activities and provide possibilities for the coming weeks.

A WEEK'S REFLECTION

Exploring the spirituality expressed by black women allows those of us concerned about the struggles of black women to envision what it means to live out one's faith on a daily basis. A study of the "black church" by contrast immediately lends itself to a critique of the institutional practices of a religious organization, without careful attention to the everyday lives of its members. As an institution the black church has been historically characterized as either heavily involved in the political struggles of black people or passively disengaged from politics. These characterizations are most often based upon the pastor's sermons, the types of announcements given during service, the money raised by the church for political organizing, and the accessibility of the church edifice for political meetings. While early twentieth-century scholarship under this paradigm often criticized the black church's absence from political engagement, post–civil rights historiography has ascribed to the church an almost "heroic role" in the 1950s and 1960s civil rights struggles.[2] Though earlier studies marked black faith "other-worldly," concerned only about the life to come, revisionist writings have pointed out the numerous ways in which black faith inspired slave revolts, gave courage and conviction to black women during anti-lynching and women's rights campaigns, and helped inspire civil rights activism. Given the social conditions of the time, the black church out of necessity established itself as a place betwixt and between the harsh realities of a hostile white society and the pain and promise of a hopeful black community.

The women who emerge today from this tradition are no less influenced by its history and the contemporary demands of society. Their faith walk is often a struggle for personal salvation as well as social justice. To be both socially conscious and morally astute is a tension that black women have embraced since the early establishment of an African American religious tradition here in the United States. Some have narrowly defined this tension as a struggle between "accommodation" and "resistance." However, unless agentive value is placed on the labor involved in personal transformation, what is often characterized as "accommodation" does not take into consideration the work of individuals in forming productive personal lives within oppressive social structures. In other words, these critiques often do not acknowledge the work of resistance in less public spaces. The terms "accommodation" and "resistance" themselves, then, become problematic, presuming far too simple a dichotomy. Instead women's responses reflect a range of experiences and a sometimes contradictory set of beliefs.

Examining spirituality allows us to see the myriad ways in which women engage in creative agency. They assume political (or nonpolitical) identities at varying stages in their lives. For women this work often hinges on the type of familial responsibilities they bear (wife, mother, caretaker of aging seniors). It also hinges on their beliefs about male/female roles in leadership. These perceptions influence not only their public work, but also their private lives. While work in private areas often goes unexamined by scholars, on the assumption that it is nonpolitical, the day-to-day struggles of women's lives in Halifax reveal tremendous agency on their part as they wrestle with defining holy and satisfying personal praxis as well as just and humane political praxis. The movement between gratitude for material and nonmaterial blessings, empathy for those who are without, and righteous discontent at a system many believe perpetuates poverty and exclusion allows us to see these places of agency.

Gratitude and empathy reveal the levels of continuous and often unrecognized work that women perform ritually in public life. In these instances women are not necessarily confronting school boards or petitioning about government policies. They are instead maintaining the best possible quality of life for themselves, their families, and those in need of care. Gratitude, for them, provides the possibility of hope in the midst of sometimes depressing circumstances. The ability to acknowledge what is good—whether related to physical manifestations such as health, family, and material gain or spiritual manifestations such as salvation, joy, or peace—offers women incentive to engage in life's work. While gratitude does not make one blind to the absence of resources, it does make one grateful for the presence of what resources do exist.

Empathy works along with gratitude in developing one's sensitivity to the needs of others. While each of the women interviewed may not have all that she desires, gratitude for what she does have lets her know that she has *something* to give. In this way women of faith are transformed from victims (or objects of oppression) to actors and agents of change. Instead of operating out of a "lack" of resources, they operate from the presence of available resources. Their actions demonstrate that while the legacy of Jim Crow and sharecropping, nearly forty years removed, looms over the political and economic conditions of the county, it does not necessarily dominate the spirit of all of its people. When women like Ms. Sylvia, Carmen Moore, and Gloria McKnight care for the elderly or tend to teenage mothers, they exude a type of energy that reflects their spiritual vitality. They selflessly give to help meet another's needs.

As well as emphasizing the meaningful work involved in demonstrating gratitude and empathy, one also needs to acknowledge that exclusive emphasis upon gratitude and empathy, without consistent attention to righteous discontent, can have the unintended consequence of reinscribing oppression. In other words, the work of actually dismantling structures of oppression is key in eliminating oppression. Caring for the elderly and providing clothes for those without and support for teenage mothers are important work. Beyond this work, however, one must ask why after working hard in fields and factories for most of their lives African American men and women retire in the South and are forced to live off of less than $500 per month. When their virtually free labor has helped to build much of the economy of the South, why must they consistently suffer from limited access to health care and nursing facilities? Why have many of them lost farmland that was once a part of their family inheritance? What scholarship or employment incentives are available to African American teenagers educated in a school system that lacks the type of teaching and educational resources available to more established systems? Why are prisons and industrial hog farms presented to a region like Halifax as "viable" economic development when these industries bring possible environmental danger to communities already in tremendous need of rejuvenation? Demanding an answer to these types of questions forms the work of righteous discontent for the people in Halifax County. To engage these challenges, the work of righteous discontent has historically relied upon the presence of a black public sphere.

As Higginbotham, Gregory, Dawson, and Elsa Brown explain, the black church historically has been central in creating this space. In Halifax County, this alternative sphere resides largely in grassroots organizations like CCT and social and political organizations like the Halifax

County Black Caucus and the Coalition for Progress. The church, however, remains a place for the expression of concerns related to African American progress in the county as well as a sphere for the celebration of faith and eschatological hope. While the intensity of the church's involvement in the area of politics has declined since its civil rights heyday, the church for many is still an important place to address social concerns. It offers a space for announcements, activities, and education.

Contrary to what Gregory observed about the restructuring of a specifically *black* public sphere in New York, the space created by these institutions in Halifax County has not undergone rigorous challenge and change. Realities of largely segregated school facilities, white majority rule in electoral politics, and inequitable labor conditions point not only to the history of racialized exclusion but to the continued need to organize around these issues. Unlike some other parts of North Carolina, where Latino and East Asian populations have grown, Halifax County, because of slow economic growth, has not readily attracted other minority populations. Politics in the county often remain highly polarized between white and black constituents. While within these groups there are often diverging methods for engagement (more radical or more conservative), the political issues themselves generally divide along preexisting racial lines.

Nationally, however, the church's response to race-based concerns in a post–civil rights era seems to be shifting, given the growth of a substantial black middle class and the expansion of black ministries within non-African American denominations, particularly on television. As evidenced by televangelist Frederick Price's year-long discussion of race and the church, people's experiences and perceptions of racism vary across economic backgrounds and regional locations. In an area like Halifax, where race is a polarizing factor in government, education, and church life, what influence do television ministers and their ministries have on the viewing audience? How do they influence how people perceive community concerns and their day-to-day realities?

RELIGIOUS INFLUENCES

Women in Halifax listen to ministers on television because they are more inclined to "teach" as opposed to "preach" their messages. They "break the scriptures down" in a way that is accessible and applicable to women's everyday experiences. These ministers offer counsel for a range of day-to-day concerns such as resolving breaches in family relationships, accessing material wealth, and overcoming emotional scars. In many ways television ministers are easily accessible counselors for people of all classes and educational backgrounds looking for resolutions to personal problems. In addition, the grounding of the ministers' messages in biblical text affirms for many the sacredness of the process and the hope that their viewers are growing closer to God as they apply the messages.

While these messages offer an assortment of assistance in overcoming personal struggles, the ministries tend to simultaneously encourage a type of individualism, materialism, and simplistic multiculturalism that depart from historic discourses in more socially oriented black church teachings. Emphasis upon multiculturalism often leads away from contemporary critiques of how race is used as a social, economic, and political organizing principle. Multiculturalism focuses more on the universalism of the gospel message versus any particular racialized experiences of the gospel. In other words, one cannot or does not talk about racism because the idea is that believers are all "one" in Christ. To talk about race under this rubric would reinscribe difference. Emphasis upon acquiring material possessions also informs much of televangelism. Such positions often carry with them a focus upon individual transformation that may eclipse the problems with social structures or institutions that may be affecting all. For example, encouraging individuals to work hard and tithe, as a means of becoming wealthy, may not take into consideration the possibility of unfair employment conditions where, for example, the placement of high-income industries in white communities hinders minority earning potential.

For all of their attention to the individual, however, television ministries do affirm the agency involved in personal transformation. These acts of personal transformation are evident as women engage private struggles that speak to the influence of spirituality on issues such as intimacy and tithing. Tithing to a large extent challenges contemporary notions of materialism, empowers women to manage their finances, and allows them to help build institutions like the church and establish resources for scholarships, elder care, and other benevolent projects that their church might assume. At the same time, however, women who tithe often still wrestle with the realities of limited and overdrawn budgets. Debt is a problem even for those who believe that God provides for their every need. This complicated relationship with money represents only one among their many personal dilemmas.

To undergo the types of emotional and psychological changes necessary to leave abusive situations or define more self-affirming boundaries in sexual relationships requires tremendous work when one considers the obstacles placed there by the conditions of oppression. Confronting the challenges of abuse, abandonment, and sexual misuse of women in a male-dominated society, especially when these challenges are aggravated by low wealth, involves a spiritual transformation that gives precedence to what women consider to be God's vision of their life versus anyone else's vision, including that of spouses and other loved ones. This reorientation in focus makes mute negative or nonaffirming voices and aims to give final authority in decisions regarding sexual involvement to God's leading. Often during this process negative self-images resulting from societal expectations or personal rejection are discarded.

This work, while not necessarily visible to public scrutiny, not only adds tremendous value to an individual's sense of identity and strength; it also inevitably affects the communities in which women live. When, for example, women assume authority over their finances, refusing to spend unnecessarily and committing a portion of their resources to their church, they not only begin to prioritize management of their finances, but they also contribute valuable resources to an institution with tremendous potential for social change.

In many instances the church is caught between what Lincoln and Mamiya define as its priestly and its prophetic responsibilities. Only to the extent that real progress is made, particularly as it relates to the manifestation of racialized equality and justice, can the church as a "black public sphere" afford to deemphasize its prophetic ministry. In regions of the country like Halifax, however, the questions of progress linger. As the local black church moves forward in pursuit of more priestly endeavors and answers the many questions developing as a result of television ministries, the church must also continue to ask itself whether its actions are leading to progressive change. Is progress real or is there a mere veneer of progress? As the women's lives and the lives of their communities demonstrate, progress is an ideal yet unfolding.

NEXT WEEK'S VISION

What is telling about the black public sphere is that it has been slow to tackle issues pertinent to women specifically. While many of the organizers within the church and in grassroots activist organizations are women, few discussions center directly around women's issues. Though many of the problems women face tend to be gendered in particular ways—child care, elderly care, domestic violence, living wages—few tackle these issues in gender-specific terminology with an allying praxis to address them. The questions of race are forthright while the questions of gender seem slow to emerge. The labor involved in finding solutions to these questions, however, is not simply women's work. The work of confronting gender oppression is as much the responsibility of men as of women.

The black church has historically done well in emphasizing the need for individual transformation, a rejuvenation of self that places one in right relationship with God and one's neighbors. The ongoing work of the church will involve understanding how parishioners' individual struggles connect to larger structural problems. For example, understanding how one woman's domestic violence situation connects with another woman's experience of sexual abuse may help shed light on the ways in which these experiences are often validated by the media's objectification of women as well as by some of the discourses of female subjugation in the church. Thus, while at the same time helping the individual recover from her victimization, a larger critique of social structures and a more conscious review of church pedagogy might help stem the tide of violence against all women both within and outside of the church.

Similarly, the frequent silence of the black church on issues of sexuality is largely to the detriment of young women and teenagers who have babies and are often left with the enormous responsibility of raising them as single parents. To speak about gender, then, means to discuss the outcomes of sexual involvement and to encourage men and women to develop loving and committed monogamous relationships. It is also to teach men and women the value of their bodies. Such conversations must inevitably create spaces for the discussion of lesbian, gay, and bisexual concerns and how the church as the body of Christ should respond to those in the congregation who are often ignored or silenced because of homophobia.

Eventually, these issues will be forced onto the table in many churches because of the growth of television ministries. As people listen to new doctrines via television, they will bring new questions to their local bodies, which will then be charged with the responsibility of responding. Television as it has in secular spaces, in other words, will force open a discussion in many congregations about sexuality, abuse, women in ministry, and a host of other topics that African American churches have been hesitant to discuss.

How these ministries influence not only people's doctrinal views, but also their political views and affiliations will be of interest to those concerned with African American progress. Scholarly assessments of this genre are needed in order for us to more clearly understand the influence of television ministries on people's lives. Traditional studies of black churches as local and national bodies will have to expand their focus to include the international influence of satellite-transmitted religious programming in black communities across the globe. What, for example, does it mean for people in postcolonial African countries who struggle with poverty and lack access to land and a means of production to hear the messages of prosperity? What influence will this doctrine have on political engagement and social practice? These are but a few questions that the growth of African American televangelism will raise on an international level. As local communities connect up with larger national and international communities, the questions of race and gender will become more complex while at the same time more illuminating.

Finally, when one raises the questions related not only to women's personal activism but also to their public activism, the emphasis upon spirituality becomes salient because it allows us to explore the actual role of faith in activism without assigning particular responsibility to a religious institution. In other words, if the black church is not active in political change, this does not mean that the women and men who are members of the black church are not involved in political change. In the Concerned Citizens of Tillery, members come from both politically active and nonactive church communities; nevertheless, their faith motivates and inspires their activism within the context of CCT. Meetings are never held without prayer, scripture reading, and the singing of hymns. Testimonies are given about God's work in members' individual lives as well as God's work in the political struggles in which they are engaged. If they have a successful lobbying trip to Washington, D.C., thanks will be given to God for safe travel and a productive day. Faith is present even when the institution of the church is not.

Ultimately, this final point asks whether or not black churches are or should be the central locations for political organizing and mobilization in black communities. Stephen L. Carter argues in his work *God's Name in Vain: The Wrongs and Rights of Religion in Politics* that the central aim of religion in politics is to provide a prophetic witness of God to the world. This witness, he maintains, is not necessarily demonstrated in organizing political rallies or forming political alliances with specific parties. The witness is in giving public voice to the issues and concerns at the heart of God. To engage in electoral politics, he continues, risks religious organizations being usurped by political agendas versus the faith agendas set forward in their belief systems. In other words, for religious institutions and religious leaders to become the main voices of political parties and coalitions is for them to compromise the legitimacy of their ministry of faith. Politics, Carter argues, is about winning and coercion.[3]

Using Martin Luther King Jr. and Fannie Lou Hamer as models, he asserts that their prophetic witness as spokespersons for what is right in God's eyes gave them a type of legitimacy that caused them to seek a higher goal than mere political victories, God's kingdom on earth. Their ideologies transcended the political, calling for individuals to affirm and respond to a sense of justice that mediates from the depths of one's soul. For Carter, "the religious voice at its most pure is the voice of the witness."[4]

The church in Halifax County, as well as the black church nationally, will continue to negotiate its place in the world of political activism, redefining old boundaries and establishing new directives. The struggles of its people will vary from urban centers to rural countrysides, causing difficulty in establishing a monolithic agenda. The work of "the church" will then reside in the spirit and the spirituality of its people. Black women in Halifax help us to identify what this spirit looks like. Their faith journeys through abusive relationships, single parenting, educational challenges, and protest marches against industrial hog farms remind us of Anna Julia Cooper's resolution, "When and where I enter . . . the whole race enters with me." Their faith negotiates their existence and helps us to see the complexities of race, class, and gender at the turn of another century. Another Sunday, a new week, has begun.

NOTES

FIRST SUNDAY

1. In order to maintain confidentiality I employ pseudonyms throughout the text when discussing people, churches, businesses, and most other organizations associated with Halifax County. When referencing national figures, primarily television ministers and elected officials, I use actual names, given that their ministries and offices are dynamically public. I also use actual names when referring to people in my hometown, Sumter, South Carolina.

2. For more on the history of women in ministry see Bettye Collier-Thomas, *Daughters of Thunder: Black Women Preachers and Their Sermons, 1850–1979* (San Francisco: Jossey-Bass, 1997). See also Vashti McKenzie, *Not without a Struggle: Leadership Development for African American Women in Ministry* (Cleveland: United Church Press, 1996). This book places in historical perspective the experience of women in ministry and offers advice for contemporary female ministers who struggle with their dual roles.

3. See Marcia L. Dyson, "When Preachers Prey," *Essence*, May 1998, 120–122.

4. A number of scholars have begun to write about the many labors that women perform in the church. Cheryl Townsend Gilkes, *If It Wasn't for the Women* (Maryknoll, N.Y.: Orbis Books, 2001), explores the breadth and depth of labor performed by "community workers" and "church women" who resist structures of oppression located outside of their communities as well as build networks and institutions of support within them. Many of these women, Gilkes notes, work overtime in their dedication to the church, while the church participates in a type of "ambivalent patriarchy" that supports women's work for it but denies women leadership in its major offices.

5. Jacquelyn Grant, "Black Women and the Church," in *But Some of Us Are Brave*, ed. Gloria T. Hull, Patricia Bell Scott, and Barbara Smith (Old Westbury, N.Y.: Feminist Press, 1982), 141–152.

6. See Milton Sernett, *Black Religion and American Evangelicalism* (Metuchen, N.J.: Scarecrow, 1975).

7. See Benjamin Elijah Mays and Joseph William Nicholson, *The Negro's Church* (New York: Institute of Social and Religious Research, 1933). For an analysis of this ideology see Hans A. Baer and Merrill Singer, *African-American Religion in the Twentieth Century: Varieties of Protest and Accommodation* (Knoxville: University of Tennessee Press, 1992).

8. Sernett, *Black Religion*, 322. Vincent Harding, Joseph R. Washington, and James Cone are among the pioneers in this movement. Scholars interpreting the tension between accommodation and resistance have historically couched these debates in terms of locating an African American cultural identity. See Eugene Genovese, *Roll, Jordan, Roll: The World the Slaves Made* (New York: Vintage Books, 1972); Albert Raboteau, *Slave Religion: The "Invisible Institution" in the Antebellum South* (New York: Oxford University Press, 1978); Charles Joyner, "'Believer I Know': The Emergence of African-American Christianity," in *African American Christianity: Essays in History*, ed. Paul E. Johnson (Berkeley: University of California Press, 1994); Peter Paris, *The Spirituality of African Peoples* (Minneapolis: Fortress Press, 1995); and Willie James Jennings, "Wrestling with a Wounded Word: Reading the Disjointed Lines of African American Spirituality," in *Spirituality and Social Embodiment*, ed. L. Gregory Jones and James J. Buckley (Oxford: Blackwell, 1997). The prevailing argument is that the more salient the presence of "African" culture in African American religious ritual, the more resistant it must be to European indoctrination. Conversely, it is argued that the more salient European practices in African American religious ritual, the less resistant and the more acculturated it is. For example, historian Albert Raboteau situates his critique of the study of African American religion within Africanist debate against "the myth of the Negro past." For Raboteau the styles of singing, dancing, and ecstatic behavior found in African-based religions such as Candomble, Santeria, Vaudou, and Shango influenced the worship styles of African slaves in America. The beliefs and practices carried out by slaves before the institutional development of the "black church" formed an invisible institution different from the Western religion prescribed to them.

The degree to which African American Christianity has been impacted by African "retentions" has thus been a continual subject of debate within the pages of research on African American culture. Anthropologists such as Melville J. Herskovits and Zora Neale Hurston supported arguments for continuity, while E. Franklin Frazier, of the Chicago school of sociology, argued for a distinct break from African religion. In discussing these debates over retentions, Genovese (*Roll, Jordan,* 209) prefers to take the middle ground, suggesting that African American religion is a sort of amalgamation of "African, European, classic Judeo-Christian, and Amerindian—but pre-eminently it emerged as a Christian faith both black and American." Genovese's concession, however, does not resolve the rigorous debates that have arisen around Herskovits's and Frazier's interpretations of race and culture—concepts which ultimately inform our understanding not only of religion, but also of economics and politics. For a discussion of the history of these debates in anthropology see Audrey Smedley, *Race in North America: Origin and Evolution of a Worldview* (Boulder: Westview Press, 1993); Carol C. Mukhopadhyay and Yolanda T. Moses, "Reestablishing 'Race' in Anthropological Discourse," *American Anthropologist* 99:3 (1997): 517–533; Faye V. Harrison, "The Persistent Power of 'Race' in the Cultural and Political Economy of Racism," *Annual Review of Anthropology* 24 (1995): 47–74; and Lee D. Baker, *From Savage to Negro: Anthropology and the Construction of Race, 1896–1954* (Berkeley: University of California Press, 1998).

Theophus Smith, "The Spirituality of Afro-American Traditions," in *Christian Spirituality: Post-Reformation and Modern,* ed. Louis Dupre and Don E. Saliers (New York: Crossroads, 1989), offers an understanding of spirituality consistent with the cultural dynamics of black faith. According to Smith, there are three major dynamics of African American spirituality: transformative, aesthetic, and political. The transformative dynamic "includes the transformations of self and world that are sought in specifically religious processes." Here Smith refers to experiences such as spirit possession and communal healing, which can alter a person's physical as well as mental state. The aesthetic dynamic pertains to the cultural forms of African American worship. These include "ritual structures" found in black music, black preaching, and vernacular speech. Finally, the spiritual political dynamic reflects "the biblical hermeneutic of figuralism," whereby the application of biblical narrative to their particular situations empowers people to act. In this process of typology, "biblical types or figures" are linked to "postbiblical persons, places and events."

9. Scholars who study African American religion often celebrate activism in the church tradition and question any scholarship that ignores the presence of political mobilization. Thus, there is an assumption among many scholars that African American religion must demonstrate some degree of social and political activism or relevance. For these scholars, individual restoration—i.e., psychic healing, spiritual transcendence—is not the only, or necessarily the most desired, end of African American religious practice. Religion, instead, should be relevant in tangible public ways to the community as a whole. See Gayraud S. Wilmore, *Black Religion and Black Radicalism: An Interpretation of the Religious History of Afro-American People* (New York: Doubleday, 1973), vii.

10. Ibid.

11. See J. H. Jackson, *A History of Christian Activism: The History of the National Baptist Convention, USA, Inc.* (Nashville: Townsend, 1980), and Baer and Singer, *African American Religion.*

12. See Evelyn Brooks Higginbotham, *Righteous Discontent: The Women's Movement in the Black Baptist Church, 1880–1920* (Cambridge: Harvard University Press, 1993), 18.

13. See Genovese, *Roll, Jordan,* 183.

14. Ibid.

15. In his work *Weapons of the Weak* (New Haven: Yale University Press, 1985), James Scott outlines everyday forms of resistance that poor people in Latin America engage in order to work against oppression. He argues that because men and women are not always able to fight in overtly political or confrontational ways, they engage daily in small acts of resistance.

16. See Gilkes, *If It Wasn't for the Women.*

17. Ortner's discussion of practice extends notions of practice set forth by earlier theorists in that her work "traces the shift from a notion of practice seen as apolitical 'action' and 'interaction' to a notion of practice as always embedded in relations of power and inequality." See Nicholas B. Dirks, Geoff Eley, and Sherry B. Ortner, eds., *Culture/Power/History: A Reader in Contemporary Social Theory* (Princeton: Princeton University Press, 1994), 15. Ortner's work has also been informed by subaltern and feminist theories which take into consideration not only the dynamics of power in society but also the agency of individuals.

18. Ibid.

19. African American religious studies is one field that has helped to bring about a reworking of practice theory. Scholars in African American studies were early critics of the role of the black church in society. According to them, the church needed to be engaged in questions of power and agency. The presumed lack of such engagement became a central element of criticism. Their critiques were largely based upon their assumption that black religion was not a social system of mere ritual and symbol, but a key site for reconfiguring relations of power in society. This logic, along with feminist and other non-Western theories of practice, has helped to center practice theory not only on power itself, but also on the ways in which subjects respond to or refashion power relations.

20. See R. Marie Griffith, *God's Daughters: Evangelical Women and the Power of Submission* (Berkeley: University of California Press, 1997).

21. See Higginbotham, *Righteous Discontent;* Elsa Barkley Brown, "Negotiating and Transforming the Public Sphere: African American Political Life in the Transition from Slavery to Freedom," *Public Culture* 7 (1994): 107–146; and Steven Gregory, "Race, Identity, and Political Activism: The Shifting Contours of the African American Public Sphere," *Public Culture* 7 (1994): 147–164.

22. The black public sphere has been dubbed an "alternative" public sphere to that described by Jürgen Habermas. For Habermas the public sphere was an elite space, set apart from the state, wherein people could engage in rational and critical debate about political issues affecting their lives. The historical exclusion of certain groups from the broader public sphere mandated the creation of alternative spheres. Not only race, but class as well as gender biases encouraged the creation of alternative spheres wherein varying views and opinions could be fully expressed.

23. See Higginbotham, *Righteous Discontent,* and Judith Weisenfeld and Richard Newman, eds., *This Far by Faith: Readings in African American Women's Religious Biography* (New York: Routledge, 1996).

24. Robin D. G. Kelley, *Yo' Mama's Disfunktional! Fighting the Culture Wars in Urban America* (Boston: Beacon, 1997).

25. See Steven Gregory, "We've Been Down This Road Already," in *Race,* ed. Steven Gregory and Roger Sanjek (New Brunswick: Rutgers University Press, 1996), and Michael C. Dawson "A Black Counterpublic?: Economic Earthquakes, Racial Agenda(s), and Black Politics," *Public Culture* 7 (1994): 195–223.

26. See Gregory, "We've Been Down This Road."

27. Cynthia Eller, *Living in the Lap of the Goddess: The Feminist Spiritual-*

ity Movement in America (New York: Crossroad, 1993), 6, outlines five major characteristics of feminist spirituality—"valuing women's empowerment, practicing ritual and / or magic, revering nature, using the feminine or gender as a primary mode of religious analysis, and espousing the revisionist version of Western history favored by the movement."

28. See Robert Wuthnow, *Sharing the Journey: Support Groups and America's New Quest for Community* (New York: Free Press, 1994).

29. Ibid., 18.

30. Eller, *Living,* 186.

31. Dirks, Eley, and Ortner (*Culture/Power/History,* 7) clarify that these desires are not innocent. They also are implicated in power and relations of power. It can, however, be argued that notions of love, tenderness, and communion are the very elements of community that lead to social organization and community protest. They are not in and of themselves "antithetical to power."

32. Emilie Townes, *Womanist Justice, Womanist Hope* (Atlanta: Scholars Press, 1993), 2. See also Higginbotham, *Righteous Discontent,* and Collier-Thomas, *Daughters of Thunder.*

33. For further discussion of the stereotypes historically ascribed to black women, see Joy James, *Shadowboxing: Representations of Black Feminist Politics* (New York: St. Martin's Press, 1999); Gloria Wade-Gayles, *No Crystal Stair: Visions of Race and Gender in Black Women's Fiction* (Cleveland: Pilgrim Press, 1997); and Patricia Hill Collins, *Black Feminist Thought: Knowledge, Consciousness, and the Politics of Empowerment* (New York: Routledge, 1991, rpt. 2000).

34. See Howard Winant, *Racial Conditions: Politics, Theory, Comparisons* (Minneapolis: University of Minnesota Press, 1994).

35. Consistent with some of the women's interpretations, theologians Henry and Ella Mitchell suggest that "true spirituality involves a belief system about God and Creation which controls ethical choices/behavior. . . . Black spirituality adds only a typical testimony that God as Holy Spirit is real and present with persons, so that the influence on human action is not legalistic coercion but personal influence." See Henry Mitchell and Ella Mitchell, "Black Spirituality: The Values in That Ol' Time Religion," *Journal of the Interdenominational Theological Center* 17 (Fall 1989/Spring 1990): 98–109.

36. In John 4: 23–24 Jesus responds to a Samaritan woman's question about why he, a Jew, is speaking with a Samaritan woman. Samaritans and Jews were in major political conflict at that time about whether the holy site for worship existed in Mount Gerizim or Jerusalem. See Craig S. Keener, *The IVP Bible Background Commentary: New Testament* (Downers Grove, Ill.: InterVarsity Press, 1993), 273. In this exchange Jesus replies that a time will come when true worshippers will worship God in spirit and truth. "But the hour is coming, and is now here, when the true worshipers will worship the Father in spirit and truth, for the Father seeks such as these to worship him. God is Spirit, and those who worship him must worship in spirit and truth." In distinguishing between spirituality and religion my informant invokes this passage of scripture to suggest that spirituality is more authentic than religiosity.

37. See Flora Wilson Bridges, *Resurrection Song: African-American Spirituality* (Maryknoll, N.Y.: Orbis Books, 2001), 2.

38. See Collins, *Black Feminist Thought*, 23.

39. See Deborah King, "Multiple Jeopardy, Multiple Consciousness: The Context of a Black Feminist Ideology," in *Words of Fire: An Anthology of African-American Feminist Thought*, ed. Beverly Guy-Sheftall (New York: New Press, 1995), 297.

40. Ibid., 298.

41. See W. E. B. Du Bois, ed., *The Negro Church* (Atlanta: Atlanta University Press, 1903); Mays and Nicholson, *The Negro's Church*; E. Franklin Frazier, *The Negro Church in America* (New York: Schocken, 1964, rpt. 1974); and C. Eric Lincoln and Lawrence H. Mamiya, *The Black Church in the African American Experience* (Durham: Duke University Press, 1990).

42. Karen Baker-Fletcher, *A Singing Something: Womanist Reflections on Anna Julia Cooper* (New York: Crossroad, 1994); Katie Cannon, *Black Womanist Ethics* (Atlanta: Scholars Press, 1988); Marcia Y. Riggs, ed., *Can I Get a Witness? Prophetic Religious Voices of African American Women: An Anthology* (Maryknoll, N.Y.: Orbis Books, 1997).

43. Aldon D. Morris, *The Origins of the Civil Rights Movement: Black Communities Organizing for Change* (New York: Free Press, 1984); Paula Giddings, *When and Where I Enter: The Impact of Black Women on Race and Sex in America* (New York: William Morrow, 1984).

44. James Clifford and George J. Marcus, eds., *Writing Culture: The Poetics and Politics of Ethnography* (Berkeley: University of California Press, 1986).

45. See Graciela Hernandez, "Multiple Subjectivities and Strategic Positionality: Zora Neale Hurston's Experimental Ethnographies," in *Women Writing Culture*, ed. Ruth Behar and Deborah A. Gordon (Berkeley: University of California Press, 1995).

46. See Clifford and Marcus, *Writing Culture*, 7.

47. See Irma McClaurin, ed., *Black Feminist Anthropology: Theory, Politics, Praxis, and Poetics* (New Brunswick: Rutgers University Press, 2001).

48. These four sets of interviews were used by all five researchers on the project in order to maintain the consistency of our findings. "Lifetime participation" and "non-participation" interviews covered questions about the level of involvement individuals have had in their communities, why they do or do not get involved, and what their experiences have been. "Drama of contestation" interviews covered questions about how people got involved in specific issues related to the environment/land use and/or education. "Informal" interviews were not conducted with a set of regimented questions in mind. Instead, we spoke with a range of people to get their general feelings about the county and their lives there.

49. Recent studies have problematized the nature of activism by exploring forms of activism that emphasize a transformation of both the individual and the community. See Paul Lichterman, *The Search for Political Community: American Activists Reinventing Commitment* (New York: Cambridge University Press, 1996), and Scott, *Weapons of the Weak*. These works challenge the notion that activism can only be public. Starn and Fox, furthermore, argue that protest is not only a physical struggle over material resources but also "necessarily involves struggle over ideas, identities, symbols and strategies." See Orin Starn and

Richard G. Fox, *Between Resistance and Revolution: Cultural Politics and Social Protest* (New Brunswick: Rutgers University Press, 1997).

REVIVAL: STRANGE MEETINGS

1. See Pat Mainardi, *The Politics of Housework* (London: Allison and Busby, 1980), 17–22. In this work Mainardi argues that there is a difference between liberated women and women's liberation. The first one signals true freedom from the domains that have been assigned to women, mainly housework (cooking, cleaning); the second brings only promises of change often left unfulfilled by men who claim to support women's liberation. While the women cleaning the kitchen that day after Aunt Eula's funeral did not engage in this type of debate and rarely challenge the gendered dynamics of such work, questions must be raised about the "backbone" work that women perform in churches. Even though they turn these spaces into social bonding spaces, there is little difference between the demands placed upon women at home and at church.

2. Much of the organizing time for CCT was spent protesting the USDA's policy regarding small farmers and minority farmers in particular. I discuss this struggle in greater detail in "Tuesday."

MONDAY

1. W. E. B. Du Bois, *The Souls of Black Folk* (New York: Vintage Books, 1990 [1903]), 56.

2. Bruce J. Schulman, *From Cotton Belt to Sunbelt: Federal Policy, Economic Development, and the Transformation of the South, 1938–1980* (Durham: Duke University Press, 1994).

3. Robert Bullard, ed., *In Search of the New South: The Black Urban Experience in the 1970s and 1980s* (Tuscaloosa: University of Alabama Press, 1989).

4. See William H. Chafe, "Epilogue from Greensboro, NC: Race and the Possibilities of American Democracy," in *Democracy Betrayed*, ed. David S. Cecelski and Timothy B. Tyson (Chapel Hill: University of North Carolina Press, 1998), 280.

5. Weisenfeld and Newman, eds., *This Far by Faith*, 2.

6. The register of deeds was a man Welch appointed during his tenure as a county commissioner.

7. See Robert B. Robinson, ed., *Roanoke Rapids: The First Hundred Years, 1897–1997* (Lawrenceville, N.J.: Brunswick, 1997).

8. Paul Luebke, *Tar Heel Politics: Myths and Realities* (Chapel Hill: University of North Carolina Press, 1990).

9. Ibid., 2.

10. Ibid.

11. See Phillip J. Wood, *Southern Capitalism: The Political Economy of North Carolina, 1880–1990* (Durham: Duke University Press, 1986); Linda Flowers, *Throwed Away: Failures of Progress in Eastern North Carolina* (Knoxville: University of Tennessee Press, 1990).

12. Luebke, *Tar Heel Politics,* 71. See also David Harvey, "Class Relations,

Social Justice and the Politics of Difference," in *Place and the Politics of Identity*, ed. Michael Keith and Steve Pile (New York: Routledge, 1993).

13. Flowers, *Throwed Away*, 183. Flowers cites an article entitled "Sun Belt Outlook May Turn Cloudy," from the Raleigh, N.C. *News and Observer*, July 7, 1985.

14. Flowers, *Throwed Away*, 183.

15. Luebke, *Tar Heel Politics*, 80.

16. Over the past 100 years anthropologists have debated the dynamics of race and racial classification systems and racism. Regardless of racist claims to white superiority, both culturally and biologically, revisionist anthropology has pointed to the inherent flaws in these arguments. (See Mukhopadhyay and Moses, "Reestablishing 'Race' in Anthropological Discourse.") Differences between whites and blacks in educational attainment and economic progress are rooted not in biological differences but rather in the nation's historic exclusion of minorities from full and uninterrupted participation in the nation's political and economic system. "Commonsense" understandings of race and racialized inequalities must thus give way to the insights offered by accurate historiography.

17. See Daniel M. Johnson and Rex R. Campbell, *Black Migration in America: A Social Demographic History* (Durham: Duke University Press, 1981), 9.

18. Ibid.

19. Ibid., 40.

20. See Higginbotham, *Righteous Discontent*, 4.

21. See Derrick Bell Jr., "The Racial Imperative in American Law," in *The Age of Segregation: Race Relations in the South, 1890–1945*, ed. Robert Haws (Jackson: University of Mississippi Press, 1978), 12.

22. Ibid., 13.

23. See St. Clair Drake and Horace R. Cayton, *Black Metropolis: A Study of Negro Life in a Northern City* (Chicago: University of Chicago Press, 1945, rev. 1993).

24. Bullard, ed., *In Search of the New South*, 5.

25. See Carol Stack, *Call to Home: African Americans Reclaim the South* (New York: Basic Books, 1996).

26. Bullard, ed., *In Search of the New South*, 6.

27. See David D. Stull, Michael J. Broadway, and Ken C. Erickson, "The Price of a Good Steak: Beef Packing and Its Consequences for Garden City, Kansas," in *Structuring Diversity: Ethnographic Perspectives on the New Immigration*, ed. Louise Lamphere (Chicago: University of Chicago Press, 1992).

28. Interviews with seniors in the community often reflected appreciation of industry work because in the days of sharecropping it represented a welcome alternative. The uncertainty of wages as well as the harsh and unfair treatment from white overseers is a part of the past few chose to remember. Under the sharecropping system, the landowner always took his share from the top and gave laborers what little, if any, remained, leaving workers in perpetual poverty. See Wood, *Southern Capitalism*.

29. Stull, Broadway, and Erickson, "The Price of a Good Steak."

30. Ibid., 51, 47.

31. See Leslie Bartlett, Thad Gulbrandsen, Marla Frederick, and Enrique Murrillo, "The Marketization of Education: Public Schools for Private Ends," *Anthropology and Education Quarterly* 33:1 (2002): 13.

32. Ibid., 13.

33. Ibid., 15.

34. See Lani Guinier, *Tyranny of the Majority: Fundamental Fairness in Representative Democracy* (New York: Free Press, 1994).

35. In Charlotte and in Durham, for example, boards looking to appoint a police chief and a school superintendent, respectively, were placed under scrutiny for the racial division of their votes. In both cases white candidates won over black candidates by votes divided along racial lines.

36. See Guinier, *Tyranny of the Majority,* 1–20.

37. See the unsigned article "Quorum Busters" in *Governing: The Magazine of States and Localities,* November 1997, 32–33. The article highlights Enfield officers as well as elected officials from other parts of the country, from Arkansas to Tennessee, who have boycotted government meetings in protest of the lack of attention given to minority concerns.

TUESDAY

1. This practice of documenting only public activities, as outlined in Anthony Giddens's discussion of agency, makes the assumption that "all social practices are situated activities"—in other words, they are affected by the dynamics of time and space. See Anthony Giddens, *Central Problems in Social Theory: Action, Structure, and Contradiction in Social Analysis* (Berkeley: University of California Press, 1979). Here Giddens cautions against the tendency to draw analogies between time and change vis-à-vis timelessness and stability, whereby change becomes an indicator of time and stability becomes an indicator of timelessness. Space, likewise, should not be seen as merely the "'environment' of social activity." Instead, one should see both time and space as integral to social activity (201–202). As Giddens notes, agency is a feature of action that acknowledges that "at any point in time, the agent 'could have acted otherwise' either positively in terms of attempted intervention in the process of 'events in the world', or negatively in terms of forbearance" (55–56).

2. While the women in my research consistently refer to God as "He," revisionist work in theological studies encourages what is considered "inclusive language." Ideas of a "Mother-Father God" as well as references to God as "She" make up this discourse. In the view of theologians who embrace this ideology, inclusive language allows women to identify with God, even or especially in cases in which their male father figure was abusive or negligent.

3. Reference to Isaiah 64:6. One's self-proclaimed righteousness is but "filthy rags." True righteousness, according to the scripture, comes from God.

4. Lesley Gill, *Precarious Dependencies: Gender, Class, and Domestic Service in Bolivia* (New York: Columbia University Press, 1994), 125.

5. Cornel West, *Race Matters* (Boston: Beacon Press, 1993), 15.

6. Tanya Luhrmann, "God as the Ground of Empathy," *Anthropology Today* 16:1 (February 2000): 19–20.

7. Ibid., 20.

8. Ibid.

9. See Stack, *Call to Home,* for a larger discussion of the return migration patterns of African Americans to the South and the types of community change organizations of which they have become a part.

10. During an earlier interview I had with this particular commissioner, he stated that this type of informal access to politicians is what African American communities have gone without historically. He takes pride in seeing himself as a grassroots politician who can be approached by those with concerns in unprescribed places: church services, funerals, grocery stores, etc.

REVIVAL: READING CHURCH HISTORY

1. Raboteau, *Slave Religion,* 138.

2. Arguing against the idea that antebellum churches were "invisible institutions," Mechal Sobel points to the large number of white church minutes that note the presence of black churches or gatherings on white plantations. See Mechal Sobel, *Trabelin' On: The Slave Journey to an Afro-Baptist Faith* (Princeton: Princeton University Press, 1979, rpt. 1988). "These data substantiate the thesis that the so-called hidden institution, the black church of the slave period, was not hidden at all; that the black church was a known and well-established institution; and that it can be seen again after a long period of obfuscation" (xvii).

3. Peter Paris, *The Social Teaching of the Black Churches* (Philadelphia: Fortress Press, 1985), 6.

4. Sobel, *Trabelin' On,* 181.

5. Historically, many of these churches were not "radical" in their approach to the social structures that hindered African American progress. Indeed, some social scientists point to the myriad ways in which the church operated as an engine of social control in the midst of the harsh conditions of slavery and Jim Crow. In *Trabelin' On* (157), Sobel explains that "in many cases, Southern whites called upon Black preachers to impose order in the black community. In one respect, this call was a privilege, for the blacks wanted to be self-policing." Citing Wilmore, *Black Religion and Black Radicalism,* and Genovese, *Roll, Jordan,* however, Lincoln and Mamiya (*The Black Church in the African American Experience,* 201) reiterate the idea that the "mere fact of black survival in a total system of dehumanization and exclusion is by itself a significant political act."

6. See Wilmore, *Black Religion and Black Radicalism.*

7. See Sobel, *Trabelin' On,* 156.

8. See Frazier, *The Negro Church in America.*

9. See Beverly Guy-Sheftall and Jo Moore Stewart, *Spelman: A Centennial Celebration* (Atlanta: Spelman College, 1981).

10. The founding of other national Baptist conventions occurred largely as a result of schisms in preexisting bodies—among them, the National Baptist Convention of America, founded in 1915, and the Progressive National Baptist Convention, founded in 1961. Among Pentecostals, the Church of the Living God was organized in 1889, the Church of Christ (Holiness) in 1907, and the

Church of God in Christ in 1897. See Lincoln and Mamiya, *The Black Church in the African American Experience*. Various other sects of Methodists, Pentecostals, and Baptists also emerged during this period.

11. See Wilmore, *Black Religion and Black Radicalism*.

12. Ibid., 135–166. See also Randall K. Burkett, "The Baptist Church in the Years of Crisis: J. C. Austin and Pilgrim Baptist Church 1926–1950," in *African American Christianity: Essays in History*, ed. Paul E. Johnson (Berkeley: University of California Press, 1994), 134.

13. See Lincoln, *The Black Church since Frazier* (New York: Schocken Books, 1974), 107.

14. Lincoln and Mamiya, *The Black Church in the African American Experience*, 36.

15. Ibid., 31.

16. I attended the AME church in the county as the guest of one of the several women whom I interviewed but did not formally include in the study. Close to ninety, she has been engaged in county politics since retirement. The medium-sized brick church, located on the main thoroughfare between Roanoke Rapids and Weldon, has a small, aging population. She explained that while there may be AME Zion churches in the area, her church is the only African Methodist Episcopal church in Halifax County.

17. This church is one of two predominantly white Adventist churches in the county. I was invited to attend a showing of a film on eschatology by another woman in the larger research pool. The final days of life on earth and the coming of God's Kingdom were discussed via a satellite presentation from another Seventh Day Adventist church outside of North Carolina.

18. This tradition in rural areas carries over from the wartime decline in the number of pastors and the need for available pastors to cover more than one church. Furthermore, the financial situations of some congregations force them to limit the number of services in order to make the cost of church operation more affordable.

WEDNESDAY

1. See Anne Moody, *Coming of Age in Mississippi: The Classic Autobiography of Growing Up Poor and Black in the Rural South* (New York: Laurel Books, 1976); Pauli Murray, *Proud Shoes: The Story of An American Family,* (New York: Harper, 1956); Melba Pattilo Beals, *Warriors Don't Cry: A Searing Memoir of the Battle to Integrate Little Rock's Central High* (New York: Pocket Books, 1994); Elaine Brown, *A Taste of Power: A Black Woman's Story* (New York: Pantheon Books, 1992); Angela Davis, *Angela Davis: An Autobiography* (New York: International Publishers, 1974); and Assata Shakur, *Assata: An Autobiography* (Westport, Conn.: L. Hill, 1987).

2. Vicki Crawford, "Beyond the Human Self: Grassroots Activists in the Mississippi Civil Rights Movement," in *Women in the Civil Rights Movement: Trailblazers and Torchbearers, 1941–1965*, edited by Vicki L. Crawford, Jacqueline Anne Rouse, and Barbara Woods (Indianapolis: Indiana University Press, 1993), 13.

3. Charles Payne, "Men Led, but Women Organized: Movement Participation of Women in the Mississippi Delta," in ibid., 8.

4. See Nancy Naples, "Activist Mothering: Cross-generational Continuity in the Community Work of Women from Low-income Neighborhoods," *Gender and Society* 6:3 (1992): 441–463; and Jenny Irons, "The Shaping of Activist Recruitment and Participation: A Study of Women in the Mississippi Civil Rights Movement," *Gender and Society* 12:6 (1998): 692–709. According to Nancy Naples, women brought distinct and essential organizing tools to the Civil Rights Movement—tools based on their socially constructed roles as nurturers, caregivers, and domestic organizers. They, for example, housed, fed, and emotionally supported students who journeyed to the South to participate in Freedom Summer. Naples has noted that such acts reflect "activist mothering," which encompasses not only the women's approach to outside activists, but also the care given to children and those in need in the community.

5. Giddings, *When and Where I Enter;* Collins, *Black Feminist Thought.*

6. Payne, "Men Led, but Women Organized," 6.

7. Higginbotham, *Righteous Discontent,* 9.

8. Ibid., 11.

9. Gregory, "Race, Identity, and Political Activism," 149.

10. Robert Bellah et al., *Habits of the Heart: Individualism and Commitment in American Life* (Berkeley: University of California Press, 1985, rpt. 1996).

11. The North Carolina Public Spheres project, for example, looks at the development of nonprofit, tax-exempt organizations and the type of activist-oriented work they engage throughout the state.

12. Black women's participation in the public is crucial. Their participation contributes not only to the "quantity" of the public sphere, but also to the "quality" of the public. In *Structural Transformations* Jürgen Habermas argues that the challenge in creating a truly democratic public sphere comes from maintaining its two-sided constitution, namely "the quality or form of rational-critical discourse" and the "quantity, or openness to, popular participation." See Craig Calhoun, ed., *Habermas and the Public Sphere* (Cambridge: MIT Press, 1992), 4. Critics of Habermas point to the overwhelming need to increase the quantity of participation and the range of what one considers "quality" participation. Black women's voices contribute to both the quality and quantity of the public by illuminating issues and concerns that may otherwise go unnoticed by a predominantly white and male populace unaffected by and often unconcerned with the issues confronting black communities.

13. Each year for nearly a decade, the church has sponsored a large production during Easter weekend commemorating the crucifixion and resurrection of Jesus. The extravagant program involves dozens of people from the church and community. Cast as disciples, weeping women at the cross, angels, Roman guards, Jesus, the actors and production staff meet regularly for two months prior to Easter weekend. As director, Cleveland oversees the process of screening actors, organizing rehearsal schedules, filtering music, and deciding upon staging.

14. To examine further this question of youth and the church, see Lincoln and Mamiya, *The Black Church in the African American Experience.* The sec-

tion titled "'In My Mother's House': The Black Church and Young People" deals specifically with the efficacy of the church in reaching contemporary youth.

15. See Gilkes, *If It Wasn't for the Women,* 24–25.

16. Ibid.

17. Lincoln and Mamiya define priestly functions as those that "involve only those activities concerned with worship and maintaining the spiritual life of members; church maintenance activities are the major thrust." Prophetic functions on the other hand, "refer to involvement in political concerns and activities in the wider community." See Lincoln and Mamiya, *The Black Church in the African American Experience,* 12.

18. The member eventually became the first African American school board member in the Roanoke Rapids school district. His candidacy early on in the election was a highly debated issue because of his stance against school merger. The church itself, however, never publicly voiced support one way or another although discussion of it took place beyond the walls of the sanctuary.

19. During my fieldwork tenure the county paper featured a story about one private academy admitting its first African American student.

20. Gilkes, *If It Wasn't for the Women,* 16.

21. See Winant, *Racial Conditions,* 29–36.

22. See David S. Cecelski, *Along Freedom Road: Hyde County, North Carolina and the Fate of Black Schools in the South* (Chapel Hill: University of North Carolina Press, 1994), 8–9.

23. In December 1996 black farmers demonstrated outside the United States Department of Agriculture (USDA) in order to bring to the attention of Secretary of Agriculture Dan Glickman and President Clinton their experience of discrimination from the agency. The farmers soon filed a class-action lawsuit against the government indicating specific causes for their concern. In response Secretary Glickman appointed an in-house team of investigators, the Civil Rights Action Team (CRAT), to investigate the farmers' complaints. In January 1997, CRAT set up listening forums in eleven locations throughout the country to hear the concerns of farmers and others who interact with the USDA. "Many farmers told of years of bias, hostility, greed, ruthlessness, rudeness, and indifference not only by USDA employees, but also by the local county committees that provide access to USDA's Farm Service Agency programs." See Civil Rights Action Team, *Civil Rights at the United States Department of Agriculture* (Washington, D.C.: United States Department of Agriculture, 1997), 3. Minority farmers were negatively affected primarily by excessive delays in the processing of their loan applications (which, given the need for timely sowing and harvesting, can have a dramatic impact on the success of one's crops). The time for processing loans for minorities and women far exceeded the average processing time for white male farmers. Furthermore, the approval rates differed by race. In 1996, the CRAT reports, "only 67 percent of African-American loans were approved in Louisiana, compared to 83 percent of nonminority loans. Alabama showed a similar disparity—only 78 percent of African American loans approved, compared to 90 percent of nonminority loans" (21).

24. This, scholars argue, is how white privilege operates. Whites have the

privilege of not having to constantly worry about their children being falsely accused of a crime and punished with a vengeance. Nor do they have to worry that
the prosecutor or judge will insist upon filing a case against them even in the absence of hard evidence, especially not against a student standout. Anthropologist John Hartigan argues that privilege operates by allowing whites to "benefit
from a host of apparently neutral social arrangements and institutional operations, all of which seem to whites at least to have no racial bias." "From the terms
or subjects of debate that comprise political campaigns to the placement and
funding of freeway projects or the placement of waste dumps, limits determining access to home financing, and the varied practices that constitute and reproduce medical professions in the United States, a set of institutional routines and
'white cultural practices' are evident in establishing and maintaining privileges
generally associated with being white. Indeed, whites benefit from being white
whether or not, as individuals, they hold supremacist notions, harbor racist sen-
timents, or are made anxious by the physical presence of peoples of color": John
Hartigan Jr., "Establishing the Fact of Whiteness," *American Anthropologist*
99:3 (September 1997): 496.

25. See Paul Gilroy, *The Black Atlantic: Modernity and Double Consciousness* (Cambridge: Harvard University Press, 1993), 30.

26. See Paul Gilroy, *Small Acts: Thoughts on the Politics of Black Culture*
(New York: Serpent's Tail, 1993), 55.

27. For more information on the growth of the hog industry and shifts in
North Carolina's agricultural landscape, see Steve Wing, Dana Cole, and Gary
Grant, "Environmental Injustice in North Carolina's Hog Industry," *Environ-
mental Health Perspectives* 108: 3 (March 2000): 225–231; and Richard H.
Olson and Thomas A. Lyson, eds., *Under the Blade: The Conversion of Agri-
cultural Landscapes* (Boulder: Westview Press, 1999).

28. See Bob Edwards and Anthony Ladd, "Environmental Justice, Swine
Production and Farm Loss in North Carolina," paper presented at the 2nd An-
nual National Black Land Loss Summit Academic Conference, Halifax, N.C.,
February 2, 1998. See also Olson and Lyson, eds., *Under the Blade*.

29. Researchers in the Department of Epidemiology, School of Public Health
at the University of North Carolina, Chapel Hill, examined the location of approximately 2,500 intensive hog production facilities, or CAFOs (confined ani-
mal feeding operations), across North Carolina and found that "these facilities
are located disproportionately in communities with higher levels of poverty,
higher proportions of nonwhite persons and higher dependence on wells for
household water supply." The health concerns that such placements raise are ex-
acerbated because CAFOs are locating in areas that already have "the highest
disease rates, the least access to medical care and the greatest need for positive
economic development and better educational systems": Wing, Cole, and Grant,
"Environmental Injustice," 229.

30. See Edwards and Ladd, "Environmental Justice," 19.

31. CRAT, 14.

32. In 1995 in communities outside of Halifax, heavy rains brought about
the failure of Oceanview Farms' hog waste lagoon and the consequent spill of
over 22 million gallons of pig sludge into the New River, depleting the water's

oxygen level and killing fish and other wildlife. The river, however, was not the only thing affected by the spill. Miles of black sludge spilled into neighborhood pools, covered tobacco and soy crops, and flooded roadways. The smell and silt alone left neighbors furious about the incident. Again, in the fall of 1999, Hurricane Fran brought heavy rains and flooding which left many of the same patterns—as well as floating pig carcasses—in neighboring communities. Incidents such as these have greatly increased the anti-pork industry sentiment in the Seniors group.

33. Letter sent from the Open Minded Seniors of CCT, dated May 20, 1997.

34. See Dirks, Eley, and Ortner, *Culture/Power/History.*

THURSDAY

1. Dennis N. Voskuil, "The Power of the Air: Evangelicals and the Rise of Religious Broadcasting," in *American Evangelicals and the Mass Media,* ed. Quentin J. Schultze (Grand Rapids, Mich.: Zondervan, 1990), 69–95. See also Quentin Schultze, *Televangelism and American Culture: The Business of Popular Religion* (Grand Rapids: Baker Book House, 1991), 55.

2. The now defunct Praise the Lord (PTL) ministry of Jim and Tammy Faye Bakker was the first satellite-transmitted religious broadcast to launch in the United States.

3. Schultze, *Televangelism,* 13. A major thesis in Schultze's work is that the reciprocal influence that religion and American culture have on each other is creating a Christianity wherein it is difficult to distinguish popular entertainment from religion.

4. For further discussion of the rise of the self-help industry as it relates to television programming see Mimi White, *Tele-Advising: Therapeutic Discourse in American Television* (Chapel Hill: University of North Carolina Press, 1992).

5. Baer and Singer, *African American Religion in the Twentieth Century,* 58.

6. Ibid., 62.

7. Ibid., 58.

8. Ibid., 59.

9. Tamelyn Tucker-Worgs, "Get on Board, Little Children, There's Room for Many More: The Black Megachurch Phenomenon," *Journal of the Interdenominational Theological Center* 29: 1 and 2 (Fall 2001/Spring 2002): 177–203, 179.

10. White, *Tele-Advising,* 112.

11. While other television ministers like Kenneth Copeland, Kenneth Hagin, Robert Tilton, Pat Robertson, Paul Morton, John Hagee, and a host of others may fit more appropriately (as in a discussion of the Faith Movement within televangelism), or more controversially into the sample, the women did not name them among the ones that they watch the most.

12. Schultze, *Televangelism,* 132. For one minister, the pastor of a United Church of Christ in Cary, Christ entered the world to bring people together in community. Pointing to the fact that the twelve tribes of Israel were divided when Christ began his earthly mission, he states, ". . . He [Jesus] thought the unification of the community of Israel was so important that he called the twelve disciples, representing the twelve tribes of Israel *together.*"

13. His most popular books have likewise fallen in the realm of self-help material, particularly that related to the emotional healing of women who have experienced abuse, neglect, or some level of failure. *Woman Thou Art Loosed* (1995) was one of his first and most popular books. Since then he has published *Loose That Man and Let Him Go!* (1995); *Lay Aside the Weight: Take Control of It Before It Takes Control of You* (1997); *Woman, Thou Art Loosed!: Devotions for Healing the Past and Restoring the Future* (1998); and *Maximize the Moment: God's Action Plan for Your Life* (1999).

14. Dates and statistics are drawn from T. D. Jakes's ministry homepage http://www.tdjakes.net/ministry/index.html.

15. Tamelyn Tucker-Worgs points out that two characteristics of megachurches are their emphasis upon neo-Pentecostalism *and* their emphasis upon community development. Many black megachurches develop CDCs (community development corporations), separate, tax-exempt organizations which work to secure community development. Among the programs that some create are single-family housing facilities, large apartment complexes, homeless shelters, drug abuse centers, women's shelters, social service provision, health clinics, job training opportunities, and commercial development. "Get on Board, Little Children," 189–190.

16. See Bellah et al., *Habits of the Heart*.

17. Ibid., 37. For quote see Alexis de Tocqueville, *Democracy in America*, trans. George Lawrence, ed. J. P. Mayer (New York: Doubleday Anchor Books, 1969), 506.

18. Frederick K. C. Price, *Name It and Claim It: The Power of Positive Confession* (Tulsa: Harrison House, 1992), 7–9. For further discussion of the New Thought Movement in American history, see Donald Meyer's *The Positive Thinkers: Popular Religious Psychology from Mary Baker Eddy to Norman Vincent Peale and Ronald Reagan* (Middletown, Conn.: Wesleyan University Press, 1988 [1965]). See also Norman Vincent Peale, *The Power of Positive Thinking* (New York: Prentice-Hall, 1952) and Napoleon Hill, *Think and Grow Rich* (Greenwich, Conn.: Fawcett, 1961).

19. Susan Harding, *The Book of Jerry Falwell: Fundamentalist Language and Politics* (Princeton: Princeton University Press, 2000), 10.

20. Ibid.

21. Schultze, *Televangelism,* 132.

22. Jim Bakker with Ken Abraham, *Prosperity and the Coming Apocalypse: Avoiding the Dangers of Materialistic Christianity in the End Times* (Nashville: Thomas Nelson, 1998), 23.

23. Ibid., 32.

24. Hank Hanegraaff, *Christianity in Crisis* (Eugene: Harvest House, 1997), 186. Hanegraaff cites Robert Tilton's "Success-N-Life" television program (December 27, 1990).

25. Bakker, *Prosperity and the Coming Apocalypse,* 27.

26. Price, *Name It and Claim It,* 138.

27. Cornel West, *Prophecy Deliverance! An Afro-American Revolutionary Christianity* (Philadelphia: Westminster, 1982), 143.

28. Burkett, "The Baptist Church in the Years of Crisis," 138.

29. See Avery F. Gordon and Christopher Newfield, eds., *Mapping Multiculturalism* (Minneapolis: University of Minnesota Press, 1996).

30. Ibid., 3.

31. The MEDC complex is "an independent 501 (c)(3) founded by The Potter's House of Dallas, Inc. [the church Jakes pastors] for the purpose of economic and social development in the Southern Sector of Dallas." In 2000 the MEDC was developing a "231.9-acre learning campus that will include a youth/community center, preschool through high school complex, performing arts center, independent living retirement community, women's care center, executive retreat, business incubator, and community auditorium." Http://www.tdjakes.net/ministry/Project2000/index.html.

32. See Steve Rabey, "Seedbed for Revival? Stand in the Gap in Washington, D.C., Aims to Spark National Spiritual Awakening," *Christianity Today*, September 1, 1997, 90.

33. Baker, *From Savage to Negro,* 221.

34. Ibid., 227.

35. According to Price, Hagin gave this sermon to his 5,000-member Rhema Bible Church in Tulsa. While Hagin has apologized *if* his words were offensive to some, he has not recanted his statement. See Rhonda B. Graham, "Holy War: Rev. Fred Price Is Fighting the Church over Racism," *Emerge,* January 1999, 44–51, 46.

36. I followed several of Price's sermons, and these are just a few of the topics he covered during the period. Because some of his parishioners are white, he was careful to point out to them that he was not stating that all whites are racist. Rather, he explained, we are living under a system that is inherently racist. One of his main illustrations of that point was the story he told of how city employees were unwilling to expeditiously carry out his request for water and sewer lines for the church and the price gouging that took place during the process. He believes that the problems occurred because he was trying to erect such an enormous church, a size some thought too elaborate for a black preacher.

37. Graham, "Holy War," 51.

38. Wahneema Lubiano, ed., *The House That Race Built: Black Americans, U.S. Terrain* (New York: Pantheon Books, 1997), viii.

REVIVAL: "LOOSED WOMEN"

1. See St. Luke 13: 11–12 (New Revised Standard Version). "And just then there appeared a woman with a spirit that had crippled her for eighteen years. She was bent over and was quite unable to stand up straight. When Jesus saw her, he called her over and said, 'Woman, you are set free from your ailment.'" The New King James version reads "loosed from your infirmity."

2. Excerpts are taken from Jakes's 1993 "Woman Thou Art Loosed" message which helped set the precedent for the message I heard in Atlanta. In 2000 the conference centered around the theme of economic empowerment and liberation from debt and financial "bondage." It included a special preregistration economic empowerment luncheon with special guest Maya Angelou.

FRIDAY

1. For further discussion of the evangelical thrust of the black church, see Charles E. Booth, *Bridging the Breach: Evangelical Thought and Liberation in the African-American Preaching Tradition* (Chicago: Urban Ministries, 2000).

2. bell hooks, *Sisters of the Yam: Black Women and Self-Recovery* (Boston: South End Press, 1993), 14.

3. See Calvin O. Pressley and Walter V. Collier, "Financing Historic Black Churches," in *Financing American Religion*, edited by Mark Chaves and Sharon L. Miller (Walnut Creek, Calif.: AltaMira Press, 1999), 24. For a discussion of the need for more research on financial giving in the black church see Baer and Singer, *African American Religion*, 85.

4. Lincoln and Mamiya, *Black Church in African American Experience*, 241.

5. Dean R. Hoge et al., *Money Matters: Personal Giving in American Churches* (Louisville: Westminster John Knox Press, 1996), 13.

6. This concept comes from the Old Testament and is often espoused by preachers and lay workers when attempting to explain or encourage tithing. "Will anyone rob God? Yet you are robbing me! But you say, 'How are we robbing you?' In your tithes and offerings! You are cursed with a curse, for you are robbing me—the whole nation of you! Bring the full tithe into the storehouse, so that there may be food in my house, and thus put me to the test, says the Lord of hosts; see if I will not open the windows of heaven for you and pour down for you an overflowing blessing." Malachi 3: 8–10, New Revised Standard Version.

7. Hoge et al., *Money Matters*.

8. Pressley and Collier, "Financing Historic Black Churches," 26.

9. Ibid.

10. See Robert Wuthnow, ed., *Rethinking Materialism: Perspectives on the Spiritual Dimension of Economic Behavior* (Grand Rapids, Mich.: William B. Eerdmans, 1995), 15.

11. Roanoke Rapids has one shopping mall and a downtown that has been struggling to survive since the mall was developed. The mall has two department stores, Belks and J. C. Penney's; between them are approximately thirty other stores including Roses, a K-Mart competitor.

12. For further discussion of the black church's historical contributions as an economic institution see Du Bois, *The Negro Church*; Mays and Nicholson, *The Negro's Church*; Frazier, *The Negro Church in America*; Carter G. Woodson, *The History of the Negro Church* (Washington: Associated Publishers, 1972); Lincoln, *The Black Church since Frazier*; and Leroy Fitts, *A History of Black Baptists* (Nashville: Broadman Press, 1985). These works, while not exclusively focusing on the monetary value of these institutions, give insight into the types of financial investments that black churches have made historically. There is great need for systematic study into the influence of the black church in creating a vibrant black middle class and establishing greater economic prosperity for African American communities in general.

13. Hoge et al., *Money Matters*, 4.

SATURDAY

1. See Michael Eric Dyson, "When You Divide Body and Soul, Problems Multiply: The Black Church and Sex," in *Traps: African American Men on Gender and Sexuality*, ed. Rudolph P. Byrd and Beverly Guy-Sheftall (Indianapolis: Indiana University Press, 2001).

2. Ibid., 317.

3. Patricia Hill Collins argues that "In the United States, because race has been constructed as a biological category that is rooted in the body, controlling Black sexuality has long been important in preserving racial boundaries. U.S. notions of racial purity, such as the rule claiming that one drop of Black 'blood' determines racial identity, required strict control over the sexuality and subsequent fertility of Black women, White women, and Black men." Collins, *Black Feminist Thought*, 133. See also Angela Davis, *Women, Race, and Class* (New York: Random House, 1981).

4. Davis, *Women, Race, and Class*, 7.

5. See Wade-Gayles, *No Crystal Stair*, 3.

6. For further exploration of these stereotypes and how they operate in black women's lives see ibid.; Collins, *Black Feminist Thought*; Gail E. Wyatt, *Stolen Women: Reclaiming Our Sexuality, Taking Back Our Lives* (New York: John Wiley and Sons, 1997); James, *Shadowboxing*; and Yanick St. Jean and Joe R. Feagin, *Double Burden: Black Women and Everyday Racism* (New York: M. E. Sharpe, 1998).

7. See Kimberle Crenshaw, "Demarginalizing the Intersection of Race and Sex: A Black Feminist Critique of Antidiscrimination Doctrine, Feminist Theory, and Antiracist Politics," *The University of Chicago Legal Forum* 139 (1989): 139–167.

8. See Wyatt, *Stolen Women*, 81.

9. Her allusion here is to Proverbs 26. She is an avid reader of scripture and has adopted it as the means through which she evaluates her life.

10. Griffith, *God's Daughters*, 135.

11. In one incident, Yvette expressed the feeling that she had been "brainwashed" by preachers before coming to the point where she could read and understand scripture for herself. "I was brainwashed to the thing about women ministers. And it's just recently that I've come to accept going to different Bible classes and listening to certain women speaking and showing me different places in the Bible where women did minister." She recalled a time before coming to this understanding where she and a friend attended a church out of town for revival. When they learned that the preacher for the evening was a woman, they left. "We found out a woman was preaching. After they took up the offering, we walked on out and left." The scripture she once thought refused women the pulpit is now the same scripture she uses to affirm their place in ministry.

12. Many Baptist denominations and more conservative Protestant denominations hold rigid guidelines as to when someone can remarry. Under most circumstances remarriage after a divorce is seen as adultery if the divorce was not decreed on acceptable terms. For a discussion of these debates see Craig S. Keener, *Paul, Women and Wives: Marriage and Women's Ministry in the Letters of Paul* (Peabody, Mass.: Hendrickson, 1992).

13. See Susan Newman, *Oh God! A Black Woman's Guide to Sex and Spirituality* (New York: Ballantine Books, 2002), 32.

14. Ibid., 35.

15. Ibid. Newman gives voice to a number of concerns facing single black Christian women like Ms. Sylvia and Ms. Cleveland. She describes the struggle between the desire to be sexually active and the desire to please God. Raising historical questions regarding the cultural context in which the Bible was written and the social context in which we live, Newman suggests that "fornication" is a term used to describe biblical prostitution, not contemporary monogamous relationships between consenting adults. Her challenge to traditional doctrine makes room for Ms. Sylvia's and Ms. Cleveland's experiences, but remains controversial in most Protestant churches.

16. This silencing of black women who have survived rape perpetuated by black men is a topic that black women scholars in particular have noted. For greater discussion see Crenshaw, "Demarginalizing," and Charlotte Pierce-Baker, *Surviving the Silence: Black Women's Stories of Rape* (New York: W. W. Norton, 1998). The Anita Hill–Clarence Thomas hearings set off an even greater public discussion about the tensions between race and gender loyalties within the black community. Karla Holloway's *Codes of Conduct* and Toni Morrison's *Race-ing Justice* both address the expectations placed upon black women to remain "loyal" to the race even when they have been victimized and abused by black men. The silence beyond the rape, abuse, or harassment becomes the second form of victimization. See Karla Holloway, *Codes of Conduct: Race, Ethics, and the Color of Our Character* (New Brunswick: Rutgers University Press, 1995), and Toni Morrison, ed., *Race-ing Justice, En-gendering Power: Essays on Anita Hill, Clarence Thomas, and the Construction of Social Reality* (New York: Pantheon Books, 1992).

17. Holloway, *Codes of Conduct*, 41.

18. Ibid., 43.

19. Pierce-Baker, *Surviving the Silence*, 84.

20. See Frances E. Wood, "'Take My Yoke Upon You': The Role of the Church in the Oppression of African-American Women," in *A Troubling in My Soul: Womanist Perspectives of Evil and Suffering*, ed. Emilie M. Townes (Maryknoll, N.Y.: Orbis Books, 1993), 43.

21. See Kelly Brown Douglas, *Sexuality and the Black Church: A Womanist Perspective* (Maryknoll, N.Y.: Orbis Books, 1999).

22. Jenell Williams and Mindy Michels, "Finding Common Ground: Anti Gay Violence and Public Discourse," in *The Graduate Review*, ed. Julianna Brege (Washington, D.C.: American University Graduate Student Association, 1996).

23. Douglas, *Sexuality and the Black Church*, 88.

24. Collins, *Black Feminist Thought*, 128.

SECOND SUNDAY

1. See Renita Weems, *Listening for God: A Minister's Journey through Silence and Doubt* (New York: Simon and Schuster, 1999), 78.

2. See Barbara Diane Savage, "Biblical and Historical Imperatives: Toward

a History of Ideas about the Political Role of Black Churches," *African Americans and the Bible: Sacred Texts and Social Textures*, ed. Vincent Wimbush (New York: Continuum, 2000).

3. See Stephen L. Carter, *God's Name in Vain: The Wrongs and Rights of Religion in Politics* (New York: Basic Books, 2000), 50.

4. Ibid., 31.

BIBLIOGRAPHY

Abelman, Robert, and Stewart Hoover. *Religious Television: Controversies and Conclusions.* Norwood, N.J.: Ablex, 1990.

Andrews, William. *"Sisters of the Spirit": Three Black Women's Autobiographies of the Nineteenth Century.* Bloomington: Indiana University Press, 1986.

Baer, Hans A. "Black Mainstream Churches: Emancipatory or Accommodative Responses to Racism and Social Stratification in American Society?" *Review of Religious Research* 30 (1988): 162–176.

Baer, Hans A., and Yvonne Jones, eds. *African Americans in the South.* Athens: University of Georgia Press, 1992.

Baer, Hans A., and Merrill Singer. *African-American Religion in the Twentieth Century: Varieties of Protest and Accommodation.* Knoxville: University of Tennessee Press, 1992.

Baker, Lee D. *From Savage to Negro: Anthropology and the Construction of Race, 1896–1954.* Berkeley: University of California Press, 1998.

Baker-Fletcher, Karen. *A Singing Something: Womanist Reflections on Anna Julia Cooper.* New York: Crossroad, 1994.

Bakker, Jim, with Ken Abraham. *Prosperity and the Coming Apocalypse: Avoiding the Dangers of Materialistic Christianity in the End Times.* Nashville: Thomas Nelson, 1998.

Bartlett, Leslie, Thad Gulbrandsen, Marla Frederick, and Enrique Murrillo. "The Marketization of Education: Public Schools for Private Ends." *Anthropology and Education Quarterly* 33, no. 1 (2002): 1–25.

Beals, Melba Pattilo. *Warriors Don't Cry: A Searing Memoir of the Battle to Integrate Little Rock's Central High.* New York: Pocket Books, 1994.

Behar, Ruth, and Deborah A. Gordon, eds. *Women Writing Culture.* Berkeley: University of California Press, 1995.

Bell, Derrick A., Jr. "The Racial Imperative in American Law." In *The Age of Seg-*

regation: Race Relations in the South, 1890–1945, ed. Robert Haws. Jackson: University of Mississippi Press, 1978.

Bellah, Robert, Richard Madsen, William M. Sullivan, Ann Swidler, and Steven M. Tipton. *Habits of the Heart: Individualism and Commitment in American Life*. Berkeley: University of California Press, 1985. Reprint, 1996.

Bluestone, Barry, and Bennett Harrison. *The Deindustrialization of America: Plant Closings, Community Abandonment, and the Dismantling of Basic Industry*. New York: Basic Books, 1982.

Bookman, Ann, and Sandra Morgan, eds. *Women and the Politics of Empowerment*. Philadelphia: Temple University Press, 1988.

Booth, Charles E. *Bridging the Breach: Evangelical Thought and Liberation in the African-American Preaching Tradition*. Chicago: Urban Ministries, 2000.

Bourdieu, Pierre. *Outline of a Theory of Practice*, trans. R. Nice. Cambridge: Cambridge University Press, 1977.

Bridges, Flora Wilson. *Resurrection Song: African-American Spirituality*. Maryknoll, N.Y.: Orbis Books, 2001.

Brown, Elaine. *A Taste of Power: A Black Woman's Story*. New York: Pantheon Books, 1992.

Brown, Elsa Barkley. "Negotiating and Transforming the Public Sphere: African American Political Life in the Transition from Slavery to Freedom." *Public Culture* 7 (1994): 107–146.

Buckner, Dilla. "Spirituality, Sexuality, and Creativity: A Conversation with Margaret Walker-Alexander." In *My Soul Is a Witness: African American Women's Spirituality*, ed. Gloria Wade-Gayles. Boston: Beacon Press, 1995.

Bullard, Robert D. "The Politics of Pollution: Implications for the Black Community." *Phylon* 47 (March 1986): 71–78.

———, ed. *In Search of the New South: The Black Urban Experience in the 1970s and 1980s*. Tuscaloosa: University of Alabama Press, 1989.

Burdick, John. *Blessed Anastacia: Women, Race, and Popular Christianity in Brazil*. New York: Routledge, 1998.

Burkett, Randall K. "The Baptist Church in the Years of Crisis: J. C. Austin and Pilgrim Baptist Church, 1926–1950." In *African American Christianity: Essays in History*, ed. Paul E. Johnson. Berkeley: University of California Press, 1994.

Calhoun, Craig, ed. *Habermas and the Public Sphere*. Cambridge: MIT Press, 1992.

Cannon, Katie. *Black Womanist Ethics*. Atlanta: Scholars Press, 1988.

Carter, Stephen L. *God's Name in Vain: The Wrongs and Rights of Religion in Politics*. New York: Basic Books, 2000.

Cecelski, David S. *Along Freedom Road: Hyde County, North Carolina, and the Fate of Black Schools in the South*. Chapel Hill: University of North Carolina Press, 1994.

Chafe, William H. *Civilities and Civil Rights: Greensboro, North Carolina, and the Black Struggle for Freedom*. New York: Oxford University Press, 1980.

———. "Epilogue from Greensboro, NC: Race and the Possibilities of American Democracy." In *Democracy Betrayed*, ed. David S. Cecelski and Timothy B. Tyson. Chapel Hill: University of North Carolina Press, 1998.

Civil Rights Action Team. *Civil Rights at the United States Department of Agriculture.* Washington, D.C.: U.S. Department of Agriculture, 1997.

Clifford, James, and George J. Marcus, eds. *Writing Culture: The Poetics and Politics of Ethnography.* Berkeley: University of California Press, 1986.

Collier-Thomas, Bettye. *Daughters of Thunder: Black Women Preachers and Their Sermons, 1850–1979.* San Francisco: Jossey-Bass, 1998.

Collins, Patricia Hill. *Black Feminist Thought: Knowledge, Consciousness, and the Politics of Empowerment.* New York: Routledge, 1991. Reprint 2000.

Comaroff, John, and Jean Comaroff. *Of Revelation and Revolution: Christianity, Colonialism, and Consciousness in South Africa.* Chicago: University of Chicago Press, 1991.

Crawford, Vicki. "Beyond the Human Self: Grassroots Activists in the Mississippi Civil Rights Movement." In *Women in the Civil Rights Movement: Trailblazers and Torchbearers 1941–1965,* ed. Vicki L. Crawford, Jacqueline Anne Rouse, and Barbara Woods. Indianapolis: Indiana University Press, 1993.

Crenshaw, Kimberle. "Demarginalizing the Intersection of Race and Sex: A Black Feminist Critique of Antidiscrimination Doctrine, Feminist Theory, and Antiracist Politics." *The University of Chicago Legal Forum* 139 (1989): 139–167.

Davis, Allison, Burleigh B. Gardner, and Mary R. Gardner. *Deep South: A Social Anthropological Study of Caste and Class.* Chicago: University of Chicago Press, 1941.

Davis, Angela. *Angela Davis: An Autobiography.* New York: International Publishers, 1974.

———. *Women, Race, and Class.* New York: Random House, 1981.

Dawson, Michael C. "A Black Counterpublic?: Economic Earthquakes, Racial Agenda(s), and Black Politics." *Public Culture* 7 (1994): 195–223.

Dirks, Nicholas B., Geoff Eley, and Sherry B. Ortner, eds. *Culture/Power/History: A Reader in Contemporary Social Theory.* Princeton: Princeton University Press, 1994.

Dodson, Jualyne E., and Cheryl Townsend Gilkes. "Something Within: Social Change and Collective Endurance in the Sacred World of Black Christian Women." In *Women and Religion in America, Volume 3: 1900–1968,* ed. Rosemary Reuther and R. Keller. New York: Harper and Row, 1987.

Dollard, John. *Caste and Class in a Southern Town.* New Haven: Yale University Press, 1937.

Douglas, Kelly Brown. *Sexuality and the Black Church: A Womanist Perspective.* Maryknoll, N.Y.: Orbis Books, 1999.

Douglass, Frederick. *Narrative of the Life of Frederick Douglass: An American Slave Written By Himself.* 1845. New York: Dolphin Books, 1963.

Drake, St. Clair, and Horace R. Cayton. *Black Metropolis: A Study of Negro Life in a Northern City.* Chicago: University of Chicago Press, 1945. Revised 1993.

Du Bois, W. E. B. *The Souls of Black Folk.* New York: Vintage Books, 1990 [1903].

———, ed. *The Negro Church.* Atlanta: Atlanta University Press, 1903.

Dudley, Kathryn Marie. *The End of the Line: Lost Jobs, New Lives in Postindustrial America.* Chicago: University of Chicago Press, 1994.

Dyson, Marcia L. "When Preachers Prey." *Essence* (May 1998): 120–122.

Dyson, Michael Eric. "When You Divide Body and Soul, Problems Multiply: The Black Church and Sex." In *Traps: African American Men on Gender and Sexuality,* ed. Rudolph P. Byrd and Beverly Guy-Sheftall. Indianapolis: Indiana University Press, 2001.

Edwards, Bob, and Anthony E. Ladd. "Environmental Justice, Swine Production, and Farm Loss in North Carolina." Paper presented at the Second Annual Black Land Loss Summit, Halifax, N.C., February 1998.

Eller, Cynthia. *Living in the Lap of the Goddess: The Feminist Spirituality Movement in America.* New York: Crossroad, 1993.

Fitts, Leroy. *A History of Black Baptists.* Nashville: Broadman Press, 1985.

Flowers, Linda. *Throwed Away: Failures of Progress in Eastern North Carolina.* Knoxville: University of Tennessee Press, 1990.

Fox, Richard, and Orin Starn, eds. *Between Resistance and Revolution: Cultural Politics and Social Protest.* New Brunswick: Rutgers University Press, 1997.

Frankenberg, Ruth. *White Women, Race Matters: The Social Construction of Whiteness.* Minneapolis: University of Minnesota Press, 1993.

Frankl, Razelle. *Televangelism: The Making of Popular Religion.* Carbondale: Southern Illinois University Press, 1987.

Franklin, Raymond S., and Solomon Resnik. *The Political Economy of Racism.* New York: Holt, Rinehart, and Winston, 1973.

Frazier, E. Franklin. *The Negro Church in America.* New York: Schocken, 1964. Reprint 1974.

Fulop, Timothy E., and Albert J. Raboteau, eds. *African-American Religion: Interpretive Essays in History and Culture.* New York: Routledge, 1997.

Gates, Henry Louis, ed. *Spiritual Narratives.* New York: Oxford University Press, 1988.

Genovese, Eugene. *Roll, Jordan, Roll: The World the Slaves Made.* New York: Vintage Books, 1972.

Giddens, Anthony. *Central Problems in Social Theory: Action, Structure, and Contradiction in Social Analysis.* Berkeley: University of California Press, 1979.

Giddings, Paula. *When and Where I Enter: The Impact of Black Women on Race and Sex in America.* New York: William Morrow, 1984.

Gilkes, Cheryl Townsend. "'Togetherness and in Harness': Women's Traditions in the Sanctified Church." In *Black Women in America,* ed. Micheline R. Malson, Elisabeth Mudimbe-Boyi, Jean F. O'Barr, and Mary Wyer. Chicago: University of Chicago Press, 1988.

———. *If It Wasn't for the Women.* Maryknoll, N.Y.: Orbis Books, 2001.

Gill, Lesley. *Precarious Dependencies: Gender, Class, and Domestic Service in Bolivia.* New York: Columbia University Press, 1994.

Gilroy, Paul. *The Black Atlantic: Modernity and Double Consciousness.* Cambridge: Harvard University Press, 1993.

———. *Small Acts: Thoughts on the Politics of Black Cultures.* New York: Serpent's Tail, 1993.

Ginsburg, Faye, and Anna Lowenhaupt Tsing, eds. *Uncertain Terms: Negotiating Gender in American Culture.* Boston: Beacon Press, 1990.

Goldfield, David R. *Black, White, and Southern: Race Relations and Southern Culture, 1940 to the Present.* Baton Rouge: Louisiana State University Press, 1990.

Gordon, Avery F., and Christopher Newfield, eds. *Mapping Multiculturalism.* Minneapolis: University of Minnesota Press, 1996.

Graham, Rhonda B. "Holy War: Rev. Fred Price Is Fighting the Church over Racism." *Emerge.* January 1999: 44–51.

Grant, Jacquelyn. "Black Women and the Church." In *But Some of Us Are Brave,* ed. Gloria T. Hull, Patricia Bell Scott, and Barbara Smith. Old Westbury, N.Y.: Feminist Press, 1982.

Gregory, Steven. "Race, Identity, and Political Activism: The Shifting Contours of the African American Public Sphere." *Public Culture* 7 (1994): 147–164.

Gregory, Steven, and Roger Sanjek, eds. *Race.* New Brunswick: Rutgers University Press, 1996.

Griffith, R. Marie. *God's Daughters: Evangelical Women and the Power of Submission.* Berkeley: University of California Press, 1997.

Guinier, Lani. *Tyranny of the Majority: Fundamental Fairness in Representative Democracy.* New York: Free Press, 1994.

Guy-Sheftall, Beverly, ed. *Words of Fire: An Anthology of African American Feminist Thought.* New York: New Press, 1995.

———, and Jo Moore Stewart. *Spelman: A Centennial Celebration.* Atlanta: Spelman College, 1981.

Habermas, Jürgen. *The Structural Transformation of the Public Sphere: An Inquiry into a Category of Bourgeois Society,* trans. Thomas Burger with the assistance of Frederick Lawrence. Cambridge: MIT Press, 1989.

Hanegraaff, Hank. *Christianity in Crisis.* Eugene: Harvest House, 1997.

Harding, Susan. *The Book of Jerry Falwell: Fundamentalist Language and Politics.* Princeton: Princeton University Press, 2000.

Harrison, Faye V. "The Persistant Power of 'Race' in the Cultural and Political Economy of Racism." *Annual Review of Anthropology* 24 (1995): 47–74.

Hartigan, John, Jr. "Establishing the Fact of Whiteness." *American Anthropologist* 99:3 (September 1997): 495–505.

Harvey, David. "Class Relations, Social Justice, and the Politics of Difference." In *Place and the Politics of Identity,* ed. Michael Keith and Steve Pile. New York: Routledge, 1993.

Hernandez, Graciela. "Multiple Subjectivities and Strategic Positionality: Zora Neale Hurston's Experimental Ethnographies." In *Women Writing Culture,* ed. Ruth Behar and Deborah A. Gordon. Berkeley: University of California Press, 1995.

Herskovits, Melville. *The Myth of the Negro Past.* Boston: Beacon Press, 1941.

Higginbotham, Evelyn Brooks. "Beyond the Sound of Silence: Afro-American Women in History." *Gender and History* 1 (1989): 50–67.

———. *Righteous Discontent: The Women's Movement in the Black Baptist Church, 1880–1920.* Cambridge: Harvard University Press, 1993.

Hill, Napoleon. *Think and Grow Rich.* Greenwich, Conn.: Fawcett, 1961.

Hoge, Dean R., Charles E. Zech, Patrick H. McNamara, and Michael J. Donahue. *Money Matters: Personal Giving in American Churches.* Louisville: Westminster John Knox Press, 1996.

Holloway, Karla F. C. *Codes of Conduct: Race, Ethics, and the Color of Our Character.* New Brunswick: Rutgers University Press, 1995.

hooks, bell. *Sisters of the Yam: Black Women and Self-Recovery.* Boston: South End Press,1993.

———. *Yearning: Race, Gender, and Cultural Politics.* Boston: South End Press, 1990.

Hurston, Zora Neale. *Mules and Men.* New York: Harper and Row, 1990.

———. *The Sanctified Church.* Berkeley: Turtle Island, 1981.

Irons, Jenny. "The Shaping of Activist Recruitment and Participation: A Study of Women in the Mississippi Civil Rights Movement." *Gender and Society* 12 (December 1998): 692–709.

Jackson, J. H. *A History of Christian Activism: The History of the National Baptist Convention, USA, Inc.* Nashville: Townsend, 1980.

Jakes, T. D. *Lay Aside the Weight: Take Control of It before It Takes Control of You.* Tulsa: Albury, 1997.

———. *Loose That Man and Let Him Go!* Tulsa: Albury, 1995.

———. *Maximize the Moment: God's Action Plan for Your Life.* New York: G. P. Putnam's Sons, 1999.

———. *Woman, Thou Art Loosed!: Devotions for Healing the Past and Restoring the Future.* Tulsa: Albury, 1998.

James, Joy. *Shadowboxing: Representations of Black Feminist Politics.* New York: St. Martin's Press, 1999.

Jennings, Willie James. "Wrestling with a Wounded Word: Reading the Disjointed Lines of African American Spirituality." In *Spirituality and Social Embodiment,* ed. L. Gregory Jones and James J. Buckley. Oxford: Blackwell, 1997.

Johnson, Daniel M., and Rex R. Campbell. *Black Migration in America: A Social Demographic History.* Durham: Duke University Press, 1981.

Joyner, Charles. "Believer I Know": The Emergence of African-American Christianity." In *African American Christianity: Essays in History,* ed. Paul E. Johnson. Berkeley: University of California Press, 1994.

Keener, Craig S. *Paul, Women, and Wives: Marriage and Women's Ministry in the Letters of Paul.* Peabody, Mass.: Hendrickson, 1992.

———. *The IVP Bible Background Commentary: New Testament.* Downers Grove, Ill.: InterVarsity Press, 1993.

Kelley, Robin D. G. *Yo' Mama's Disfunktional! Fighting the Culture Wars in Urban America.* Boston: Beacon, 1997.

King, Deborah K. "Multiple Jeopardy, Multiple Consciousness: The Context of a Black Feminist Ideology." In *Words of Fire: An Anthology of African-American Feminist Thought,* ed. Beverly Guy-Sheftall. New York: New Press, 1995.

Klass, Morton, and Maxine Weisgrau, eds. *Across the Boundaries of Belief: Contemporary Issues in the Anthropology of Religion.* Boulder: Westview Press, 1999.

Kostarelos, Frances. *Feeling the Spirit: Faith and Hope in an Evangelical Black Storefront Church*. Columbia: University of South Carolina Press, 1995.

Lash, Scott, and John Urry. *The Ends of Organized Capitalism*. Cambridge, U.K.: Polity Press, 1987.

Levine, Lawrence. *Black Culture and Black Consciousness*. New York: Oxford University Press, 1977.

Lichterman, Paul. *The Search for Political Community: American Activists Reinventing Commitment*. New York: Cambridge University Press, 1996.

Lincoln, C. Eric. *The Black Church since Frazier*. New York: Schocken Books, 1974.

———. *Race, Religion, and the Continuing American Dilemma*. New York: Hill and Wang, 1984.

———, and Lawrence H. Mamiya. *The Black Church in the African American Experience*. Durham: Duke University Press, 1990.

Lubiano, Wahneema, ed. *The House That Race Built: Black Americans, U.S. Terrain*. New York: Pantheon Books, 1997.

Luebke, Paul. *Tar Heel Politics: Myths and Realities*. Chapel Hill: University of North Carolina Press, 1990.

Luhrmann, Tanya. "God as the Ground of Empathy." *Anthropology Today* 16:1 (February 2000): 19–20.

Mainardi, Pat. *The Politics of Housework*. London: Allison and Busby, 1980: 17–22.

Marable, Manning. *How Capitalism Underdeveloped Black America: Problems in Race, Political Economy, and Society*. Cambridge: South End Press, 1983. Reprint 2000.

Martin, Clarice. "Biblical Theodicy and Black Women's Spiritual Autobiography." In *A Troubling in My Soul: Womanist Perspectives on Evil and Suffering*, ed. Emilie Townes. New York: Orbis Press, 1993.

Mathews, Holly F., ed. *Women in the South: An Anthropological Perspective*. Athens: University of Georgia Press, 1989.

Mays, Benjamin Elijah, and Joseph William Nicholson. *The Negro's Church*. New York: Institute of Social and Religious Research, 1933.

McCarthy Brown, Karen. *Mama Lola: A Vodou Priestess in Brooklyn*. Berkeley: University of California Press, 1991.

McClaurin, Irma, ed. *Black Feminist Anthropology: Theory, Politics, Praxis, and Poetics*. New Brunswick: Rutgers University Press, 2001.

McKenzie, Vashti. *Not without a Struggle: Leadership Development for African American Women in Ministry*. Cleveland: United Church Press, 1996.

Meyer, Donald. *The Positive Thinkers: Popular Religious Psychology from Mary Baker Eddy to Norman Vincent Peale and Ronald Reagan*. Middletown: Wesleyan University Press, 1988 [1965].

Meyer, Joyce. *Beauty for Ashes: Receiving Emotional Healing*. Tulsa: Harrison House, 1994.

_____. *Eat and Stay Thin: Simple, Spiritual, Satisfying Weight Control*. Tulsa: Harrison House, 1999.

_____. *How to Succeed at Being Yourself: Finding the Confidence to Fulfill Your Destiny*. Tulsa: Harrison House, 1999.

_____. *If Not for the Grace of God: Learning to Live Independent of Frustrations and Struggles*. Tulsa: Harrison House, 1995.

Mintz, Sidney. *The Birth of African American Culture: An Anthropological Perspective*. Boston: Beacon Press, 1976.

Mitchell, Henry, and Ella Mitchell. "Black Spirituality: The Values in That Ol' Time Religion." *The Journal of the Interdenominational Theological Center* 17 (Fall 1989/Spring1990): 98–109.

Moody, Anne. *Coming of Age in Mississippi: The Classic Autobiography of Growing Up Poor and Black in the Rural South*. New York: Laurel Books, 1976.

Morris, Aldon D. *The Origins of the Civil Rights Movement: Black Communities Organizing for Change*. New York: Free Press, 1984.

Morris, Brian. *Anthropological Studies of Religion*. Cambridge: Cambridge University Press, 1987.

Morrison, Toni, ed. *Race-ing Justice, En-gendering Power: Essays on Anita Hill, Clarence Thomas, and the Construction of Social Reality*. New York: Pantheon Books, 1992.

Mukhopadhyay, Carol C., and Yolanda T. Moses. "Reestablishing 'Race' in Anthropological Discourse." *American Anthropologist* 99:3 (1997): 517–533.

Murray, Pauli. *Proud Shoes: The Story of an American Family*. New York: Harper, 1956.

Naples, Nancy. "Activist Mothering: Cross-generational Continuity in the Community Work of Women from Low-income Neighborhoods." *Gender and Society* 6:3 (1992): 441–463.

Newman, Susan. *Oh God! A Black Woman's Guide to Sex and Spirituality*. New York: Ballantine Books, 2002.

Olson, Richard H., and Thomas A. Lyson, eds. *Under the Blade: The Conversion of Agricultural Landscapes*. Boulder: Westview Press, 1999.

Ortner, Sherry B. "Theory in Anthropology since the Sixties." *Society for Comparative Study of Society and History* 26:1 (1984): 126–166.

Paris, Peter. *The Social Teaching of the Black Churches*. Philadelphia: Fortress Press, 1985.

_____. *The Spirituality of African Peoples*. Minneapolis: Fortress Press, 1995.

Payne, Charles. "Men Led, but Women Organized: Movement Participation of Women in the Mississippi Delta." In *Women in the Civil Rights Movement: Trailblazers and Torchbearers 1941–1965*, ed. Vicki L. Crawford, Jacqueline Anne Rouse, and Barbara Woods. Indianapolis: Indiana University Press, 1993.

Peale, Norman Vincent. *The Power of Positive Thinking*. New York: Prentice-Hall, 1952.

Pierce-Baker, Charlotte. *Surviving the Silence: Black Women's Stories of Rape*. New York: W. W. Norton, 1998.

Powdermaker, Hortense. *After Freedom: A Cultural Study in the Deep South*. NewYork: Atheneum, 1968.

Pressley, Calvin O., and Walter V. Collier. "Financing Historic Black Churches." In *Financing American Religion*, ed. Mark Chaves and Sharon L. Miller. Walnut Creek, Calif.: AltaMira Press, 1999.

Price, Frederick K. C. *Name It and Claim It: The Power of Positive Confession.* Tulsa: Harrison House, 1992.

"Quorum Busters." *Governing: The Magazine of States and Localities.* November 1997, 32–33.

Rabey, Steve. "Seedbed for Revival? Stand in the Gap in Washington, D.C., Aims to Spark National Spiritual Awakening." *Christianity Today,* September 1, 1997.

Raboteau, Albert. *Slave Religion: The "Invisible Institution" in the Antebellum South.* New York: Oxford University Press, 1978.

Riggs, Marcia, ed. *Can I Get a Witness? Prophetic Religious Voices of African American Women: An Anthology.* Maryknoll, N.Y.: Orbis Books, 1997.

Robinson, Robert B., ed. *Roanoke Rapids: The First Hundred Years, 1897–1997.* Lawrenceville, N.J.: Brunswick, 1997.

Sahlins, Marshall. *Islands of History.* Chicago: University of Chicago Press, 1985.

Sanders, Cheryl. *Empowerment Ethics for a Liberated People.* Minneapolis: Fortress Press, 1995.

Savage, Barbara Diane. "Biblical and Historical Imperatives: Toward a History of Ideas about the Political Role of Black Churches." In *African Americans and the Bible: Sacred Texts and Social Textures,* ed. Vincent Wimbush. New York: Continuum, 2000.

Schor, Julie. *The Overspent American.* New York: Basic Books, 1998.

Schulman, Bruce J. *From Cotton Belt to Sunbelt: Federal Policy, Economic Development, and the Transformation of the South, 1938–1980.* Durham: Duke University Press, 1994.

Schultze, Quentin. *Televangelism and American Culture: The Business of Popular Religion.* Grand Rapids, Mich.: Baker Book House, 1991.

Scott, James. *Weapons of the Weak.* New Haven: Yale University Press, 1985.

Sernett, Milton C. *Black Religion and American Evangelicalism.* Metuchen, N.J.: Scarecrow, 1975.

Shakur, Assata. *Assata: An Autobiography.* Westport, Conn.: L. Hill, 1987.

Smedley, Audrey. *Race in North America: Origin and Evolution of a Worldview.* Boulder: Westview Press, 1993.

Smith, Theophus. "The Spirituality of Afro-American Traditions." In *Christian Spirituality: Post-Reformation and Modern,* ed. Louis Dupre and Don E. Saliers. New York: Crossroads, 1989.

Sobel, Mechal. *Trabelin' On: The Slave Journey to an Afro-Baptist Faith.* Princeton: Princeton University Press, 1979. Reprint 1988.

St. Jean, Yanick, and Joe R. Feagin. *Double Burden: Black Women and Everyday Racism.* New York: M. E. Sharpe, 1998.

Stack, Carol. *Call to Home: African Americans Reclaim the Rural South.* New York: Basic Books, 1996.

Starn, Orin, and Richard G. Fox. *Between Resistance and Revolution: Cultural Politics and Social Protest.* New Brunswick: Rutgers University Press, 1997.

Stull, David D., Michael J. Broadway, and Ken C. Erickson. "The Price of a Good Steak: Beef Packing and Its Consequences for Garden City, Kansas." In

Structuring Diversity: Ethnographic Perspectives on the New Immigration,
ed. Louise Lamphere. Chicago: University of Chicago Press, 1992.

Tocqueville, Alexis de. *Democracy in America,* trans. George Lawrence, ed. J. P.
Mayer. New York: Doubleday Anchor Books, 1969.

Townes, Emilie M. *Womanist Justice, Womanist Hope.* Atlanta: Scholars Press,
1993.

Tucker-Worgs, Tamelyn. "Get on Board, Little Children, There's Room for Many
More: The Black Megachurch Phenomenon." *Journal of the Interdenominational Theological Center* 29: 1 and 2 (Fall 2001/Spring 2002): 177–203.

Voskuil, Dennis N. "The Power of the Air: Evangelicals and the Rise of Religious
Broadcasting." In *American Evangelicals and the Mass Media,* ed. Quentin
Schultze. Grand Rapids, Mich.: Zondervan, 1990.

Wade-Gayles, Gloria, ed. *My Soul Is a Witness: African American Women's Spirituality.* Boston: Beacon Press, 1995.

———. *No Crystal Stair: Visions of Race and Gender in Black Women's Fiction.*
Cleveland: Pilgrim Press, 1997.

Washington, Joseph J., Jr. *Black Religion: The Negro and Christianity in the
United States.* Boston: Beacon Press, 1960.

Weems, Renita. *Listening for God: A Minister's Journey through Silence and
Doubt.* New York: Simon and Schuster, 1999.

Weisenfeld, Judith. *African American Women and Christian Activism: New
York's Black YWCA, 1905–1945.* Cambridge: Harvard University Press,
1997.

———, and Richard Newman, eds. *This Far by Faith: Readings in African American Women's Religious Biography.* New York: Routledge, 1996.

West, Cornel. *Prophecy Deliverance! An Afro-American Revolutionary Christianity.* Philadelphia: Westminister, 1982.

———. *Race Matters.* Boston: Beacon Press, 1993.

White, Deborah Gray. *Ar'n't I a Woman? Female Slaves in the Plantation South.*
New York: W. W. Norton, 1985.

White, Mimi. *Tele-Advising: Therapeutic Discourse in American Television.*
Chapel Hill: University of North Carolina Press, 1992.

White, O. Kendall, and Daryl White, eds. *Religion in the Contemporary South.*
Athens: University of Georgia Press, 1995.

Williams, Delores. "A Womanist Perspective on Sin." In *A Troublin' in My Soul:
Womanist Perspectives on Evil and Suffering,* ed. Emilie Townes. New York:
Orbis Press, 1993.

———. "The Color of Feminism." In *Feminist Theological Ethics,* ed. Lois K.
Daly. Louisville: Westminster John Knox Press, 1994.

Williams, Jenell, and Mindy Michels. "Finding Common Ground: Anti Gay Violence and Public Discourse." In *The Graduate Review,* ed. Julianna Brege.
Washington, D.C.: American University Graduate Student Association, 1996.

Williams, Melvin D. *Community in a Black Pentecostal Church: An Anthropological Study.* Prospect Heights, Ill.: Waveland Press, 1974.

Wilmore, Gayraud S. *Black Religion and Black Radicalism: An Interpretation of
the Religious History of Afro-American People.* New York: Doubleday, 1973.

Winant, Howard. *Racial Conditions: Politics, Theory, Comparisons*. Minneapolis: University of Minnesota Press, 1994.

Wing, Steve, Dana Cole, and Gary Grant. "Environmental Injustice in North Carolina's Hog Industry." *Environmental Health Perspectives* 108: 3 (March 2000): 225–231.

Wood, Frances E. "'Take My Yoke Upon You': The Role of the Church in the Oppression of African-American Women." In *A Troubling in My Soul: Womanist Perspectives of Evil and Suffering*, ed. Emilie M. Townes. Maryknoll, N.Y.: Orbis Books, 1993.

Wood, Phillip J. *Southern Capitalism: The Political Economy of North Carolina, 1880–1990*. Durham: Duke University Press, 1986.

Woodson, Carter G. *The History of the Negro Church*. Washington, D.C.: Associated Publishers, 1972.

Wuthnow, Robert. *Christianity and Civil Society: The Contemporary Debate*. Valley Forge, Pa.: Trinity Press International, 1996.

———. *Sharing the Journey: Support Groups and America's New Quest for Community*. New York: Free Press, 1994.

———, ed. *Rethinking Materialism: Perspectives on the Spiritual Dimension of Economic Behavior*. Grand Rapids, Mich.: Eerdmans, 1995.

Wyatt, Gail E. *Stolen Women: Reclaiming Our Sexuality, Taking Back Our Lives*. New York: John Wiley and Sons, 1997.

Index

Abernathy, Ralph, 88
Abolitionist Movement, 95
abstinence, 28, 186, 190–91, 192, 194–96, 200–201
abuse/rape, 114, 187, 188, 198, 209, 218, 240n.16
accommodation vs. resistance. *See* resistance vs. accommodation
activism: American social, 95; of black churches, 6, 8–9, 17, 27, 83, 85–88, 139–40, 212, 230n.5; Christian, 95; decline vs. shift in, 96–97; and gratitude/empathy, 64–65, 71–72, 80–81, 120; by nonprofit organizations, 97, 232n.11; personal, 168 (*see also* sexual politics; tithing); as public vs. personal transformation, 28, 226n.49; sexual politics as, 168; of spirituality, 12–13, 17, 18, 64–65, 219 (*see also* righteous discontent); tithing as, 168–69; transformation via, 28, 226n.49; by women, generally, 95–96. *See also* righteous discontent; *specific movements and organizations*
adultery, 203
African American public sphere: as alternative, 224n.22; engagement in, 94 (*see also* righteous discontent); in New York City, 27, 215; and racism, 9–10; significance of, 8–10; and women's issues, 217–18. *See also* televangelism

African American religion: accommodation tradition in, 5–6, 222n.8; activist tradition in, 223n.9; as conservative/evangelical, 167–68; criticism of, 224n.19; ethnography of and by African American women, 18–24; influences on, 5–6, 222n.8; self-help tradition in, 7. *See also* black churches
African Americans: informal access to politicians by, 230n.10; migration to the North by, 48; and the resistance/accommodation debate, 212–13, 222n.8; restitution to, 35. *See also* race/racism
African Methodist Episcopal Church. *See* AME Church
afterlife, 30–31
agency: and gratitude/empathy, 213–14; resistance as, 7, 223n.15; and spirituality, 7, 8, 10, 213; and structure/institutions, 7–8, 224n.17, 224n.19; time/space dynamics of, 229n.1; of women, generally, 7, 213, 224n.17
AIDS, 208
Allen, Richard, 86
AME Church (African Methodist Episcopal Church), 86, 87, 90, 231n.16
Angelou, Maya, 237n.2
anthropology. *See* ethnography
Anti-Lynching Movement, 95

Indexer:	Carol Roberts
Compositor:	Binghamton Valley Composition
Text:	10 / 13 Sabon
Display:	Sabon, Sackers Gothic Medium
Printer and binder:	Sheridan Books, Inc.